IMAGES of Rail

The Oregonian Railway

ON THE COVER: Whiteson, seen looking south around 1890, was a major junction point between the Oregonian Railway's narrow-gauge line from Fulquartz Landing to Sheridan and the Oregon & California (O&C) Railroad's line from McMinnville to Corvallis. Here, an O&C passenger train has stopped, blocking the narrow-gauge crossing while loading passengers at the Whiteson depot. The hotel, seen on the left, accommodated passengers needing to stay overnight at Whiteson in order to make connections between the two railroads. Things did indeed move at a more leisurely pace back then. (Author's collection.)

IMAGES
of Rail

THE OREGONIAN RAILWAY

Ed Austin

ARCADIA
PUBLISHING

ISBN 978-1-4671-3031-8

Published by Arcadia Publishing
Charleston, South Carolina

Printed in the United States of America

Library of Congress Control Number: 2013932275

For all general information, please contact Arcadia Publishing:
Telephone 843-853-2070
Fax 843-853-0044
E-mail sales@arcadiapublishing.com
For customer service and orders:
Toll-Free 1-888-313-2665

Visit us on the Internet at www.arcadiapublishing.com

Contents

ACKNOWLEDGMENTS

This book would not have been possible without the dedicated efforts of many unnamed photographers who made the effort necessary to record the early development of railroads in the Willamette Valley. Unfortunately, the names associated with many of these early photographs have been lost to time.

All of the historic photographs in this volume came from the author's personal collection, having been accumulated over a period of nearly 50 years. Unless otherwise noted, all of the contemporary photographs were taken by the author.

Greatly appreciated additional assistance came from the late Ed Culp, the late Guy Dunscomb, and Robert Lowry. These gentlemen had the foresight to record information related to Oregon railroads before the author had the foresight to be born. Thus, a significant bit of history was saved and can now be enjoyed by us all.

Additional information came from work done previously by Gerald M. Best, Leslie M. Scott, Mallory Hope Ferrell, and Tom Madden. The collective effort of these prolific writers has significantly enhanced the body of available information pertaining to some of our most esoteric and all but forgotten railroad lines.

To all of these gentlemen: THANK YOU. To you, we owe much.

INTRODUCTION

For those most familiar with the Southern Pacific (SP) Railroad, mention of SP narrow gauge brings visions of the Owens Valley and a diminutive 10-wheeler trundling along through vast open spaces. Much less well known is the extensive narrow-gauge railroad system in Oregon's Willamette Valley that came under SP ownership between 1890 and 1892. Many Southern Pacific branchlines in Western Oregon followed routes originally built as narrow gauge beginning in 1878; today, sections of the original narrow-gauge routes are still used by the Portland & Western Railroad and the Willamette Valley Railway.

In the mid-1800s, travel in Oregon was difficult at best. Travel via wagon was slow and dusty in the summer and often impossible for much of the winter. Development of the extraordinary farming potential of the Willamette Valley was highly restricted by this lack of dependable transportation. The construction of the Oregon & California Railroad initially appeared to offer relief, but expansion of O&C branchlines was slow and limited by the availability of funds.

After Henry Villard acquired control of the O&C in 1873, little attention could be given to the needs of local farmers. Villard was preoccupied with the construction of the Oregon Railway & Navigation Company east along the Columbia River and the extension of the O&C mainline south toward California.

At a meeting held at Amity on October 20, 1877, local farmers discussed the possibilities for constructing their own railroad. Interest in the project was high and a subsequent meeting on November 17 led to the incorporation of the Dayton, Sheridan & Grand Ronde (DS&GR) Railroad. The line was proposed to extend approximately 20 miles from the Yamhill River near Dayton to the farming community of Sheridan. The result would be relatively inexpensive access to Portland and markets beyond via riverboats traveling the Yamhill and Willamette Rivers.

Since the DS&GR planned no connection with the standard-gauge O&C, the line would be built to three-foot gauge to reduce costs. Grading began on June 6, 1878, and by July rails were being spiked down. The first train operated on July 29, and service all the way to Sheridan began on October 24. In the meantime, the citizens of Dallas voted a $17,000 subsidy to the DS&GR in order to have the narrow gauge build a branchline to their city. Construction of this extension began at Sheridan Junction (now Broadmead) with rails reaching Smithfield in January 1879. Grading was completed another four miles toward Dallas, but here progress halted.

Although traffic on the DS&GR was initially brisk, cash was in short supply. Some of the monies for the initial construction had been raised by selling transportation scrip, and now those shipments were not generating additional cash to continue construction. When the Pacific Rolling Mill brought suit in January 1879 to recover $93,000 it had accepted in mortgages, the DS&GR was forced into receivership.

However, the potential of the struggling narrow gauge had not gone unnoticed. William Reid clearly saw the value of a railroad system extending throughout the Willamette Valley connecting outlying farming communities with the existing water and rail network. Reid even proposed extending a narrow-gauge line over the Cascade Mountains to a connection with the Central Pacific Railroad near Winnemucca, Nevada.

Anticipating the failure of the DS&GR, Reid organized the Willamette Valley Railroad on September 9, 1878, and with backing from Scottish investors he acquired control of the narrow-gauge line on June 2, 1879. No new construction was undertaken by the Willamette Valley Railroad, and the DS&GR remained in receivership until April 2, 1880. Meanwhile, Reid renamed his proposed narrow-gauge empire, incorporating the Oregon Railway Co. Ltd.

on February 21, 1880. The properties and rights of the DS&GR were conveyed to the Oregon Railway Co. Ltd. on April 2. Now, with the existing narrow-gauge line out of receivership and a fresh influx of cash, construction resumed. The track was completed from Smithfield to Dallas on June 1, 1880, and construction began at Silverton for an extension down the east side of the Willamette Valley on April 19.

For reasons apparently connected to the railroad's Scottish financial backing, the Oregonian Railway Company Ltd. (of Scotland) was incorporated on May 4, 1880, taking over the properties and rights of the Oregon Railway Company Ltd. on December 11.

In the fall of 1880, David Graham Drummond Ogilvy, Earl of Airlie, toured the Oregon properties on behalf of the Scottish investors. Apparently impressed with what he saw, the earl ordered construction of a bridge across the Willamette River between Fulquartz and Ray's Landings to connect the Westside and Eastside Divisions. He also approved a survey across the Cascades for the proposed connection with the Central Pacific near Winnemucca.

Meanwhile, construction continued throughout the Willamette Valley. From Dallas, the line was extended south to Airlie, named for the Earl of Airlie. This extension opened for traffic on September 17, 1881. From Dayton Junction (near Dayton), track was extended via Lafayette and Ekin (renamed Dundee) to the Willamette River landing at Fulquartz. Here, the authorized bridge construction began in November 1880. On the Eastside, track was completed from Ray's Landing via St. Paul and Woodburn to Silverton on October 4, 1880. At Woodburn, the Oregonian Railway's narrow-gauge line crossed the standard-gauge O&C main line at grade.

On January 10, 1881, the Eastside Division was opened to West Scio and the line was completed to Brownsville on July 5. During the same period, grading began for an extension of the Westside Division from Dundee to Portland. Naturally, the rapid expansion of the Oregonian Railway throughout the Willamette Valley was not going unnoticed by Henry Villard.

Villard felt the dominance of his Oregon & California Railroad in Oregon was being challenged by the little narrow-gauge upstart. To eliminate this perceived threat, Villard offered the Scottish investors a lease arrangement whereby the O&C would "operate" the narrow-gauge properties as a part of the O&C system. In return, the Scottish investors would receive a fixed return on their investment. Despite arguments by William Reid, the Scots accepted Villard's offer and on October 1, 1881, the O&C took over operation of the Oregonian Railway narrow-gauge lines.

Interested primarily in eliminating the threat posed to the O&C, Villard stopped work on the Willamette River Bridge and suspended service between Ray's Landing and Woodburn. Service was also suspended between Fulquartz and Whites (Whiteson). Subsequently, the narrow-gauge lines were operated only as feeders to the Oregon & California Railroad. Although it proved advantageous to the O&C to extend the narrow gauge south from Brownsville to Coburg in 1882, the narrow-gauge lines were generally allowed to deteriorate.

When Villard's railroad empire faltered in 1884, the lease of the Oregonian Railway Ltd. was repudiated and, on May 1, control of the narrow-gauge properties returned to the Scottish investors. Given the highly deteriorated condition of the once promising narrow-gauge system, little progress could be made and Charles N. Scott was appointed receiver for the Oregonian Railway Ltd. on November 15, 1884. As receiver, Scott began to rebuild the neglected narrow-gauge system. Work resumed on the Willamette River Bridge and service was restored on the sections that had been embargoed by Villard.

The Oregonian Railway Ltd. was beginning to show signs of life. William Reid incorporated the Portland & Willamette Valley Railroad on January 19, 1885, to take over construction of the line from Dundee to Portland that had begun in 1881. Work began at Dundee Junction (near Dundee) in January 1886, and the line was completed via Newberg and Rex Hill to Oswego by December. Service to Jefferson Street Station in West Portland began on July 14, 1888.

However, despite efforts to restore the Oregonian Railway to profitability, the line was struggling to overcome deterioration incurred during the years of O&C control. After remaining in receivership for five years, the line was sold to the Oregon Western Railroad, which operated the narrow-gauge system until it was sold in foreclosure on April 4, 1890, to Richard Koehler.

Koehler was acting on behalf of the Southern Pacific Company, which now controlled the Oregon & California. Southern Pacific management foresaw the potential usefulness of the narrow-gauge routes and intended to integrate them into the SP lines in Oregon. On April 19, 1890, the Southern Pacific incorporated the Oregonian Railroad and on May 19, Richard Koehler conveyed the Oregonian Railway to the new company.

By May 1887, it had become public that it was actually C.P. Huntington who had provided much of the capital used by William Reid to extend the narrow-gauge line from Dundee to Portland and that this had been done in the interest of the Southern Pacific Company. Again acting on behalf of the Southern Pacific, Richard Koehler was appointed receiver of the Portland & Willamette Valley Railroad through foreclosure.

On August 5, 1892, the properties of the Portland & Willamette Valley Railroad were transferred to the Portland & Yamhill Railroad, which the Southern Pacific had incorporated on June 14, 1892, for that specific purpose. Thus, the Southern Pacific acquired control of the entire narrow-gauge system once planned as a major independent railroad in the Willamette Valley and Oregon.

Work on the Willamette River Bridge was halted for the final time and the line from Ray's Landing to Woodburn was abandoned. The lines from Fulquartz landing to Dundee and from Dayton Junction to Dayton were also abandoned. The remaining narrow-gauge lines were converted to standard gauge by the end of 1893, although the third rail from Dundee to Portland remained in place until 1895, allowing for dual-gauge operation over Rex Hill.

Four sections of original narrow-gauge lines became important elements of the Southern Pacific lines in Oregon: a major portion of the SP Woodburn-Springfield branch from Woodburn to Coburg, the majority of the Jefferson Street branch from Jefferson Street to Lafayette via Rex Hill, the Willamina branch from Whiteson to Sheridan via Broadmead, and the Airlie branch from Broadmead to Airlie via Dallas and Monmouth.

With changing economics and improved alternate modes of transportation, the reason for some of the original narrow-gauge routes ceased to be valid. The Airlie branch from Perrydale to Airlie was abandoned in sections between 1927 and 1934. Train service on the final segment of the original Airlie branch from Broadmead to Perrydale continued until mid-1985, after which the track was removed.

On the east side of the Willamette Valley, abandonment of sections of the Woodburn-Springfield branch began in 1976; by 1985, all of the line south of Tallman had been removed, as had the section of the original narrow-gauge route between West Stayton and Shelburn that included the Santiam River crossing.

By the late 1980s, the Southern Pacific was looking for options to shed responsibility for operation of some of its remaining branchlines in Oregon while retaining the long haul traffic that was still being generated. As a result, shortline operators began to assume operation of some of the remaining branchlines. In February 1993, operation of the original narrow-gauge route from Woodburn to West Stayton was taken over by the Willamette Valley Railroad via a lease agreement. After leasing the property for three years, the Willamette Valley Railroad purchased the line from the Southern Pacific in 1996. Today, the line is still intact but trains seldom go past Mount Angle or Silverton.

In 1993, the Willamette and Pacific Railroad was created by Genesee & Wyoming Inc. to take over operation of several Southern Pacific branchlines in Oregon. These included the former narrow-gauge route from Whiteson to Sheridan and sections of the original narrow-gauge route between Oswego and Lafayette. Both of these routes remain in service as of 2014. In 1995, Genesee & Wyoming created the Portland & Western Railroad to combine the operations of the Willamette and Pacific Railroad with other Oregon branchlines that were being leased by Genesee & Wyoming.

Thus, as we move into the 21st century, significant sections of the original narrow-gauge routes remain active, serving the commercial interests of Oregon by funneling rail traffic to the national rail network.

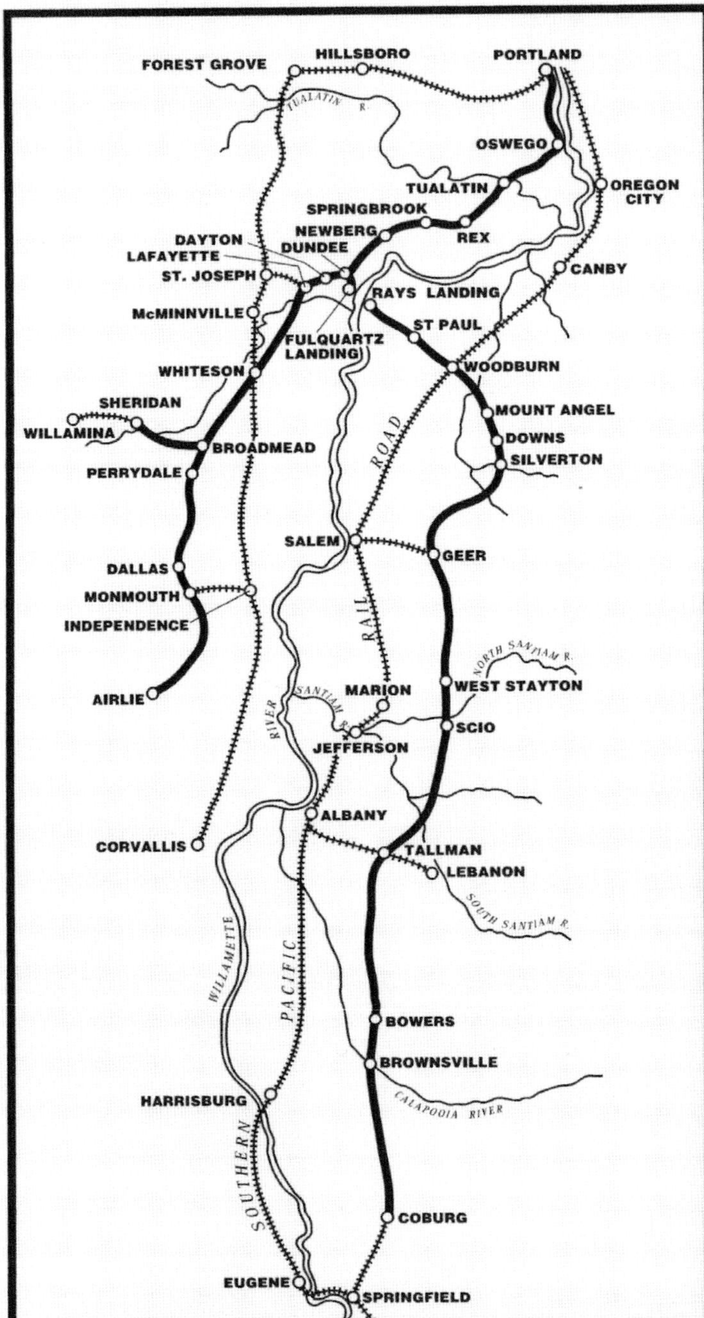

Narrow Gauge Railroad circa 1881

With Southern Pacific Railroad lines shown for reference

This map gives a simplified overview of narrow-gauge railways in the Willamette Valley around 1881. Related Southern Pacific Railroad routes are shown as crosshatched lines for reference. Not all of these SP lines existed in 1881.

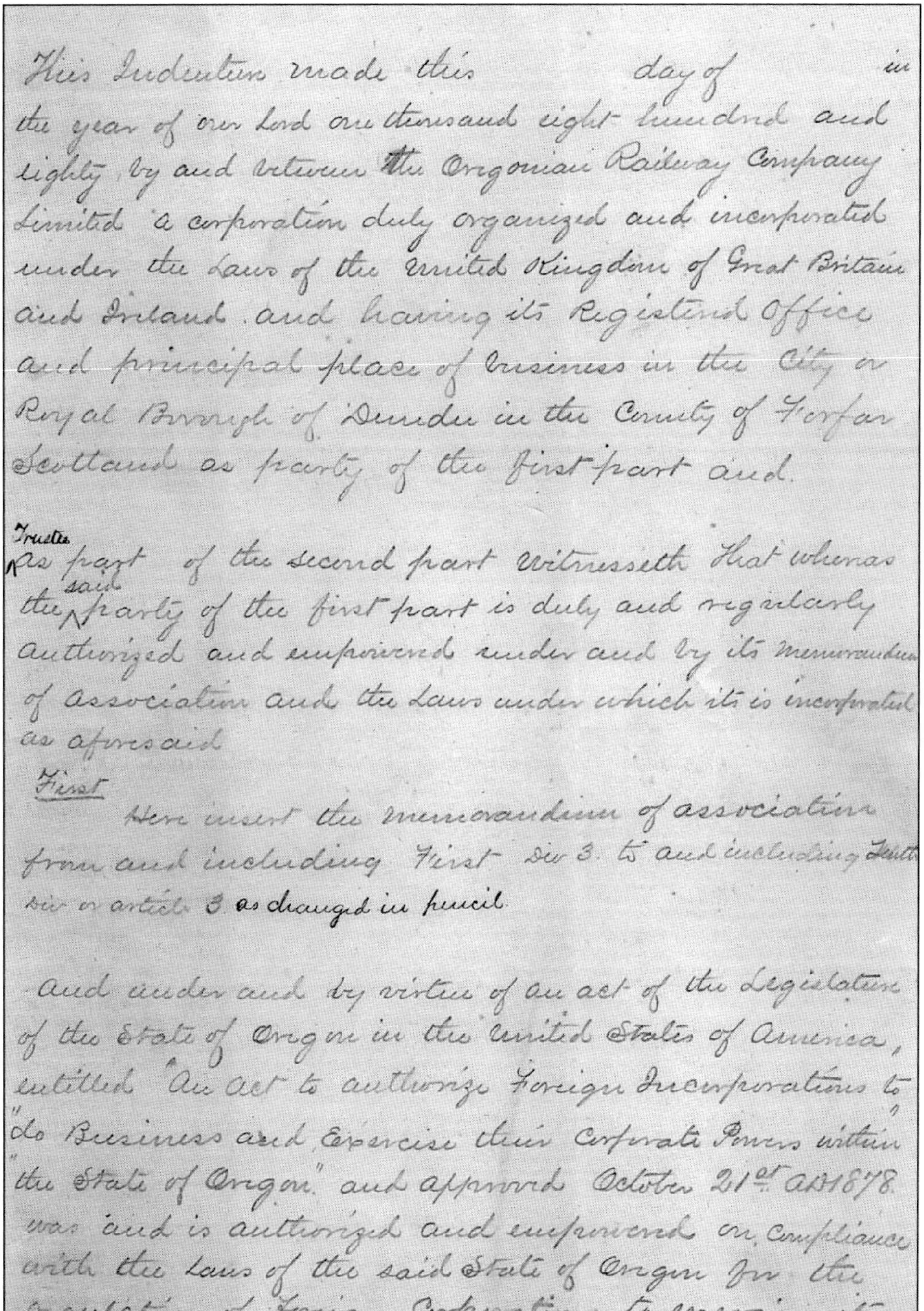
This Indenture made this day of in the year of our Lord one thousand eight hundred and eighty by and between the Oregonian Railway Company Limited a corporation duly organized and incorporated under the Laws of the United Kingdom of Great Britain and Ireland and having its Registered Office and principal place of business in the City or Royal Burgh of Dundee in the County of Forfar Scotland as party of the first part and.

Trustee as part of the second part Witnesseth That whereas the said party of the first part is duly and regularly authorized and empowered under and by its memorandum of association and the Laws under which its is incorporated as aforesaid

First

Here insert the memorandum of association from and including First div 3. to and including Tenth div or article 3 as changed in pencil

And under and by virtue of an act of the Legislature of the State of Oregon in the United States of America, entitled "An Act to authorize Foreign Incorporations to do Business and Exercise their Corporate Powers within the State of Oregon" and approved October 21st AD 1878 was and is authorized and empowered on compliance with the Laws of the said State of Oregon for the regulation of Foreign Corporations to exercise its

This is a copy of the first page of the original 16-page handwritten draft of the lease giving Henry Villard control of the Willamette Valley's narrow-gauge railways. As a result of this lease, progress on what might have become a significant narrow-gauge railroad system was effectively halted. Much of the proposed narrow-gauge route would later be constructed by the Southern Pacific Railroad as standard gauge.

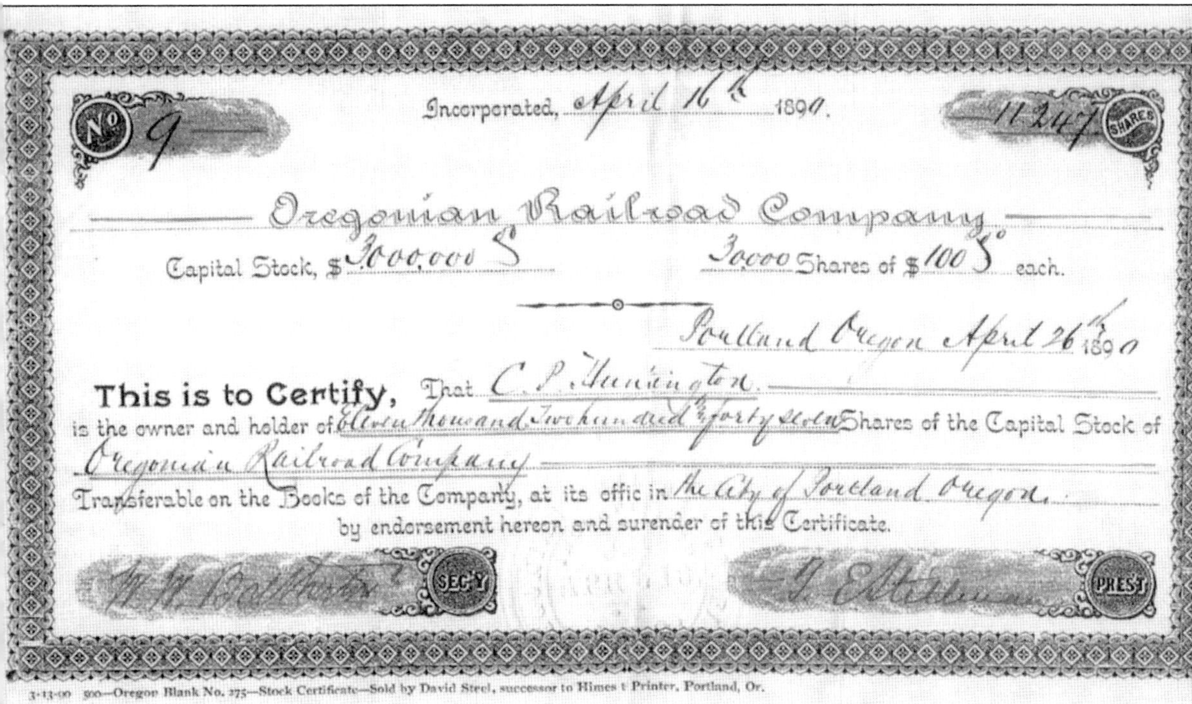

No 9 Incorporated, April 16th 1890. 11247 Shares

Oregonian Railroad Company.

Capital Stock, $3000000 $ 30000 Shares of $100 $ each.

Portland Oregon April 26th 1890

This is to Certify, That C. P. Huntington
is the owner and holder of Eleven thousand Two hundred & forty seven Shares of the Capital Stock of
Oregonian Railroad Company
Transferable on the Books of the Company, at its offic in the City of Portland Oregon
by endorsement hereon and surender of this Certificate.

SEC'Y PREST

3-13-00 500—Oregon Blank No. 275—Stock Certificate—Sold by David Steel, successor to Himes t Printer, Portland, Or.

The Southern Pacific played a significant role in the affairs of railroads in Oregon in 1890 as confirmed by the name on this stock certificate, none other than C.P. Huntington. Huntington was one of the original "Big Four" behind the Central Pacific Railroad and was a creator of the Southern Pacific Railroad. On April 26, 1890, he purchased 11,247 shares of stock in the newly forming Oregonian Railroad Company, thus acquiring nearly 40 percent ownership in the new company. Small wonder then that within a few years, remaining segments of the Willamette Valley's narrow-gauge railroad system would be incorporated into the Southern Pacific Railroad's lines in Oregon.

One

Fulquartz Landing to Sheridan and Willamina

The narrow-gauge Dayton, Sheridan & Grand Ronde Railroad was originally envisioned to run from a steamboat landing on the Yamhill River at Dayton, Oregon, approximately 20 miles to the community of Sheridan. In 1877, local farmers recognized the need for dependable year-round access beyond local markets. Ben Holladay's O&C was focused on building a standard-gauge railroad from Portland to California. For the O&C, building branch lines would have to wait for perhaps another decade or more. For farmers in outlying areas like Sheridan, commercial viability made waiting impractical; being men of action, their answer was obvious: "Build our own railroad."

Despite limited resources, subscriptions were forthcoming and construction began early in 1878. By spring, Chinese workers were actively grading the route. Rails arrived that summer and the line from Dayton to Sheridan was opened for traffic on October 24, 1878. However, financial difficulties soon beset the farmers' railroad empire and in January 1879, the Pacific Rolling Mill brought suit to recover $93,000 owed for rails, forcing the DS&GR into receivership.

Enter William Reid. Reid had seen greater potential in the narrow-gauge railroad than imagined by its builders. With backing from Scottish investors, a more expansive phase of construction was undertaken. Limits to navigation on the Yamhill River were considered an impediment to year-round operation. Reid's plans called for an extension to Fulquartz Landing on the Willamette River. Here, the narrow-gauge railroad could connect directly with steamboats traveling the Willamette Valley's major waterway.

When the Southern Pacific acquired control of the narrow-gauge lines between 1890 and 1892, sections of the original route from Fulquartz Landing to Sheridan were seen as valuable feeders to the giant among western railroads. Direct rail access to Portland had rendered the river landing at Fulquartz irrelevant, but the line between Whiteson and Sheridan fit into SP's plans. By 1893, the track had been widened to standard-gauge, and for 14 years a 56-foot turntable at Sheridan marked the western end of the SP branch.

In 1907, the Sheridan & Willamina Railroad extended track 5.4 miles from Sheridan to Willamina. This line was absorbed by the SP in June 1913, thus completing what would become the SP's Willamina Branch. An additional extension from Willamina to Grand Ronde was opened for traffic in 1921 by the Willamina & Grand Ronde (W&GR) Railroad.

Genesse and Wyoming Corporation took over the line from Whiteson to Willamina in 1993. This track is still operated by G&W subsidiary Portland & Western in 2013. A 5.2-mile section of the old W&GR was taken over by Hampton Industries in June 1995, but the mill at Fort Hill has been dismantled and today this section of track is only used to store railroad cars.

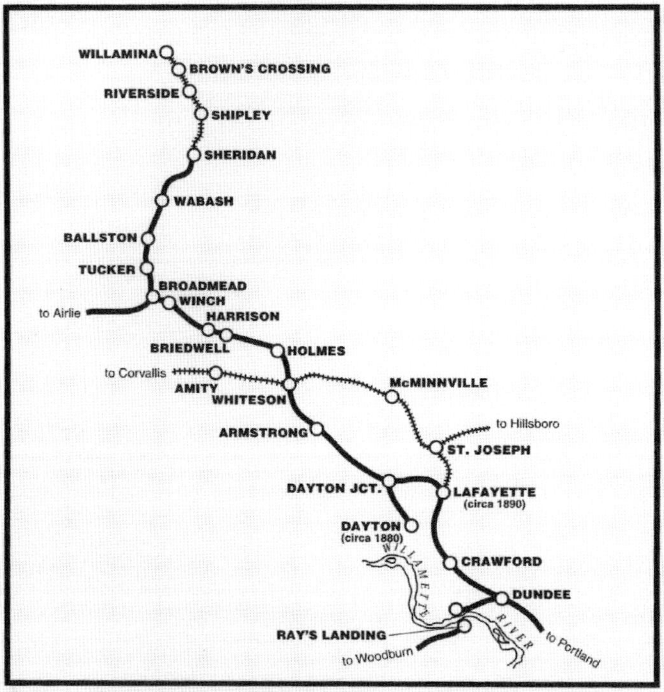

Railroads Fulquartz Landing to Sheridan & Willamina
With Southern Pacific Railroad lines shown for reference

This map gives a simplified view of the rail lines between Fulquartz Landing and Willamina. The narrow-gauge route is shown in bold. Southern Pacific lines are shown as crosshatched lines for reference. However, not all of these SP lines existed concurrently with the narrow gauge.

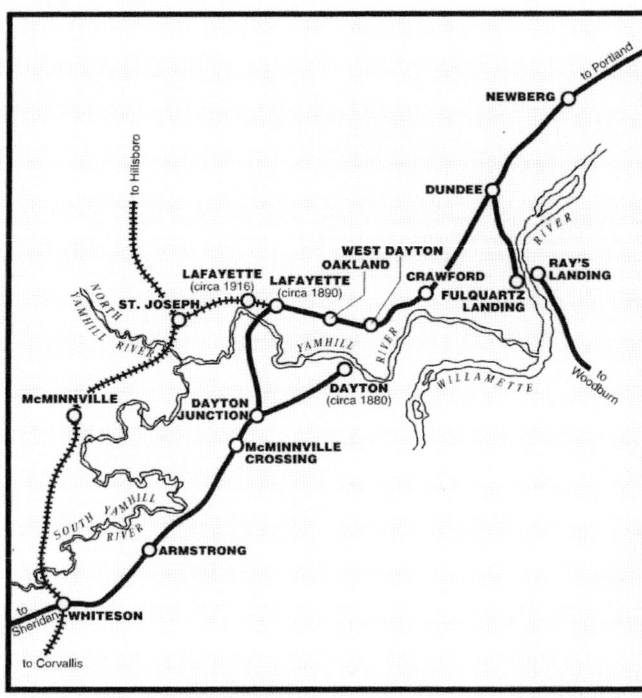

Railroads between Fulquartz Landing and Whiteson
Enlarged for clarification

This enlarged view focuses on the lines in the vicinity of Fulquartz Landing, McMinnville, and Whiteson. Several revisions to operations in this area occurred between 1880 and 1900, resulting in a rather confusing track arrangement.

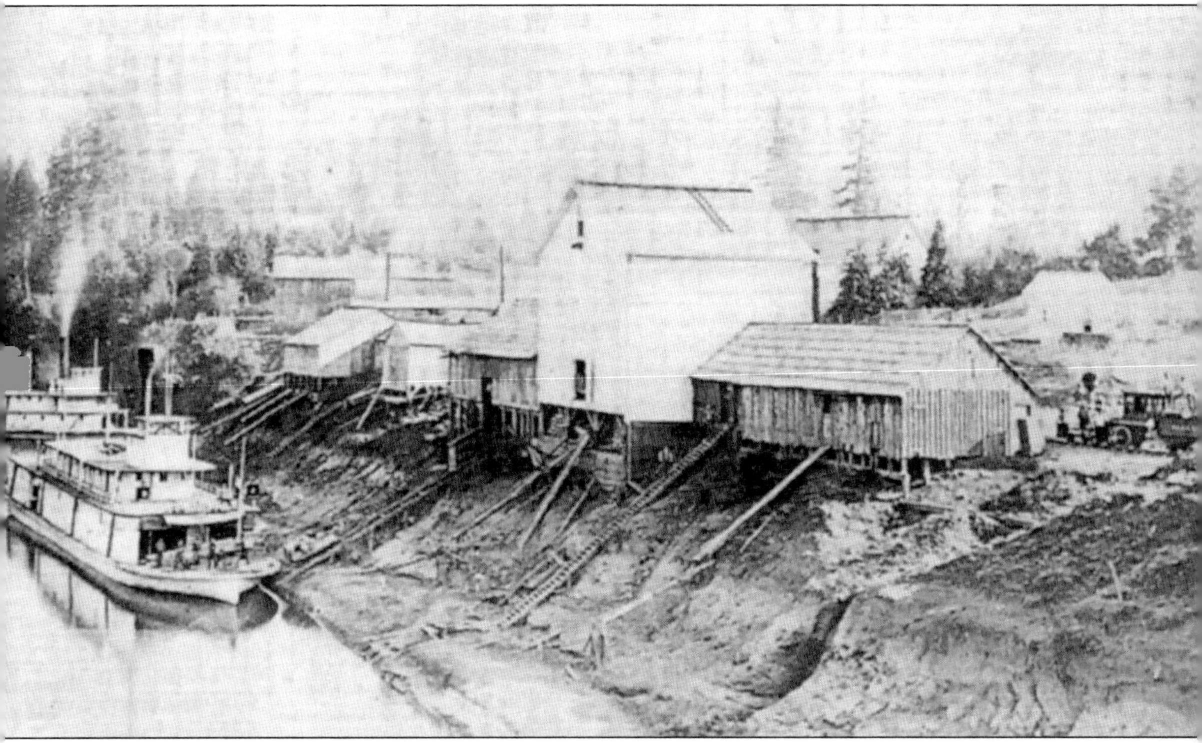

As originally planned, the Dayton, Sheridan & Grand Ronde Railroad was to extend from the steamboat landing on the Yamhill River at Dayton to the farming community of Sheridan. This extremely rare, albeit rather poor-quality photograph is the only known view showing the original terminal at Dayton. It is also the only known image showing one of the DS&GR's first two locomotives in service. The tiny, narrow-gauge 2-4-0 is visible at far right. (Courtesy Ed Culp.)

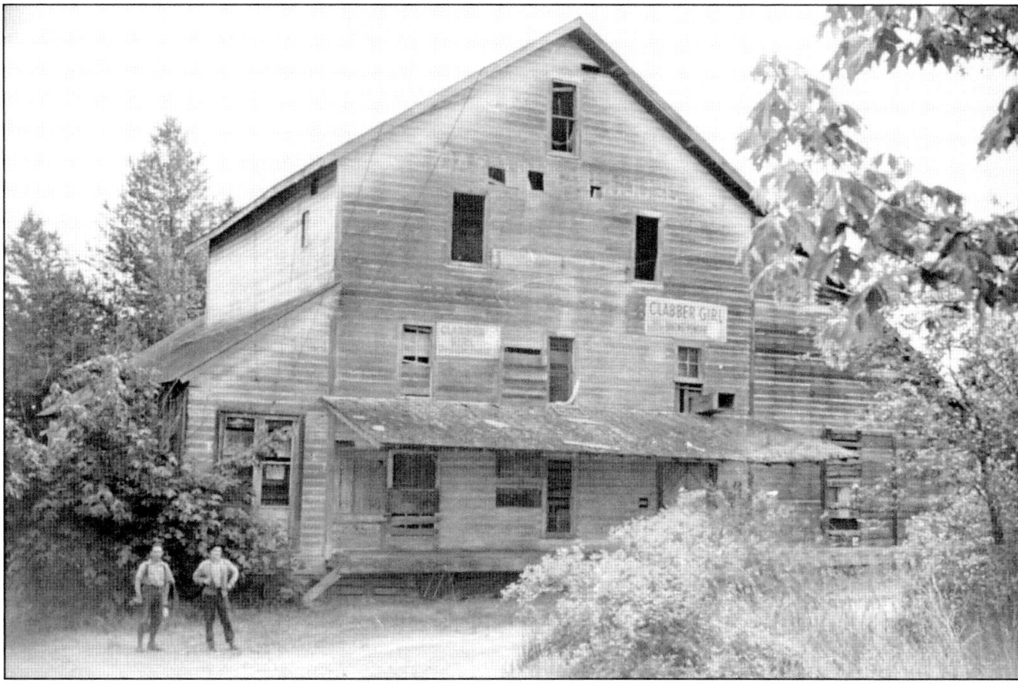

The abandoned warehouse seen in these two views predates the narrow-gauge Dayton, Sheridan & Grand Ronde Railroad by several years. Although very difficult to read, the words "Dundee Warehouse" can be seen above the upper two windows in the older view with the two men standing to the left. Apparently, the building was revitalized later but was again abandoned by the time the second photograph was taken c. 1960s.

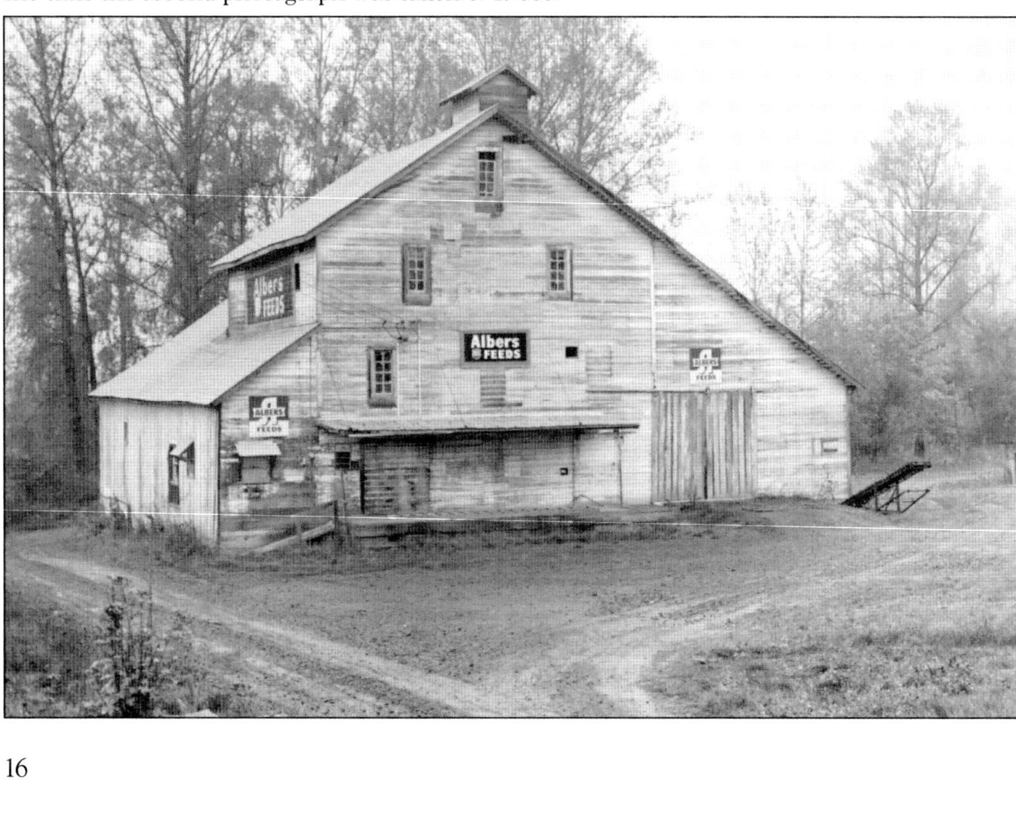

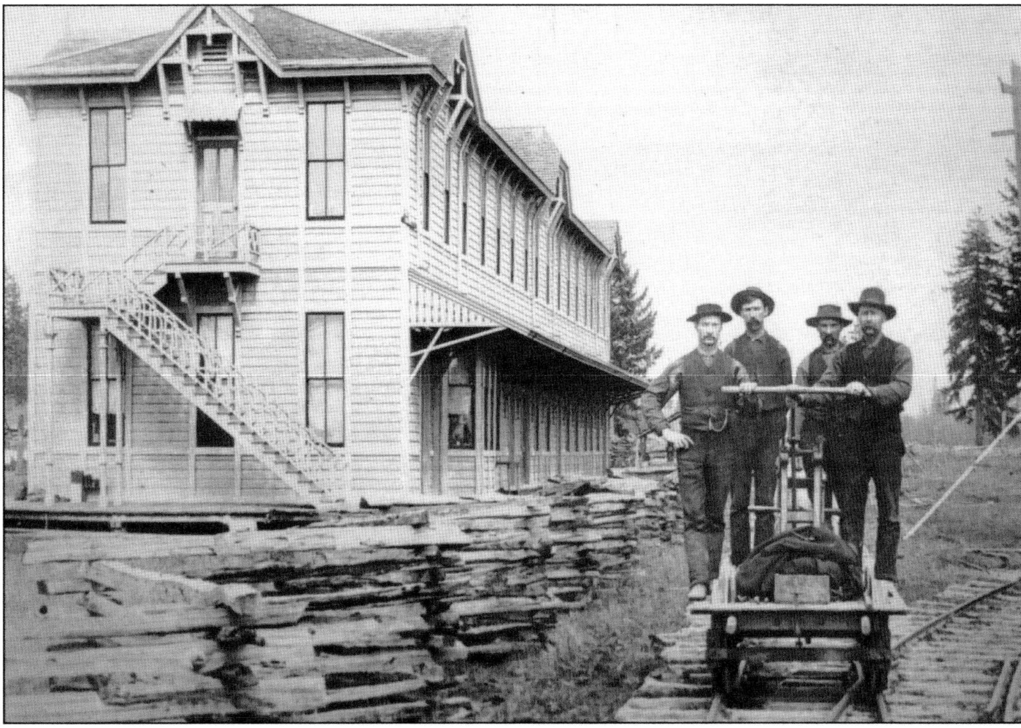

The original Dundee depot and hotel is seen here shortly after its completion in 1881. The building measured 20 feet by 80 feet and was built by the Oregonian Railway Co. Ltd. as its general headquarters. The depot, telegraph office, and dining room were on the ground floor, with 32 sleeping rooms for employees and guests upstairs. The structure was razed in 1906 and replaced by a single-story depot.

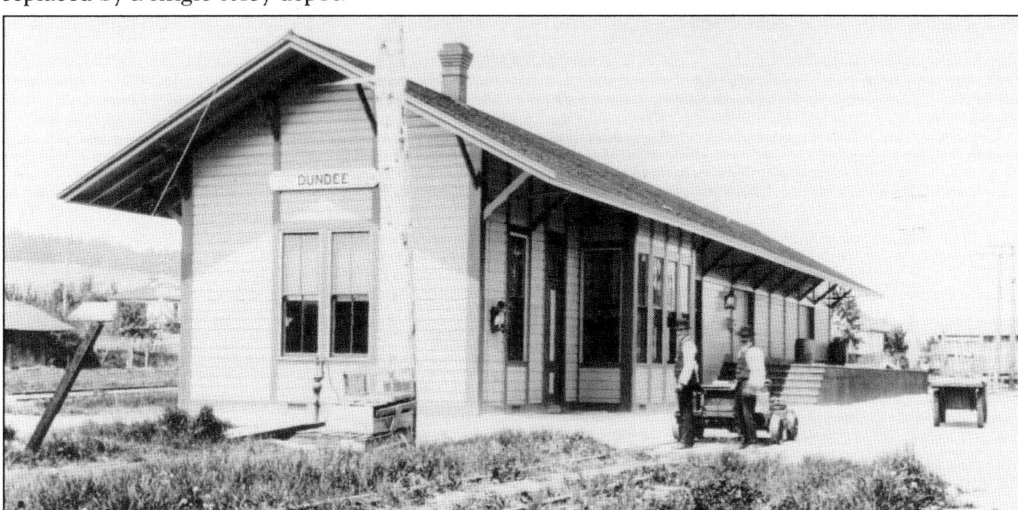

To take advantage of the natural topography, the original narrow-gauge line followed Hess Creek from Fulquartz Landing uphill to Dundee. When the narrow gauge was extended to Portland, this location became Dundee Junction but the name was shortened back to Dundee on December 8, 1912. By this time, the track was standard gauge, and the old narrow-gauge line to Fulquartz Landing had been abandoned for more than two decades.

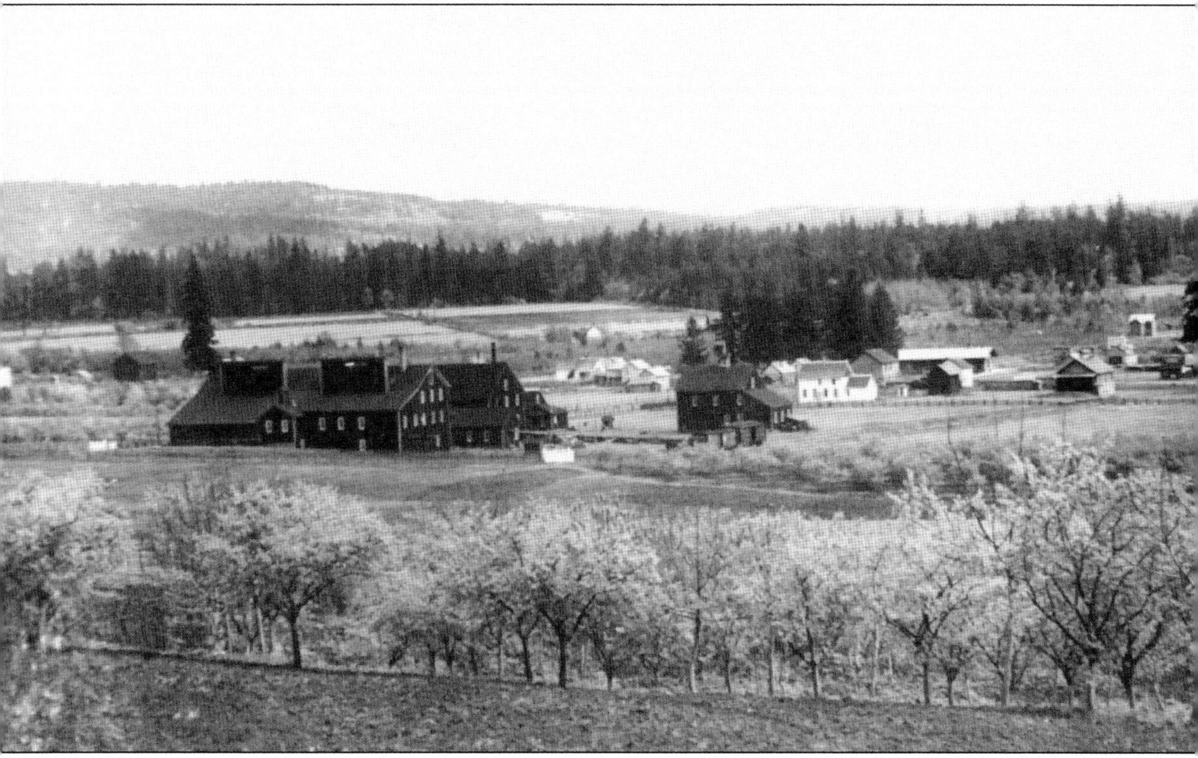

By 1900, Dundee could claim the largest prune orchard in the world and the largest walnut orchard in the United States. Both were owned by Thomas Prince, who built a substantial dryer and packinghouse on his farm in 1897. This view, taken after 1906, looks toward the southeast with Prince's operation in the foreground and Dundee in the distance. Note the boxcars spotted for loading near the center. The long, low building at right center is the Southern Pacific depot. Fulquartz Landing would be beyond the tree line in the distance.

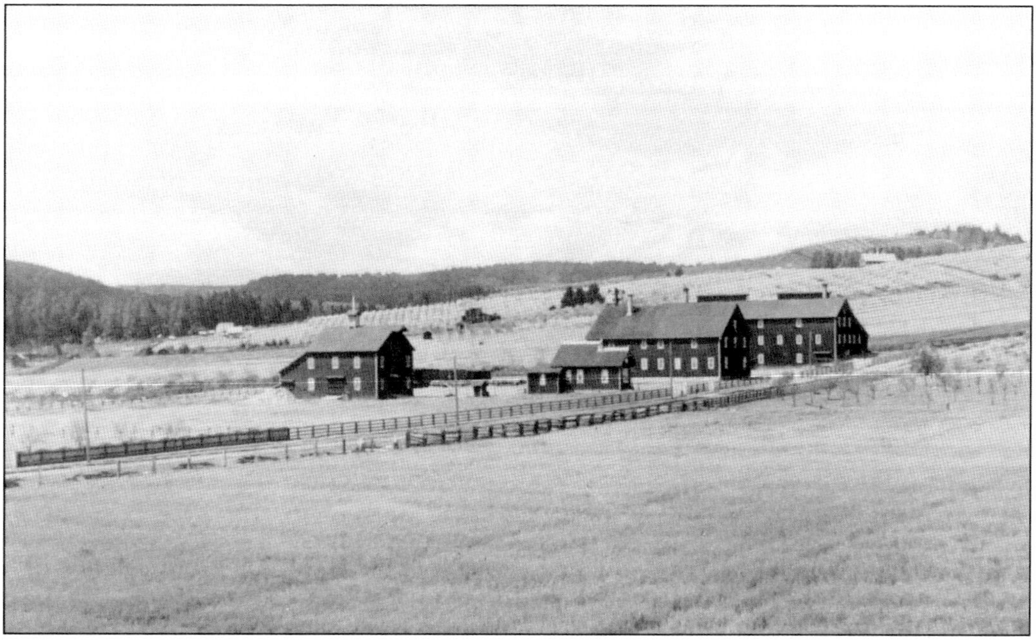

These two views give a closer look at Prince's fruit and nut dryer and packinghouse. Initially, second-growth timber on the farm supplied cordwood and railroad ties to the railroad via a spur from Dundee. Horses and mules pulled the empty cars up to the Prince farm for loading, after which gravity was in charge of the return trip to the mainline. Later, the spur served the fruit and nut loading shed as seen here.

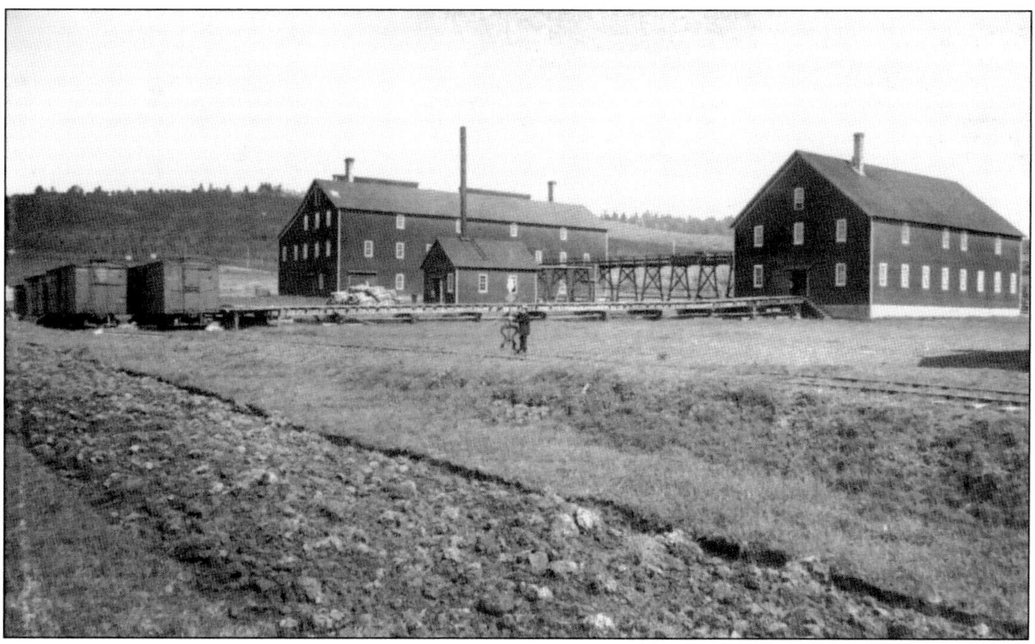

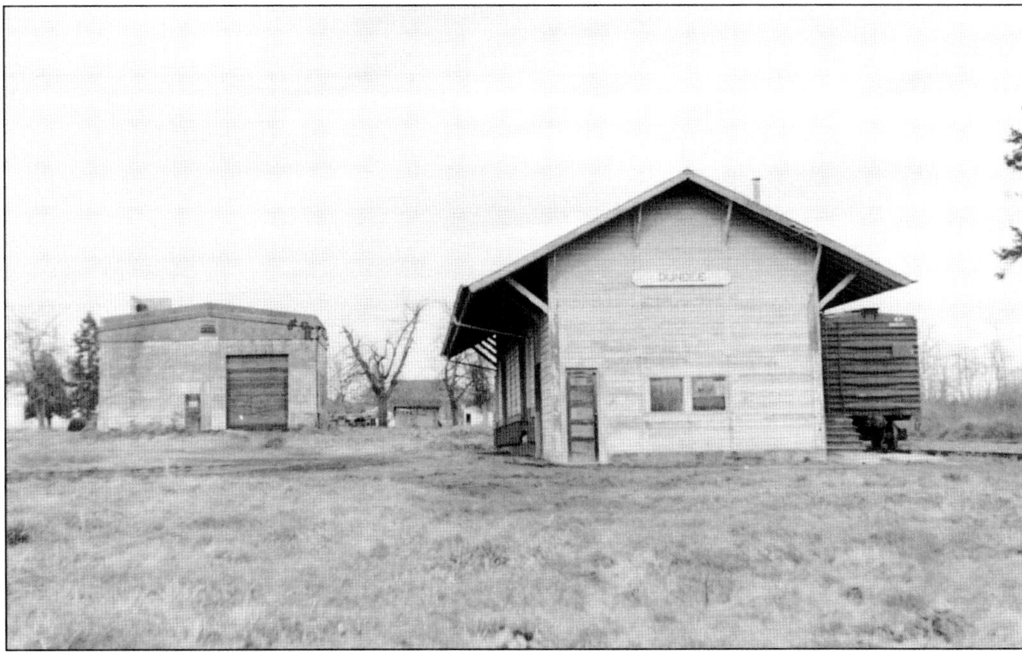

It appears the old Dundee depot was still serving as a warehouse when this photograph was taken in the early 1960s. To the left stands the concrete shell of the Red Electric substation built by the SP at Dundee to serve its electric interurban operations. Although the Red Electric ceased operation in Oregon in 1929, the old substation was still standing in 2014.

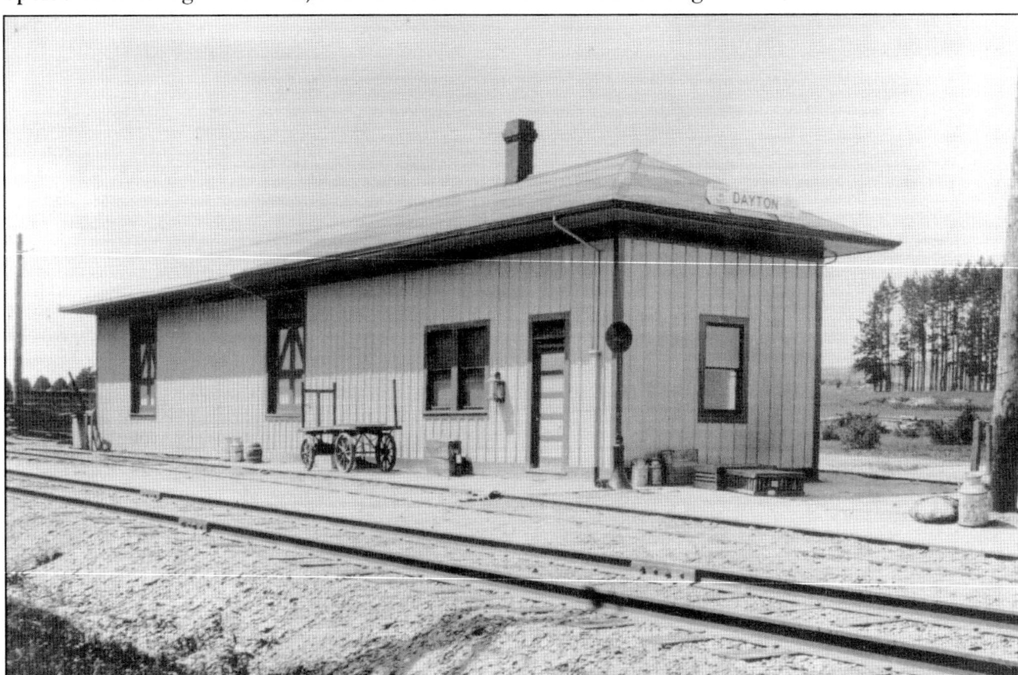

This 16-foot-by-84-foot depot served the Southern Pacific at Dayton between 1906 and 1938. From 1923 to 1932, the depot also served as a train order station in addition to its other duties. It is seen here around 1915.

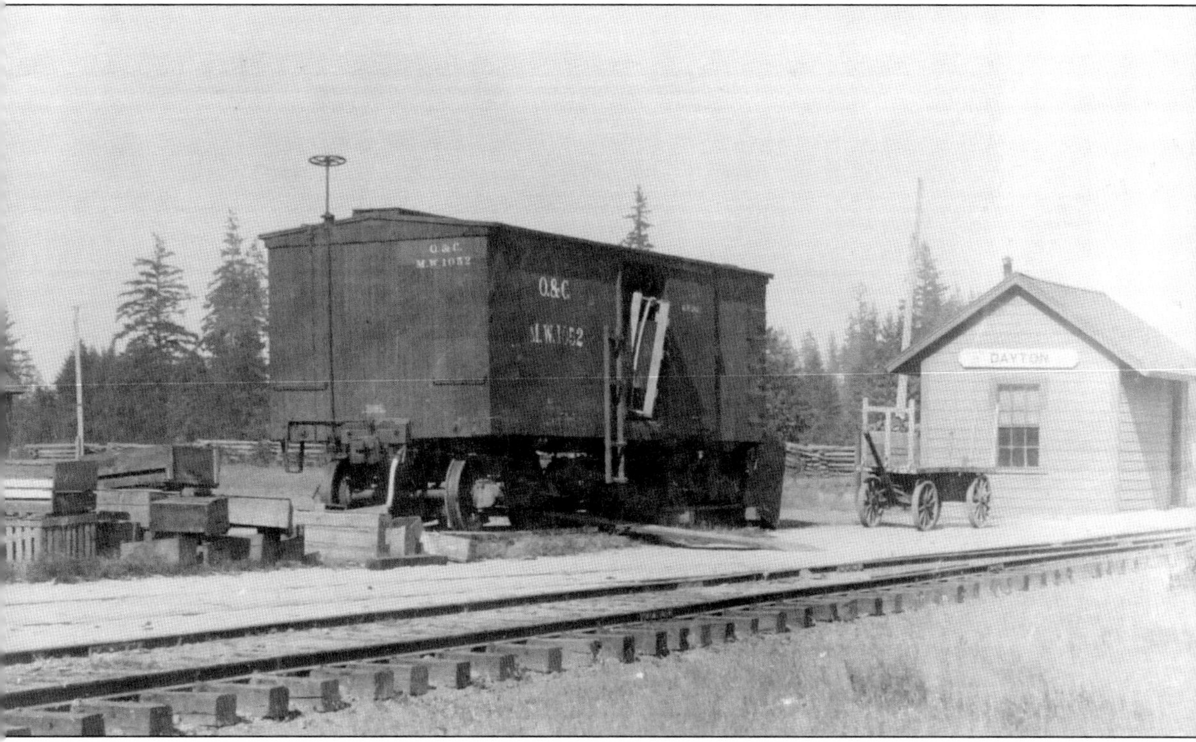

This small depot served Dayton after the railroad moved the location to this point on the line between Dundee and Lafayette. Originally, this location was referred to as West Dayton in order to avoid confusion with the community of Dayton located near the Yamhill River. "West" was dropped from the name when the narrow-gauge line to Dayton was abandoned in 1891. The small structure appears to offer little more than shelter for passengers and possibly a desk for the local depot agent. The Southern Pacific replaced this building with a more substantial depot in 1906.

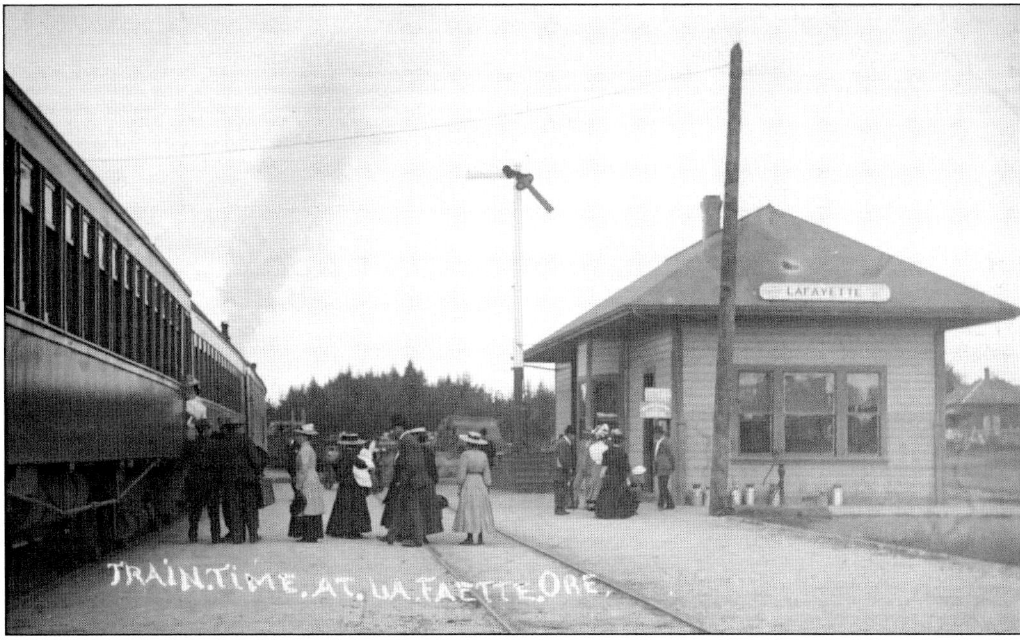

It appears the SP is doing a brisk business at Lafayette in this c. 1918 view. Originally, Lafayette was located six tenths of a mile east of this location. However, after the original route from Lafayette to Whiteson via Dayton Junction and Armstrong was abandoned in 1906, the depot site was moved to the location seen here. The depot measured 20 feet by 58 feet. Lafayette served as a train order office from 1892 until 1932. The depot seen here was closed on July 20, 1939.

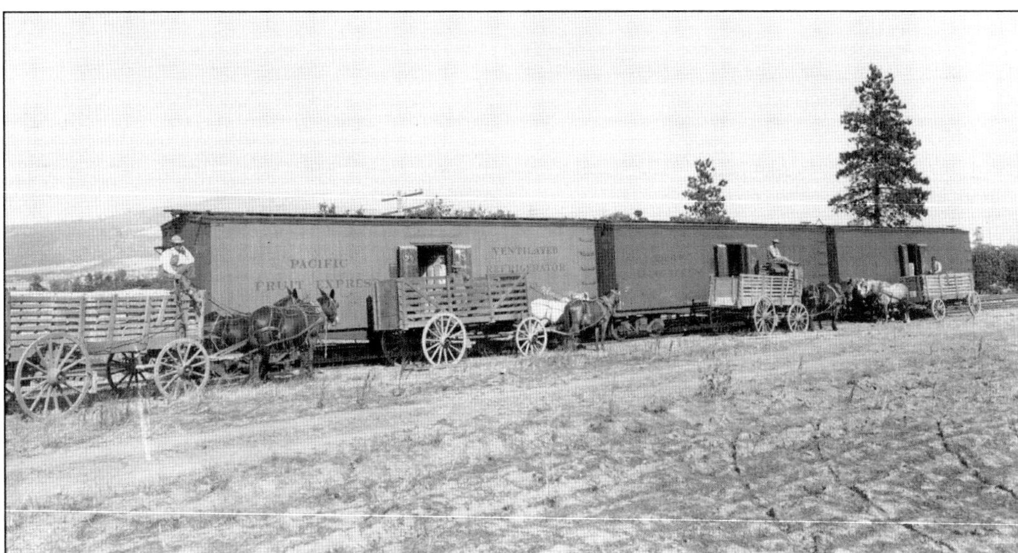

The area around Dundee and Lafayette has long been famous for its crops of fruit and nuts. However, it was the railroad that made distribution of these crops viable. To that end, we see here three refrigerator cars taking on loads probably destined for eastern markets. The teams with their wagons seem to be waiting patiently while the work is done, an emotion perhaps not shared by the driver atop the wagon to the left as he waits his turn to unload.

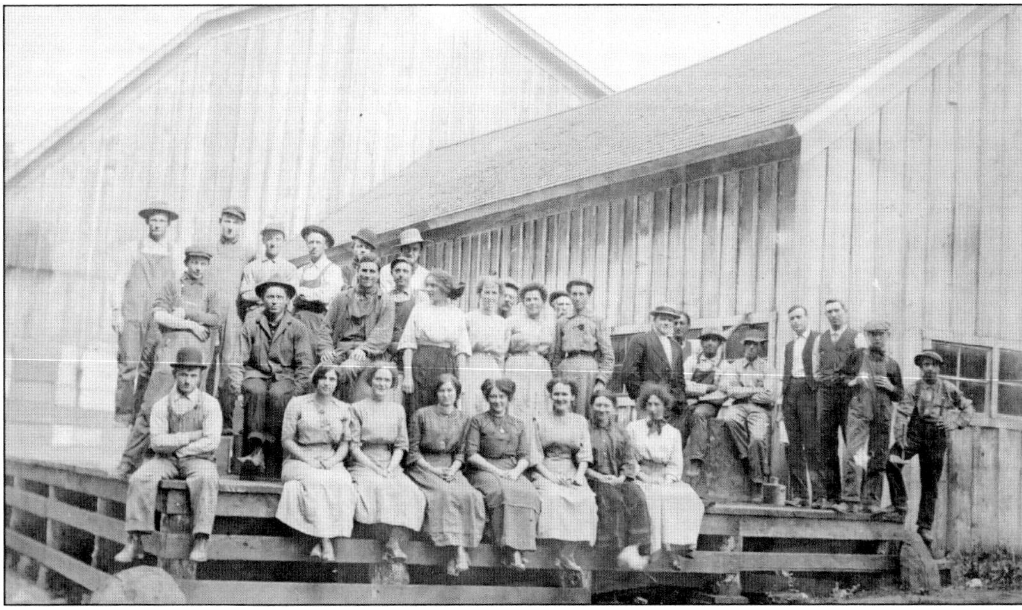

A group photograph was enough reason for the crew of this apple packinghouse at Lafayette to take a break. These were the days when labor was still cheaper than machinery and more readily available in Oregon's rural farming communities.

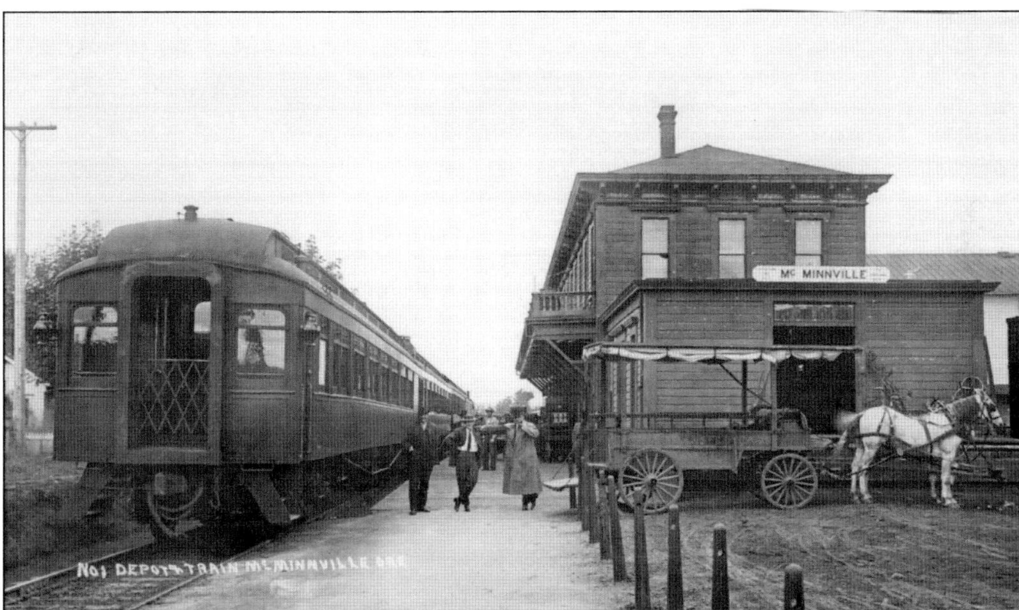

The original McMinnville depot and hotel is seen here around 1910. According to Southern Pacific records the 26-foot-by-93-foot structure was built in 1906, but it was actually built much earlier by the Western Oregon Railroad, which built the line through McMinnville in 1879. A new depot was built in McMinnville in 1912, and the old depot was converted to a freight depot. It served in this capacity until December 1964.

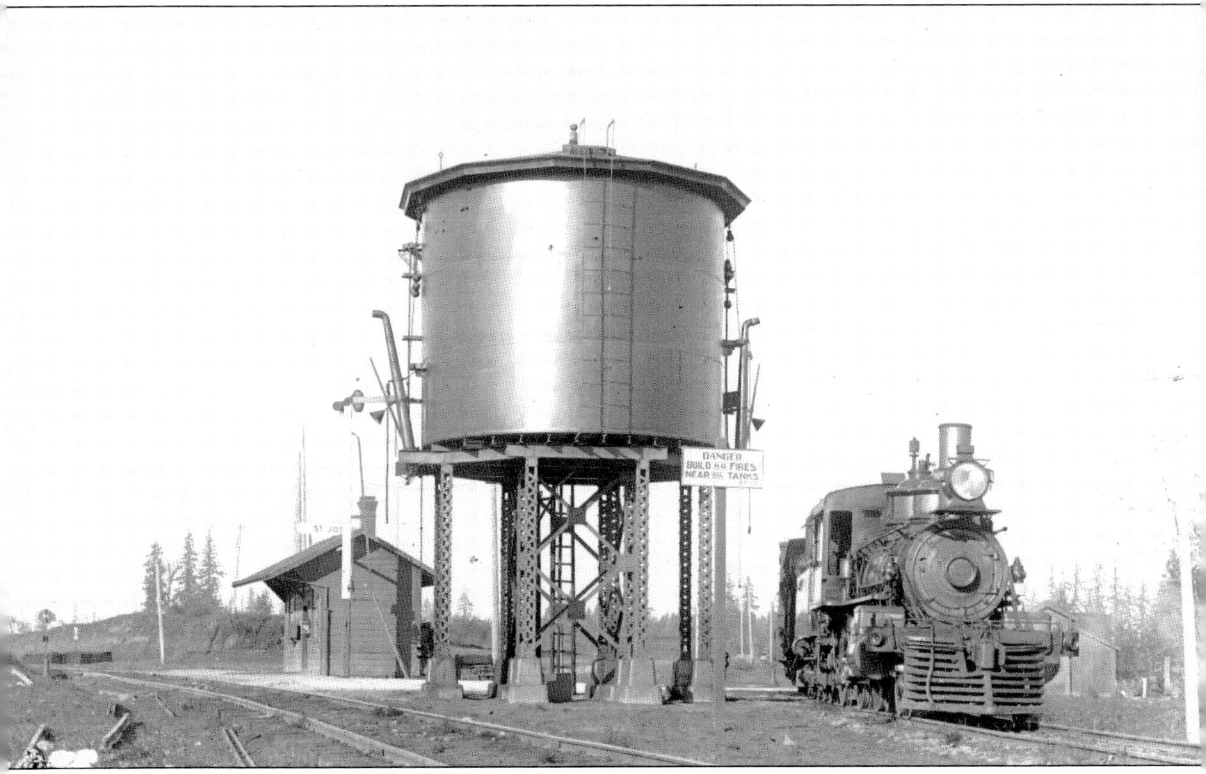

By 1872, the Oregon & California Railroad had completed a standard-gauge line south from Hillsboro to St. Joseph, where construction came to a halt. After Henry Villard acquired control of the O&C, the line from St. Joseph was extended south through McMinnville and Whiteson to Corvallis under the name Western Oregon Railroad. This section was completed in 1880. Thus, the narrow-gauge route from Lafayette to Whiteson via Dayton Junction and the O&C line from St. Joseph to Whiteson via McMinnville effectively duplicated each other. In 1906, a connection was made between Lafayette and St. Joseph that allowed the original narrow-gauge route from Lafayette to Whiteson to be abandoned and at the same time made St. Joseph a significant rail junction. Fortunately, locomotive engineer and photographer H.L. Arey captured this scene on film as his train paused at St. Joseph in 1914. Arey's train had just arrived from Lafayette and would soon continue to McMinnville and Whiteson. The 1872 O&C line from Hillsboro is seen curving to the left. (H.L. Arey photograph, author's collection.)

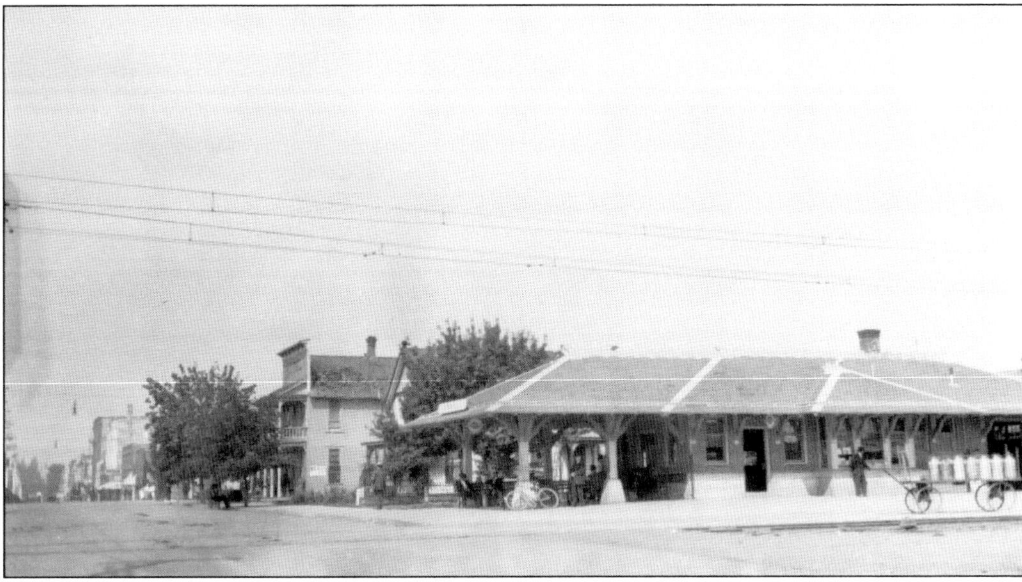

The second McMinnville depot was built in anticipation of Southern Pacific's ambitious plan to install electrified interurban service in Oregon. Electric train service between McMinnville and Portland began in 1914. Electric operation ended in 1929, but this depot is still used by the Portland & Western Railroad in 2014.

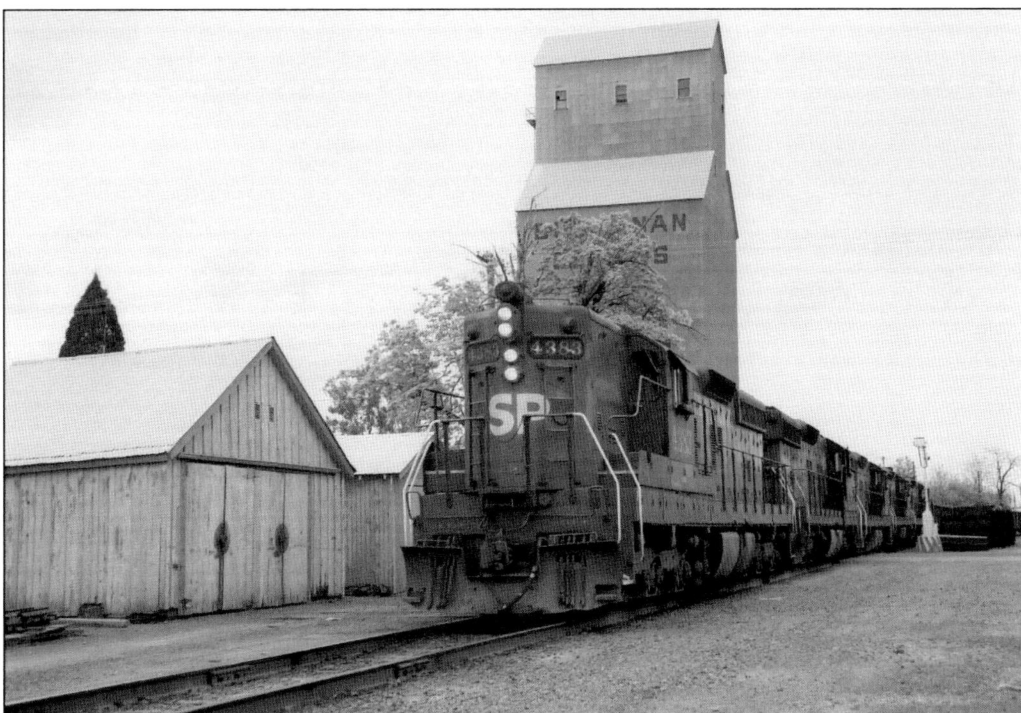

The SP's Westside Line remained a viable source of freight traffic long after the last passenger train had departed the area. Here, the SP *Westsider* is arriving at McMinnville on April 28, 1984. The five locomotives were needed to surmount Rex Hill on the original narrow-gauge route of the Portland & Willamette Valley Railroad between Oswego and Newberg.

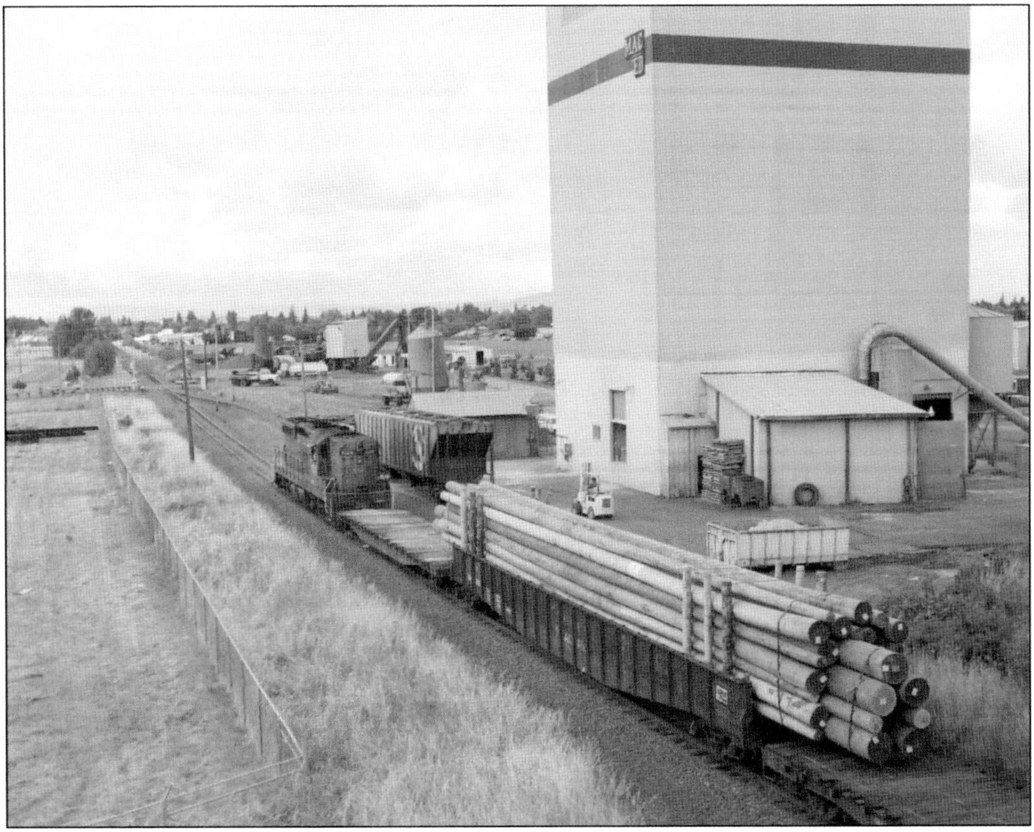

The *Willamina Turn* is returning to McMinnville from Whiteson on July 25, 1983. Note the empty flat cars required at either end of the pole load. The gondola carrying poles is 65 feet long, giving some perspective on the height of the trees from which these poles came.

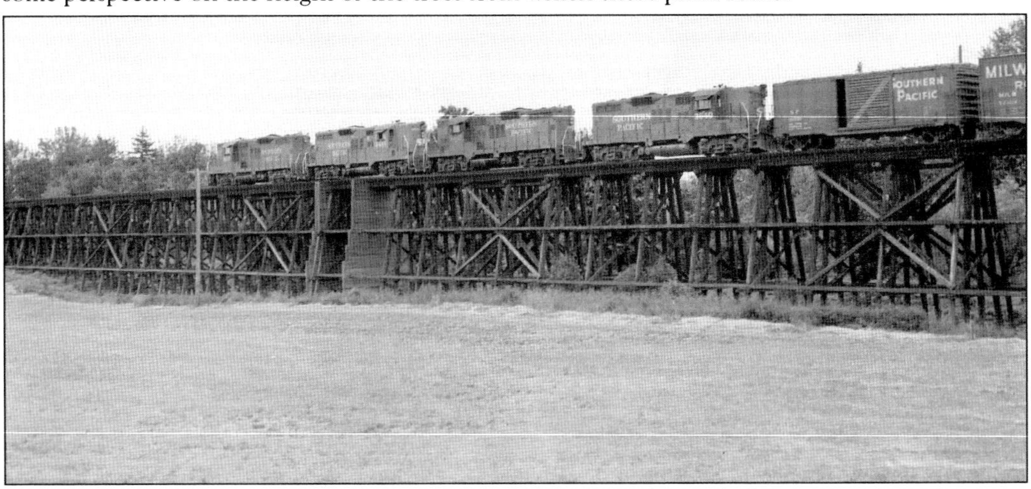

The *First Northsider* is seen on the approach to the South Yamhill River crossing between McMinnville and Whiteson on June 22, 1974. This section was built as standard gauge by the Western Oregon Railroad under the direction of Henry Villard between 1879 and 1880. The Western Oregon Railroad was controlled by the O&C and became part of the Southern Pacific Railroad in 1887.

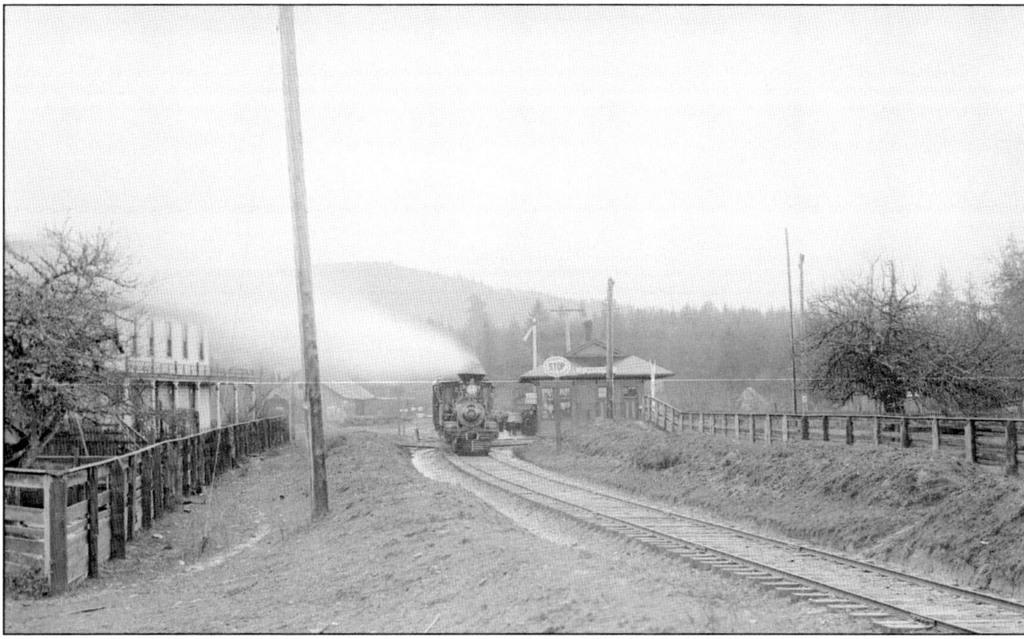

When Henry Villard extended the Western Oregon Railroad south from St. Joseph beginning in 1879, the DS&GR narrow-gauge line had already been serving Whiteson since the previous fall. Thus, when the standard-gauge line reached Whiteson, a 90 degree crossing at grade was necessary. Subsequently, Whiteson became a significant junction point between the two railroads. Here, a northbound standard-gauge passenger train has stopped at the Whiteson depot with the rear of the locomotive blocking the narrow-gauge crossing.

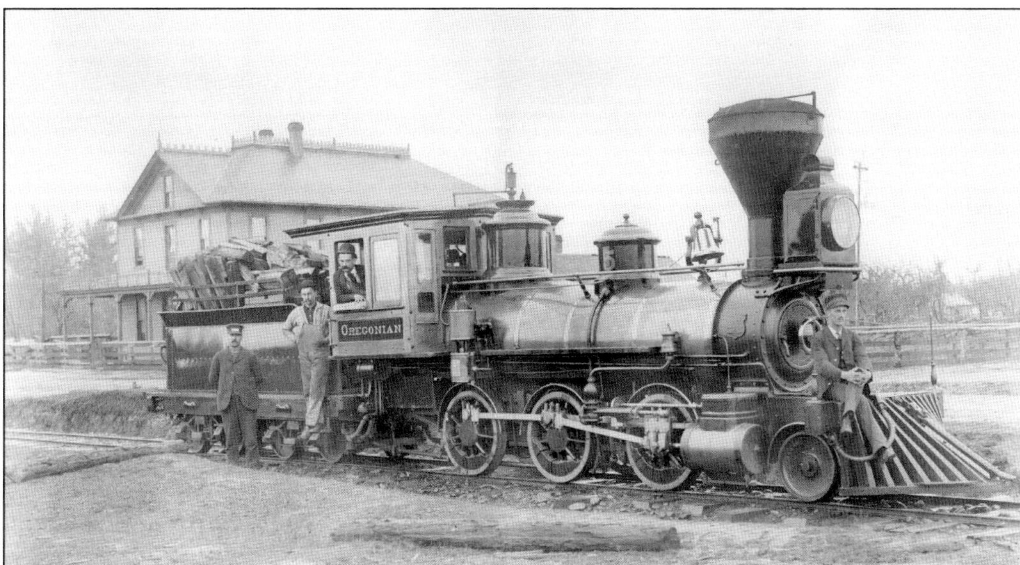

In this view, narrow-gauge 2-6-0 No. 5 is stopped at Whiteson on the track headed to Dayton Junction. Visible behind the locomotive is the south end of the hotel, the west side of which is seen to the left in the previous image. The hotel served passengers needing to stay overnight at Whiteson in order to make connections between the two railroads. Apparently the DS&GR and the O&C made little effort to coordinate their schedules, much to the advantage of the hotel.

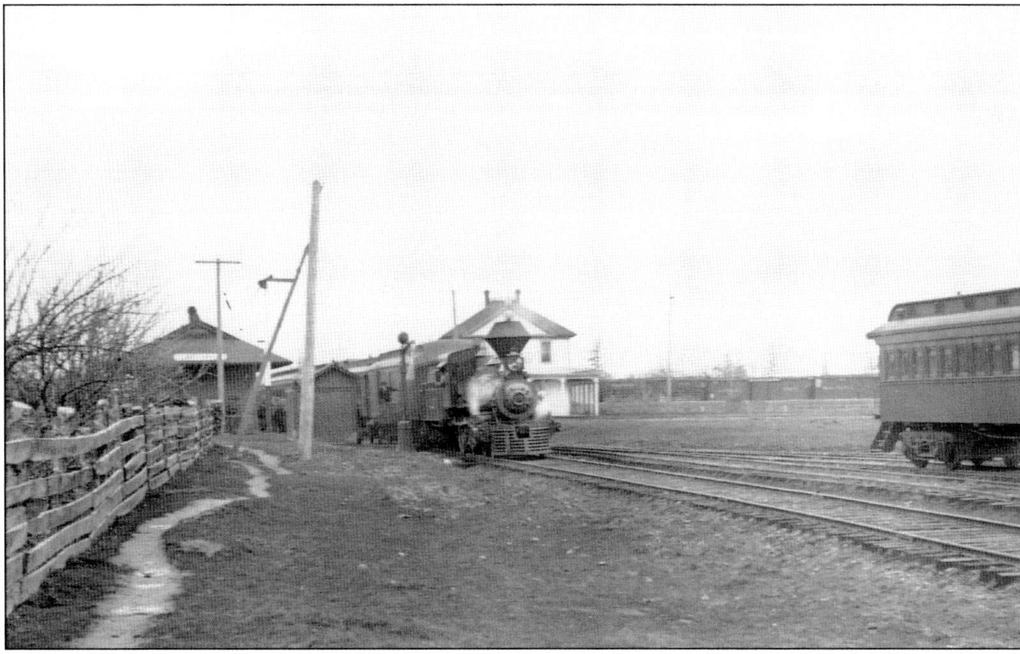

This later view finds a southbound passenger train stopped at Whiteson. The original narrow-gauge line would have crossed between the hotel and the depot near the rear of the train. The standard-gauge freight cars in the background are on a connection between the original narrow-gauge route and the SP line to Corvallis.

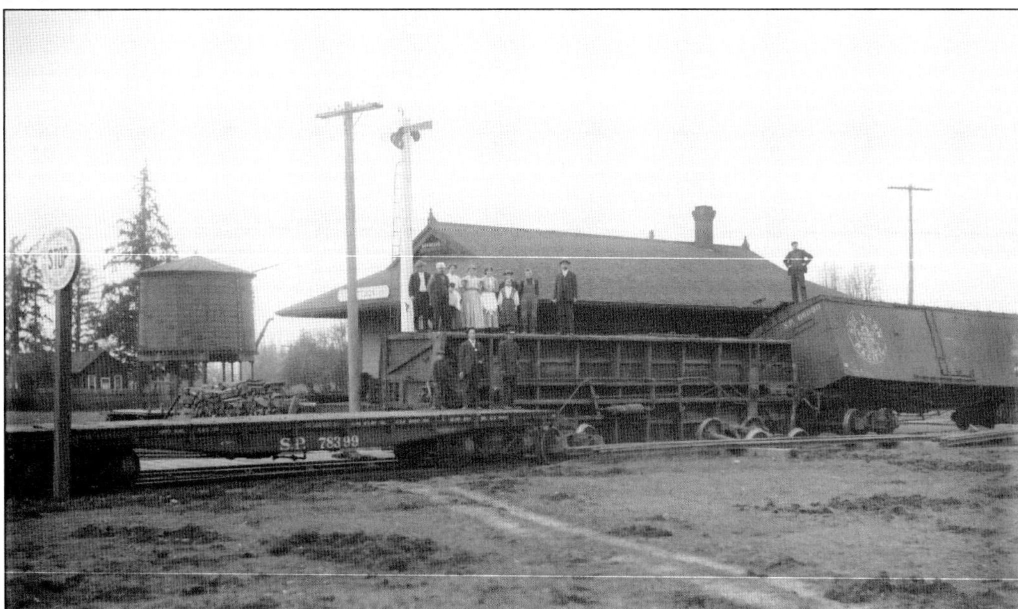

A little mishap at Whiteson in 1902 seems to have left the depot untouched, although the agent on duty at the time might have been slightly jarred. This view looks to the west toward Sheridan with the original narrow-gauge line passing to the right of the depot beyond SP boxcar No. 66030. A wye was later constructed at this point, which was still being used by the Portland & Western Railroad in 2014.

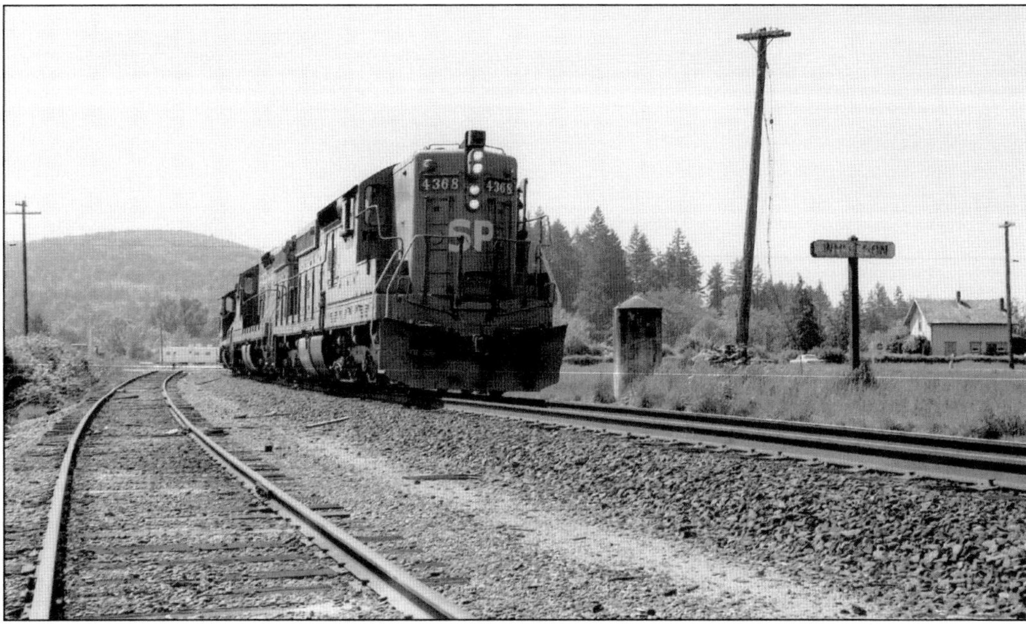

On May 12, 1979, a Westside train is rolling past the signboard at Whiteson. This job was taking empty cars north to Hillsboro, where they will be stored pending an upswing in traffic. The Whiteson depot would have been to the right behind the diesels, and the hotel would have been just out of this view to the left of the track. The original narrow-gauge line crossed here on the grade now used by Whiteson Road.

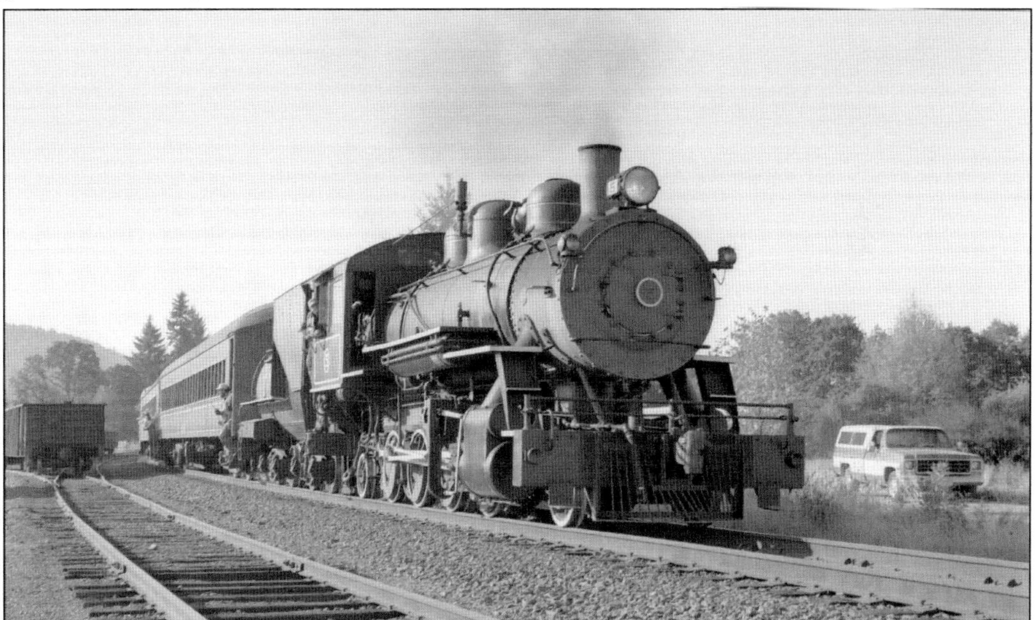

Steam returned to Whiteson on September 13, 1989, albeit only for the movies. This classy locomotive spent several days on the line between Whiteson and Corvallis filming a Hollywood movie. The name of the movie is long forgotten, but the presence of the little steamer was duly recorded by several photographers.

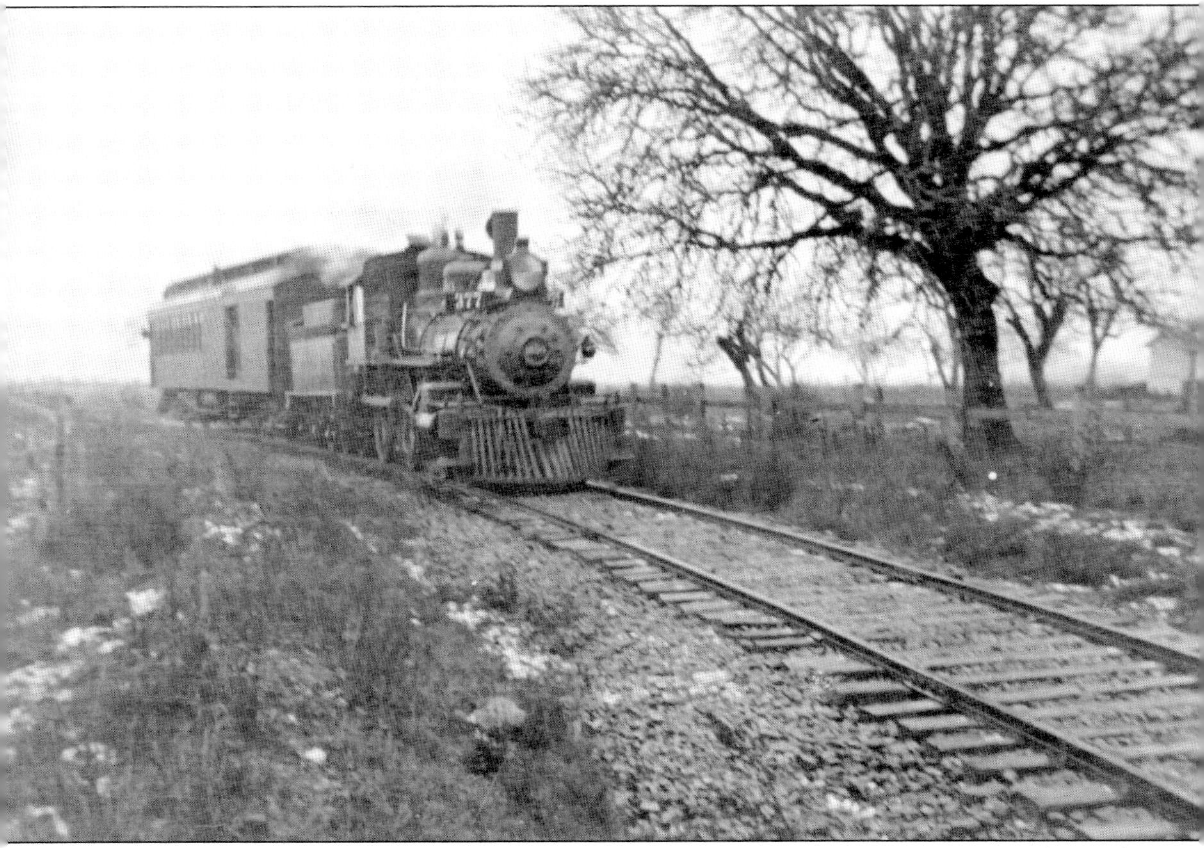

This rare action view finds engineer Charles Patrick bringing SP 4-4-0 No. 1400 and a single combine car down Ballston Hill near Wabash in January 1923. The "377" visible on the locomotive's indicator boards means that this is train No. 377, scheduled to leave Willamina at 7:25 a.m. with an 8:20 a.m. arrival at Whiteson. Here, a connection will be made with the Red Electric interurban running between Corvallis and Portland. At 9:45 a.m., No. 1400 and her combine car would return to Willamina running as train No. 378, only to repeat the trip in the afternoon as trains No. 380 and No. 379.

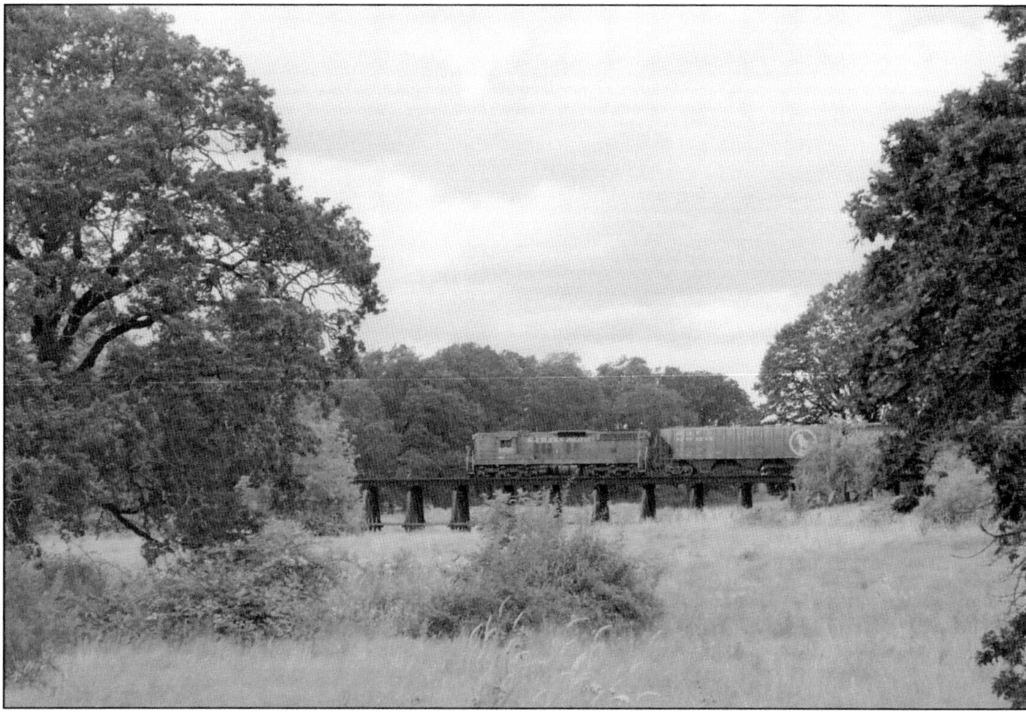

The *Willamina Turn* is seen headed west between Whiteson and Broadmead on July 25, 1983. This SP job usually worked between McMinnville and Willamina, but this day's trip would be a bit unusual. The covered hopper trailing No. 4326 is destined for Perrydale, thus necessitating a rare side trip out what remained of the old line to Airlie. Although nearly overgrown with grass and seldom used, the track was still in place from Broadmead to Perrydale until 1985.

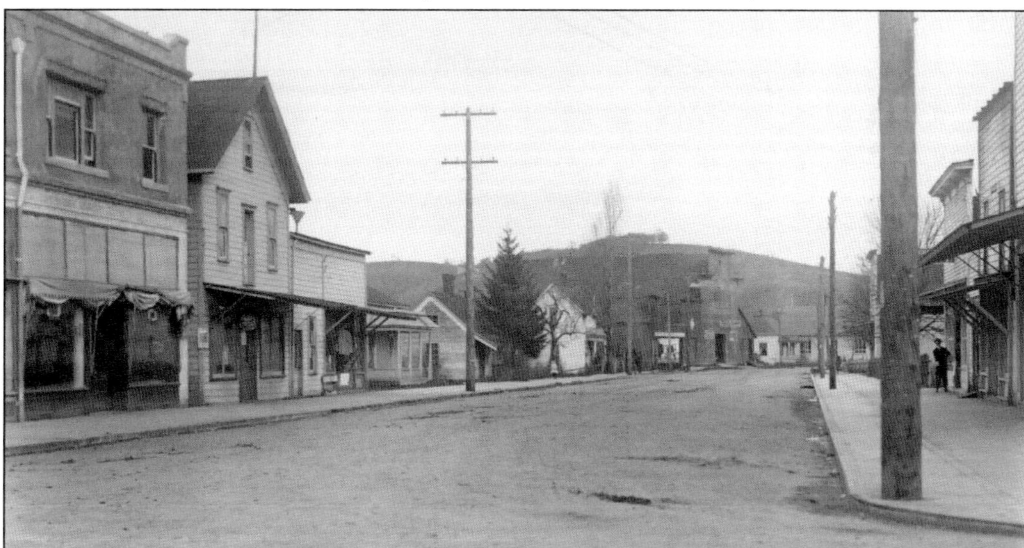

Apparently the citizens of Sheridan were camera shy when this view of Main Street was taken, or perhaps the photographer just got up very early on a Sunday. In either case, the scene depicts a typical early 20th century farming community in the Willamette Valley.

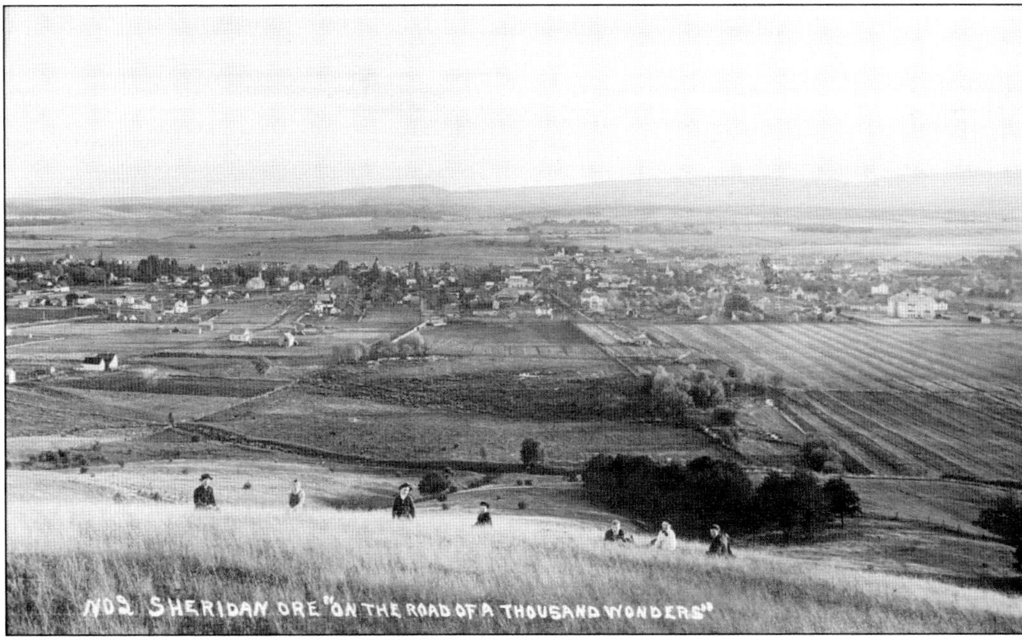

The narrow-gauge DS&GR began revenue service to Sheridan on October 24, 1878, providing local farmers access to markets in Portland and beyond via a steamboat connection at Fulquartz Landing. By 1893, the track had been converted to standard-gauge and was owned by the Southern Pacific, which had come to dominate rail service in the Willamette Valley, not to mention much of the West Coast. By the early 20th century Sheridan had grown significantly, as seen in these two panoramic views. Passenger trains now made two round trips daily between Sheridan and Whiteson, where connections could be made to Portland via Red Electric interurban trains.

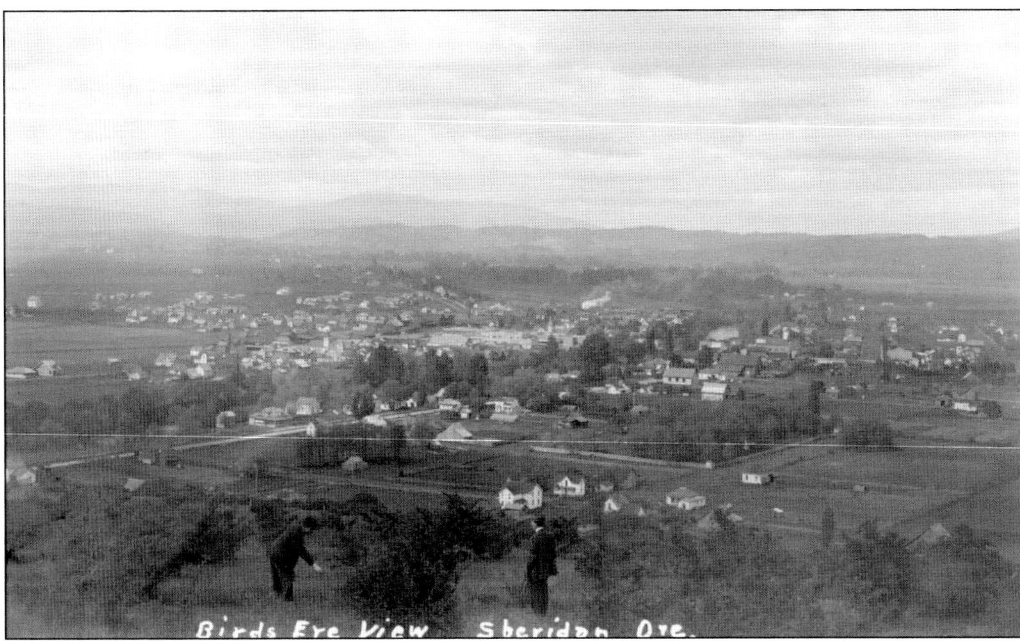

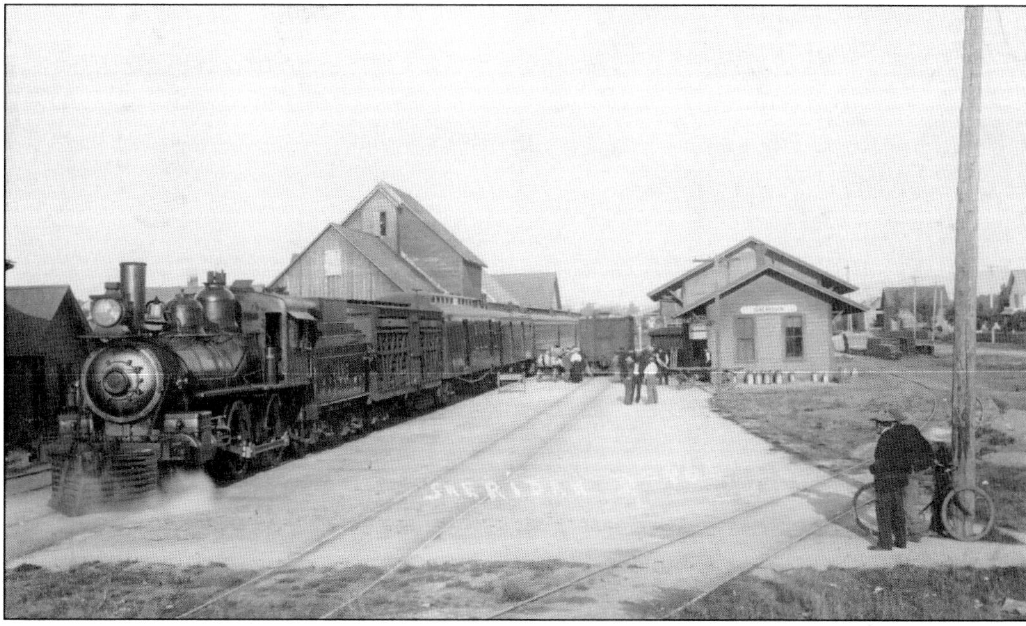

SP 4-4-0 No. 1395 was built in 1888 and is seen here leading a mixed train at Sheridan around 1908. Note the livestock car directly behind the locomotive. Slack action between the train cars was at a minimum near the front of the train, thus making for a safer ride for the animals. Next came mail and baggage cars, where employees were on their feet working. Passengers riding farther back in the train were expected to remain seated or be able to look out for themselves.

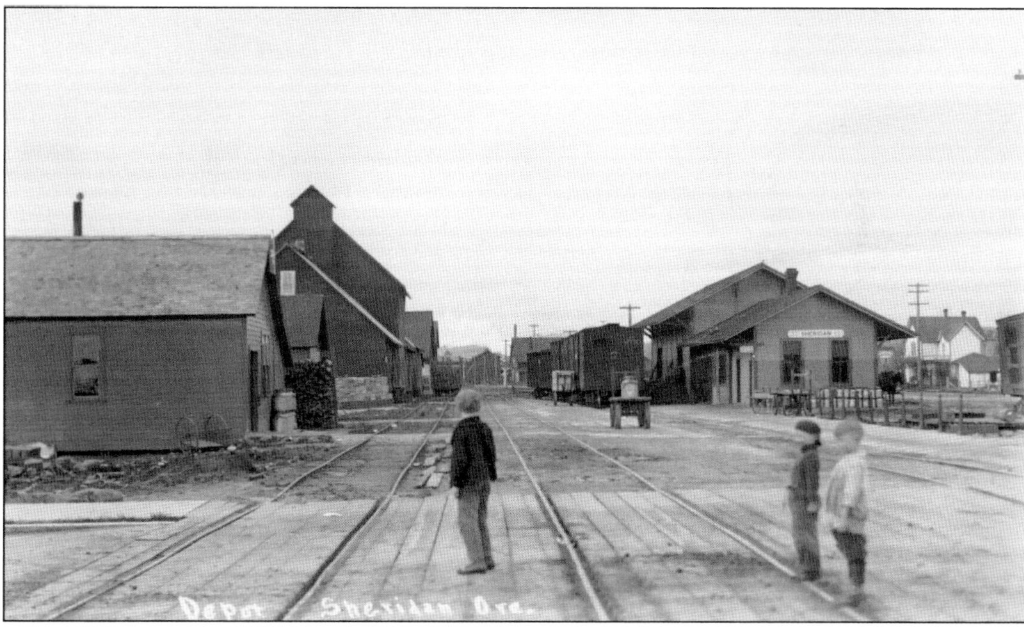

What did young boys living in Sheridan around the turn of the last century do for entertainment? Hang out where the action was, naturally, and that would be around the train depot. At a time when travel beyond the immediate area was not an everyday occurrence, the coming and going of the train was an event worthy of note. Romantic visions of a larger world could be conjured by the image of the locomotives and the men who ran them.

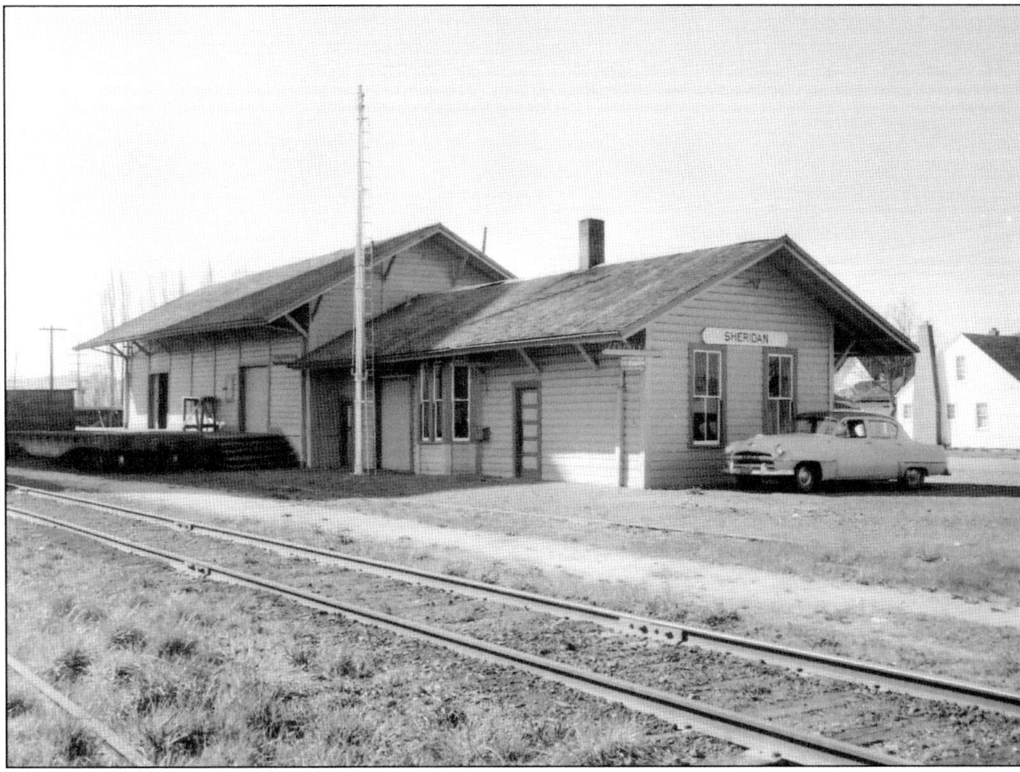

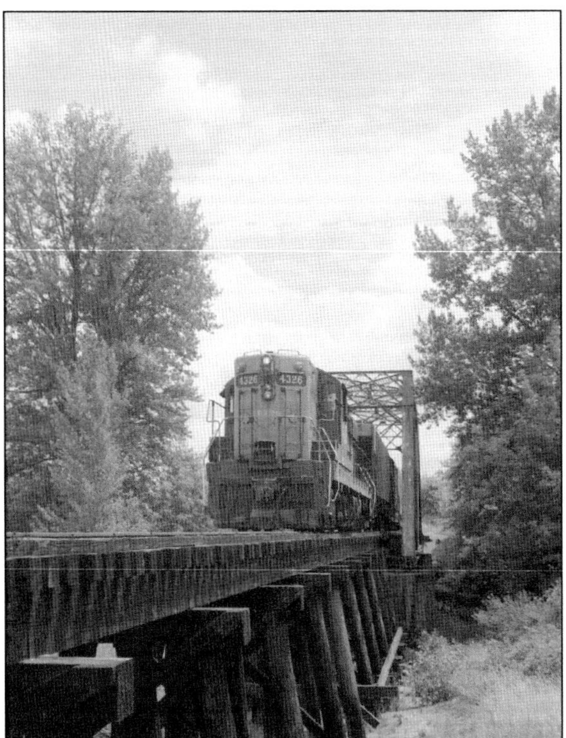

Although it would be retired in 1964, the depot at Sheridan appears well maintained in this 1959 photograph. This structure was one of four similar depots built during the narrow-gauge era between 1878 and 1882. The others were located at West Scio, Dallas, and Monmouth. However, the building seen here would hardly be recognized by folks from that time. Extensive modifications and repainting have given the building a Southern Pacific look.

The Willamina Turn is crossing the South Yamhill River just west of Sheridan on July 25, 1983. This section west from Sheridan was built in 1907 by the Sheridan & Willamina Railroad to serve lumber interests and a large brick plant located at Willamina. The Sheridan & Willamina Railroad came under Southern Pacific control in 1913 as part of an SP plan to extend electric interurban service throughout the Willamette Valley, but this plan was never fully realized.

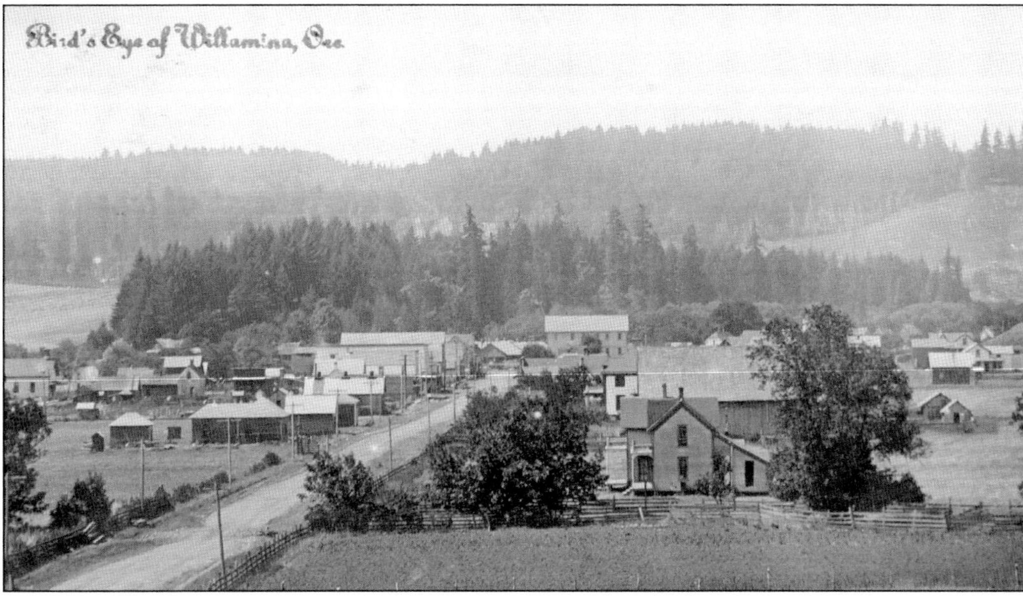

Willamina was nestled in the foothills of Oregon's Coast Range mountains, and thus, it was close to extensive stands of timber, as seen in this view looking west around 1909. The railroad would be to the left just out of view.

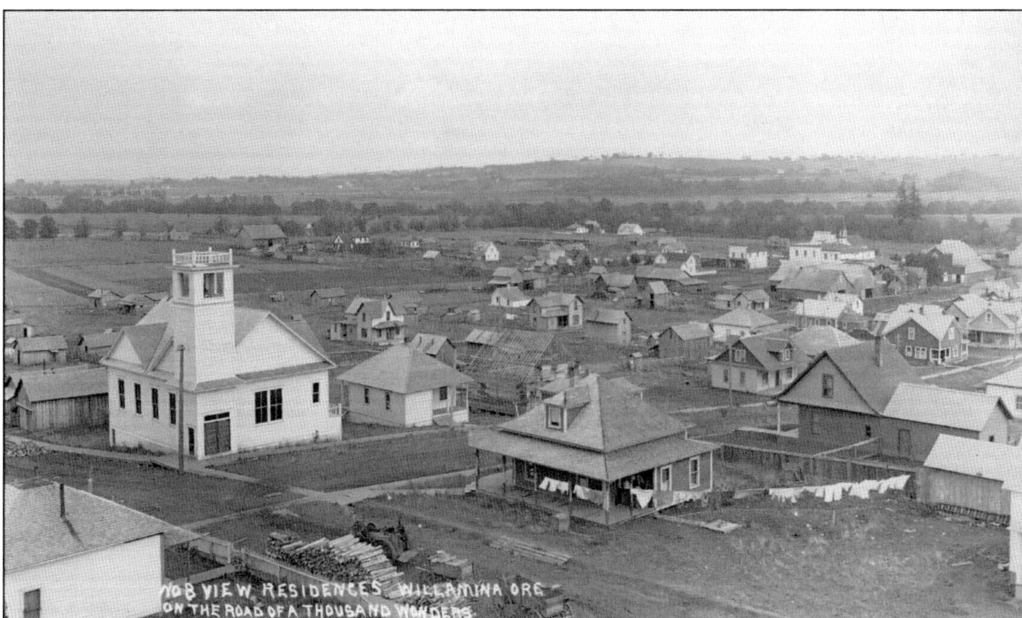

Willamina is seen here looking toward the southeast around 1912. The railroad from Sheridan enters the view in the upper left, passing above the white church tower and continuing along the south side of town.

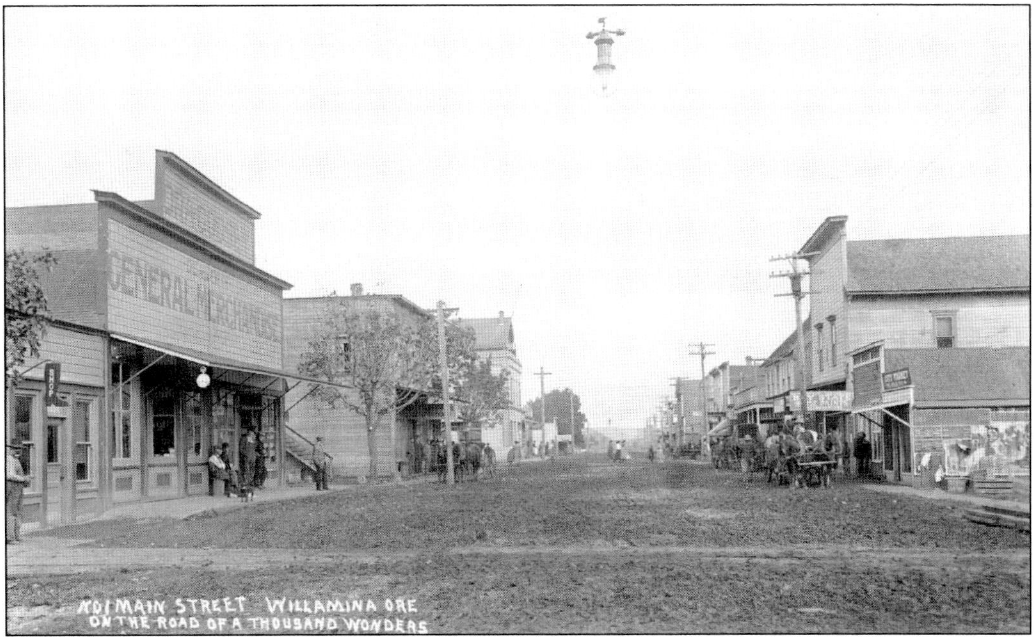

Electricity came to Willamina in 1903, thus facilitating the streetlights seen hanging overhead. However, it appears paved streets were still in the future when this photograph was taken looking east on Main Street. The combination of dirt streets and roads along with Oregon's propensity for rain made railroads a necessity at the beginning of the 20th century.

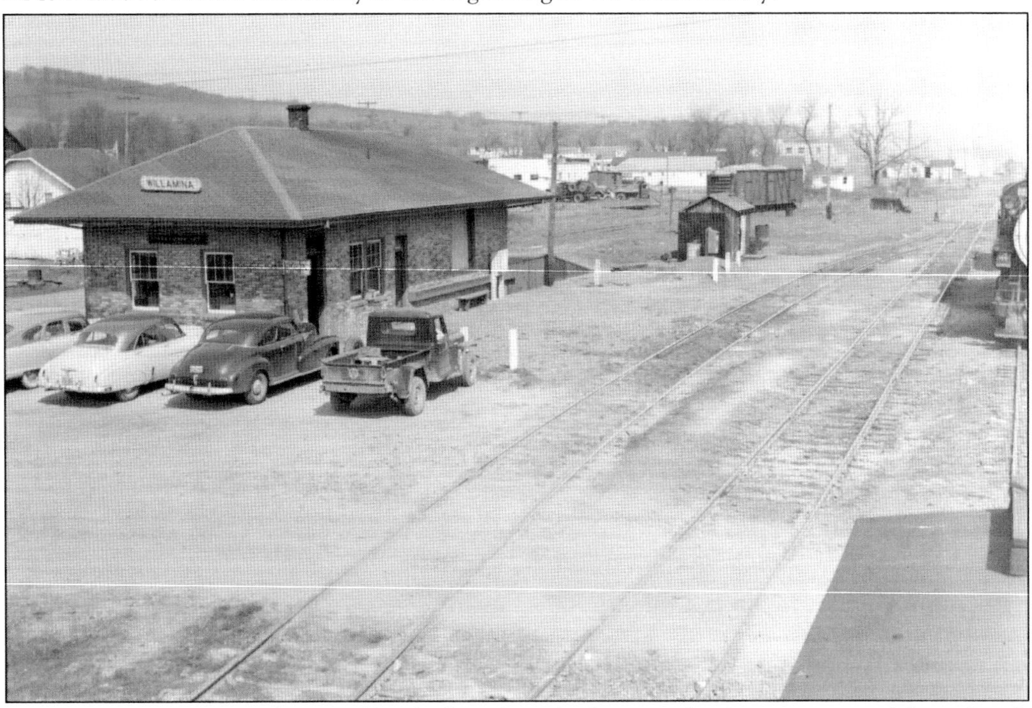

Given its proximity to a substantial brick plant that also happened to be a customer of the railroad, it is not surprising that the Willamina depot was constructed of brick. The 20-foot-by-51-foot depot was built in 1911 and served the railroad until 1977. It is seen here looking east in 1949.

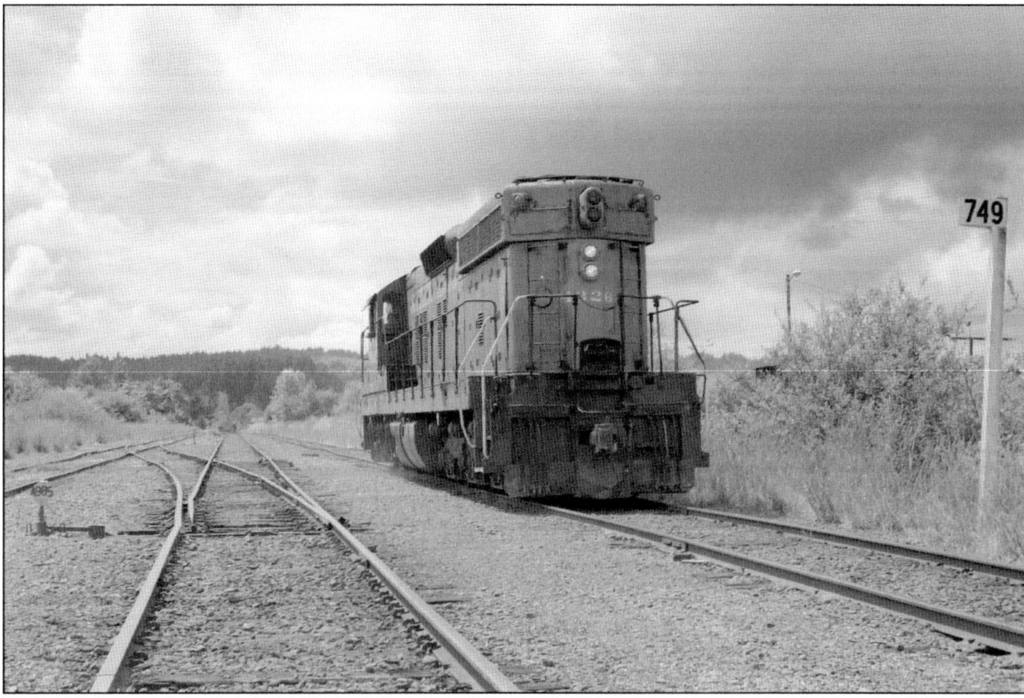

The power for the *Willamina Turn* pauses at Willamina prior to returning to McMinnville on July 25, 1983. The milepost to the right indicates that it is 749 miles from this point to San Francisco on Southern Pacific rails. At the time, San Francisco was considered milepost 0 on the SP and the distance to all other connected locations were measured from that starting point by the railroad.

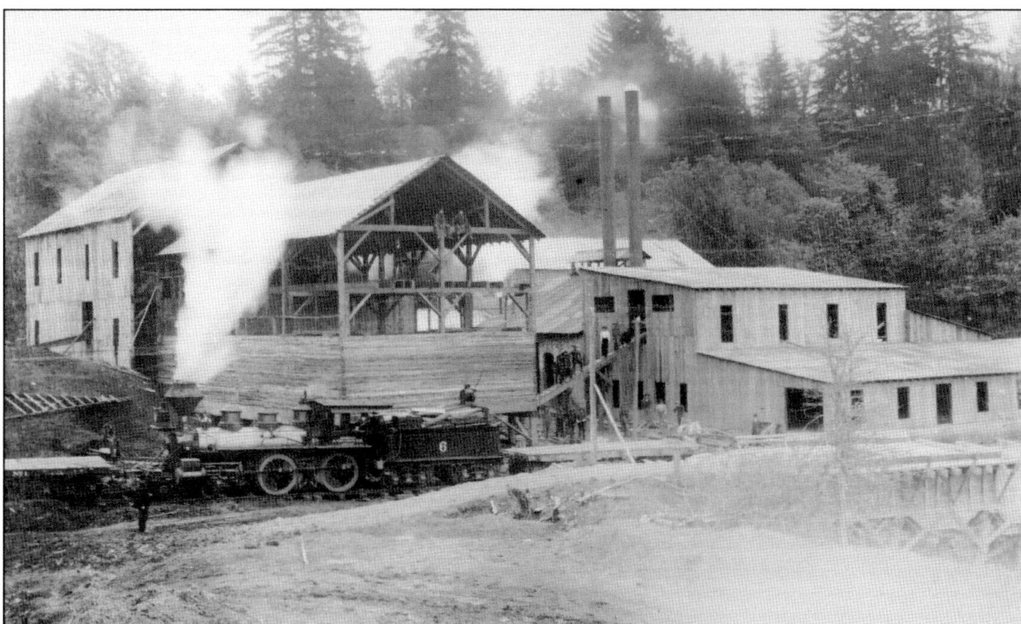

Sheridan & Willamina 4-4-0 No. 6 is working at the brick plant, which appears to be undergoing renovation in this c. 1910 view.

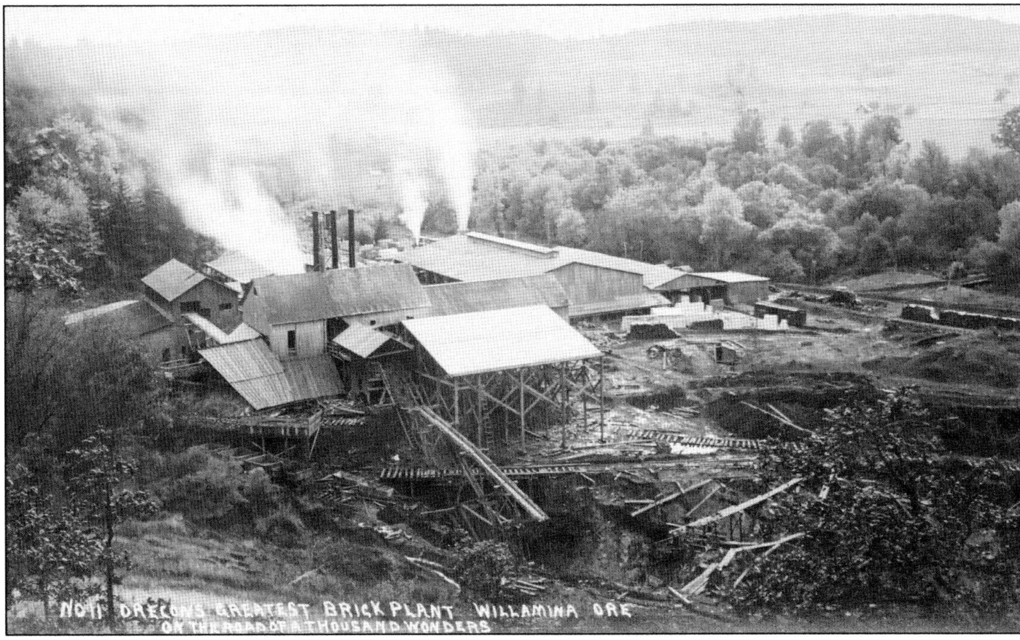

These two photographs give a good overview of the facilities at the Willamina brick plant around 1915. Note the boxcars to the right near the loading shed in these views. For many years, this plant supplied firebrick to the Southern Pacific Railroad's boiler shop at the Brooklyn roundhouse in Portland. Firebrick was a necessary component in steam locomotive boilers.

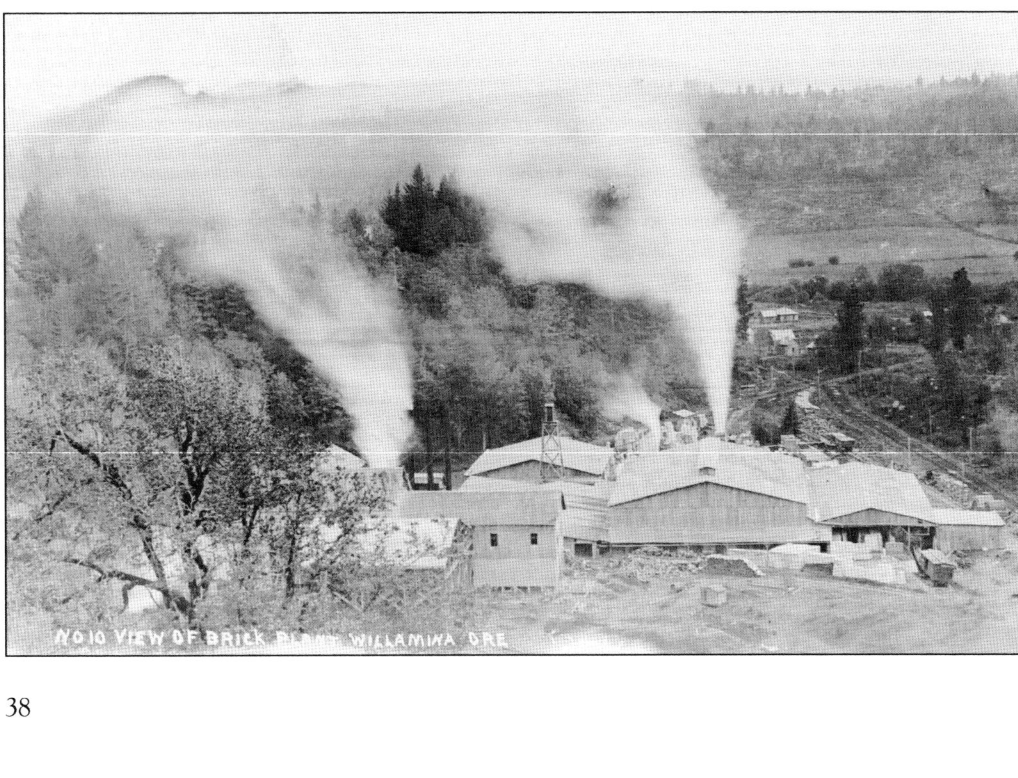

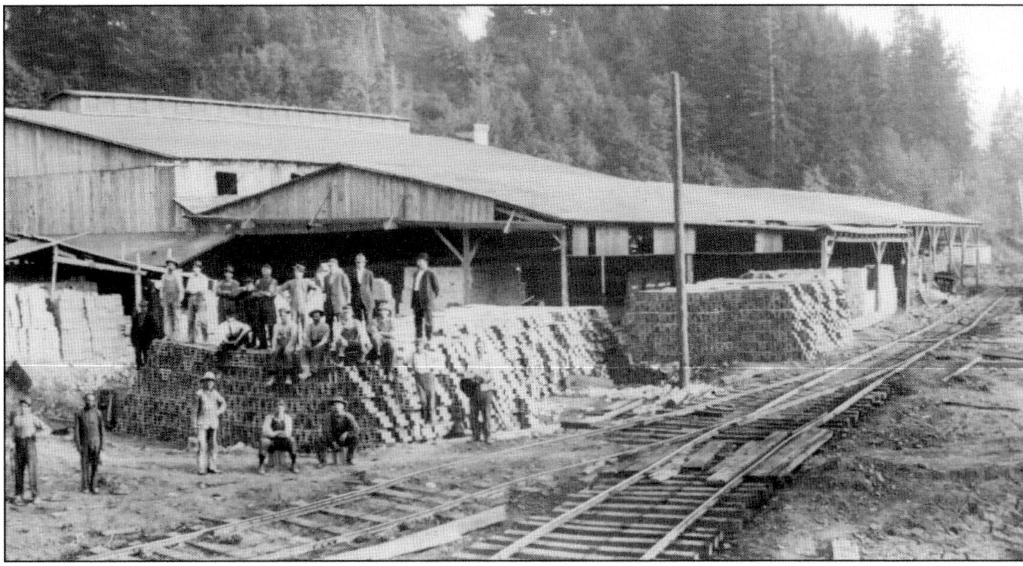

A closer view of the loading shed indicates a substantial inventory of brick is on hand and ready for shipment. Note the crude track work serving the plant.

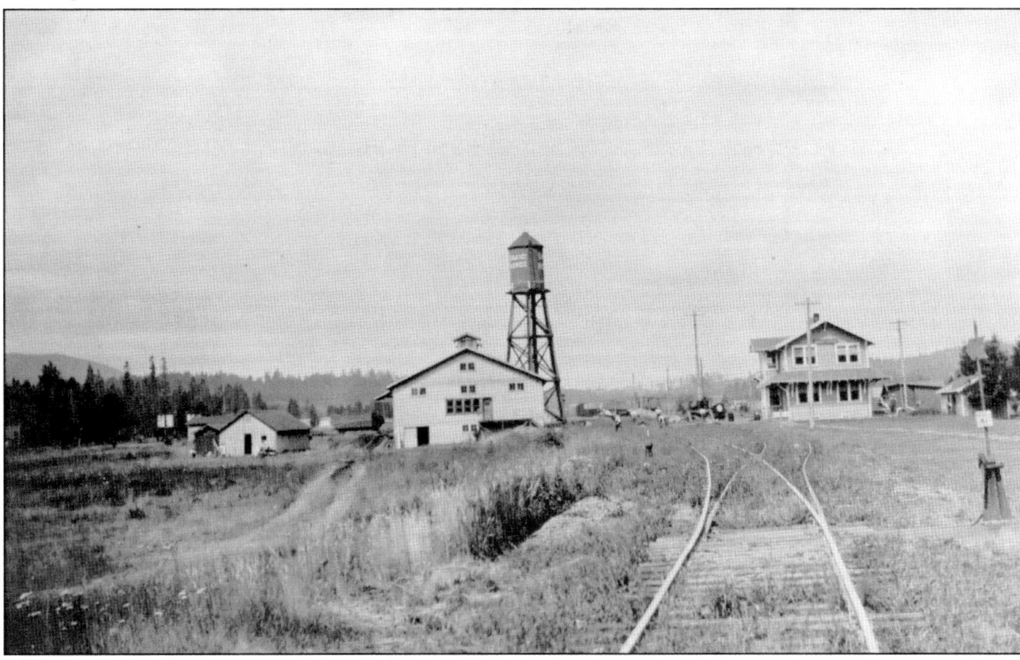

Although the Southern Pacific rails ended at Willamina, an independent shortline railroad continued west from Willamina another eight miles to Grand Ronde serving timber and lumber interests. This line was built by the Willamina & Grand Ronde Railroad between June 1920 and November 1921. During the next 20 years, the line was owned by no less than five different companies, including the Long-Bell Lumber Co. In 1944, Long-Bell was shipping 40 car loads of logs a day out of Grand Ronde. In January 1955, the line became the Northern Division of the Longview, Portland & Northern (LP&N) Railroad, at which point the LP&N owned three unconnected railroads, two in Oregon and one in Washington. This photograph looking west shows the LP&N depot and yard facilities at Grand Ronde in the late 1950s.

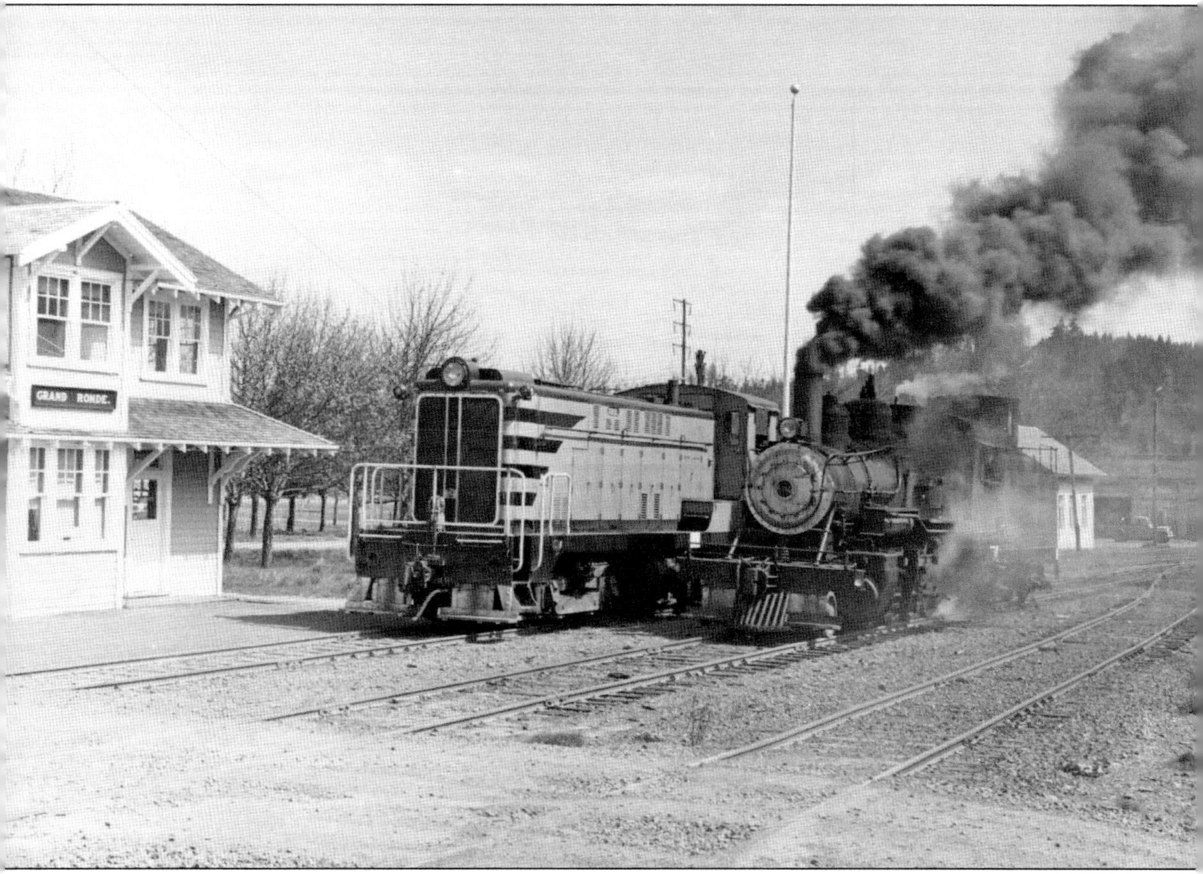

The end of steam on the LP&N symbolically took place in 1960, when Baldwin-built 2-8-0 No. 680 was replaced by Baldwin diesel No. 1001. However, this was not the end for No. 680. She remained in the engine shed at Grand Ronde until 1977, when she was sold to the Virginia & Truckee Railroad for use on its tourist operation at Virginia City, Nevada. During the 17 years No. 680 was stored at Grand Ronde she was occasionally, albeit unofficially, steamed up so as to "stretch her legs."

Two

Broadmead to Airlie

Construction of the Dayton, Sheridan & Grand Ronde Railroad began in earnest in the summer of 1878. Seeing that the narrow-gauge line would soon be a reality and recognizing the value of a rail connection to their community, citizens of Dallas voted a $17,000 subsidy to entice the DS&GR to extend a branch to their city. Construction of the line began at Broadmead (originally called Sheridan Junction) and by January 1879, the narrow-gauge rails had reached Smithfield with the grade completed another four miles south toward Dallas. At this point, financial difficulties brought construction to a halt.

Construction of the DS&GR had been backed by selling transportation scrip. Now, local farmers were paying for transportation using the scrip they had received in return for their initial investments. The result was a lack of cash, which ultimately forced the fledgling narrow-gauge line into receivership.

William Reid, having foreseen great potential in the narrow-gauge railroad, took advantage of the line's financial difficulty and with backing from Scottish investors, gained control of the DS&GR in June 1879. The influx of cash from Scotland allowed construction to resume and the extension from Smithfield to Dallas was completed on June 1, 1880. The track was extended south from Dallas to Airlie by September 1881.

By now, Henry Villard had become concerned that the expansive plans being projected by the Oregonian Railway could challenge his Oregon & California Railroad for dominance of transportation in Oregon's Willamette Valley. Thus, Villard was forced to gain control of the—in his view—upstart narrow-gauge intruder. This he successfully accomplished effective October 1, 1881. During the period the O&C controlled the Oregonian Railway until May 1, 1884, service continued on the line from Broadmead to Airlie, albeit to suit the needs of the O&C. Following the collapse of Villard's railroad empire attempts were made to revitalize the now highly deteriorated narrow-gauge system, but they were ultimately unsuccessful.

On April 4, 1890, the Oregonian Railway was sold in foreclosure to Richard Koehler acting on behalf of the Southern Pacific Company, which now controlled the O&C. Acquisition of the narrow-gauge system provided the SP with valuable feeder lines throughout the Willamette Valley, and the track from Broadmead to Airlie was one such line. The line from Broadmead to Airlie was converted to standard gauge by 1893 and subsequently operated as the SP's Airlie Branch. With changing economics, the line to Airlie became less useful and the track between Perrydale and Airlie was abandoned in sections starting in 1927. By 1934, only the section from Broadmead to Perrydale remained active. Train service on this segment continued until mid-1985, after which the last rails were removed. Today, little trace of the original narrow-gauge line remains.

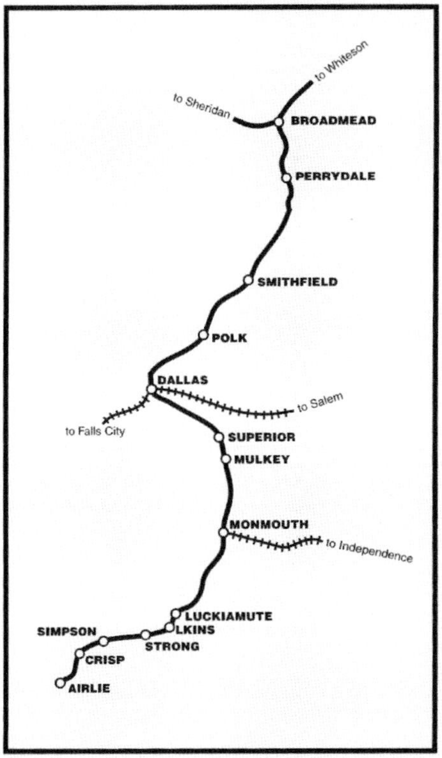

Railroad Broadmead to Airlie

With Southern Pacific Railroad lines shown for reference

This map gives a simplified overview of the narrow-gauge railway from Broadmead to Airlie. Significant station points are indicated, although not all of these were necessarily in use during the years the line was narrow gauge. Related Southern Pacific Railroad routes are shown as crosshatched lines for reference. Again, however, not all of these SP lines existed concurrently with the narrow gauge. Today, none of the original narrow-gauge line from Broadmead to Airlie remains.

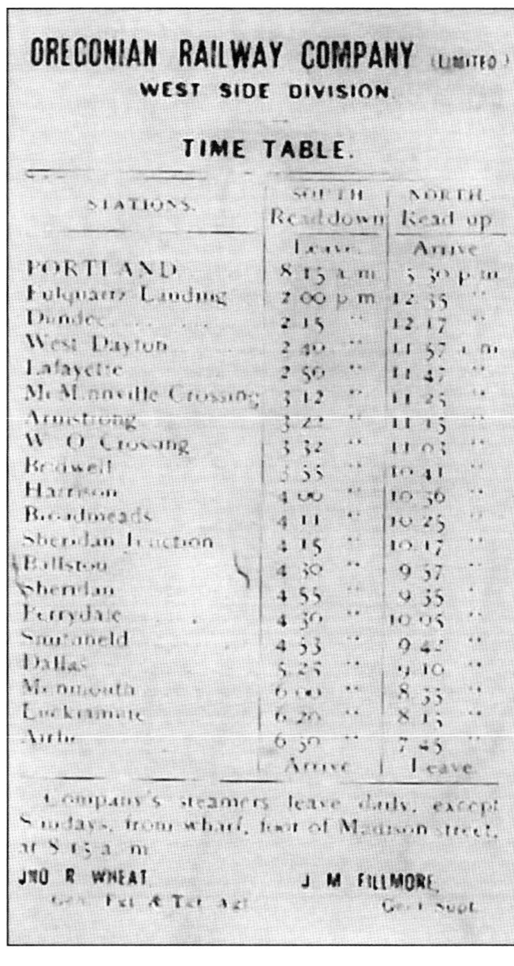

OREGONIAN RAILWAY COMPANY (LIMITED)

WEST SIDE DIVISION

TIME TABLE.

STATIONS.	SOUTH Read down	NORTH Read up
	Leave.	Arrive
PORTLAND	8 15 a m	5 30 p m
Fulquartz Landing	2 00 p m	12 35 "
Dundee	2 15 "	12 17 "
West Dayton	2 40 "	11 57 a m
Lafayette	2 50 "	11 47 "
McMinnville Crossing	3 12 "	11 25 "
Armstrong	3 22 "	11 15 "
W O Crossing	3 32 "	11 03 "
Broadwell	3 55 "	10 41 "
Harrison	4 00 "	10 36 "
Broadmeads	4 11 "	10 25 "
Sheridan Junction	4 15 "	10 17 "
Ballston	4 30 "	9 57 "
Sheridan	4 55 "	9 35 "
Perrydale	4 30 "	10 05 "
Smithfield	4 53 "	9 42 "
Dallas	5 25 "	9 10 "
Monmouth	6 00 "	8 55 "
Luckiamute	6 20 "	8 15 "
Airlie	6 50 "	7 45 "
	Arrive	Leave

Company's steamers leave daily, except Sundays, from wharf, foot of Madison street, at 8 15 a m

JNO R WHEAT, Gen Frt & Tkt Agt
J M FILLMORE, Gen'l Supt

Although undated, this timetable gives a good idea of operations on the line to Airlie around the 1880s. An 8:15 a.m. departure from Portland via steamboat would get one to Fulquartz Landing by 2:00 p.m. From there, the Oregonian Railway traveled to Airlie, arriving at 6:50 p.m. This must have seemed a marvel of modern times to folks who only a few years earlier had attempted the same trip by wagon.

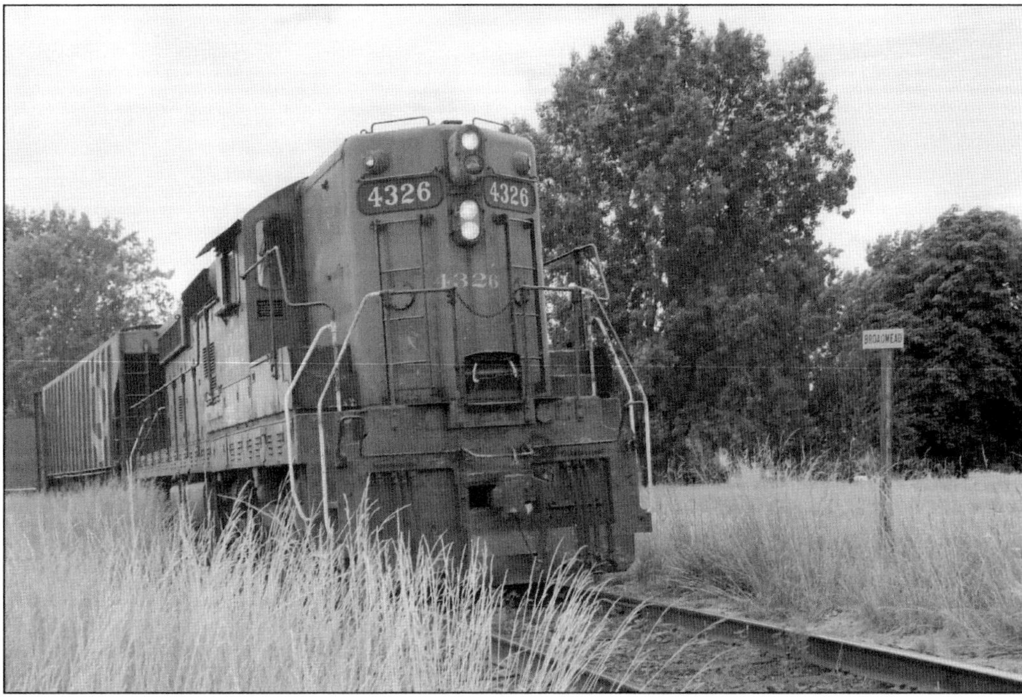

The original Oregonian narrow-gauge line to Airlie left the line between Whiteson and Sheridan at Broadmead heading south through Dallas and Monmouth. Segments of the line were successively abandoned by the Southern Pacific between 1927 and 1934 until the only remaining section extended barely two miles to Perrydale. Service on this short section continued into the mid-1980s. In these two views, SP No. 4326 is easing around the wye at Broadmead on July 25, 1983. By this date, trains seldom ventured out the line to Perrydale. This run, with engineer Winters, would turn out to be one of the last trips over this former narrow-gauge route.

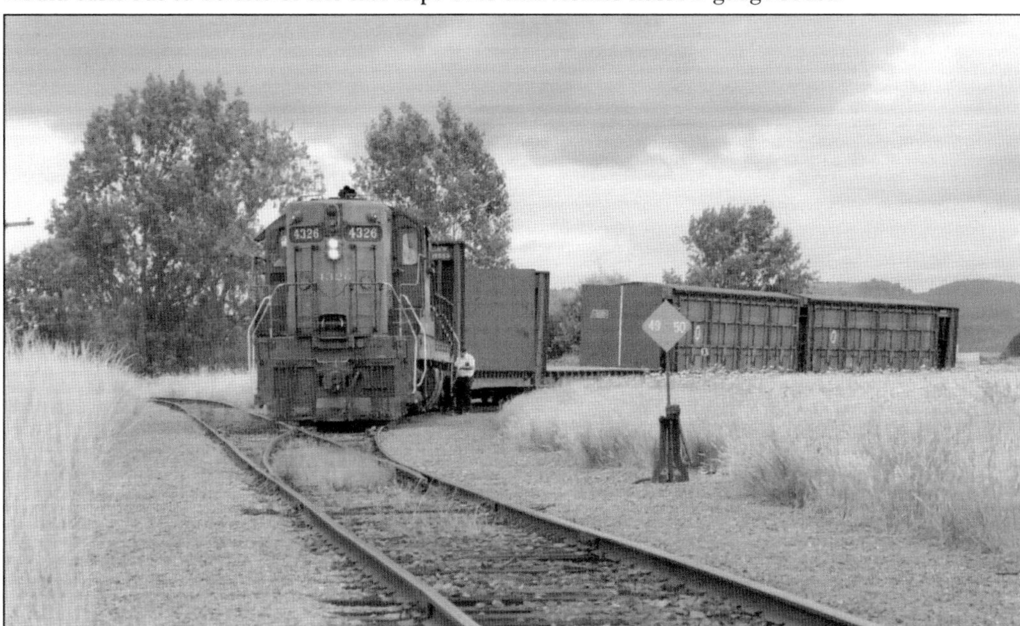

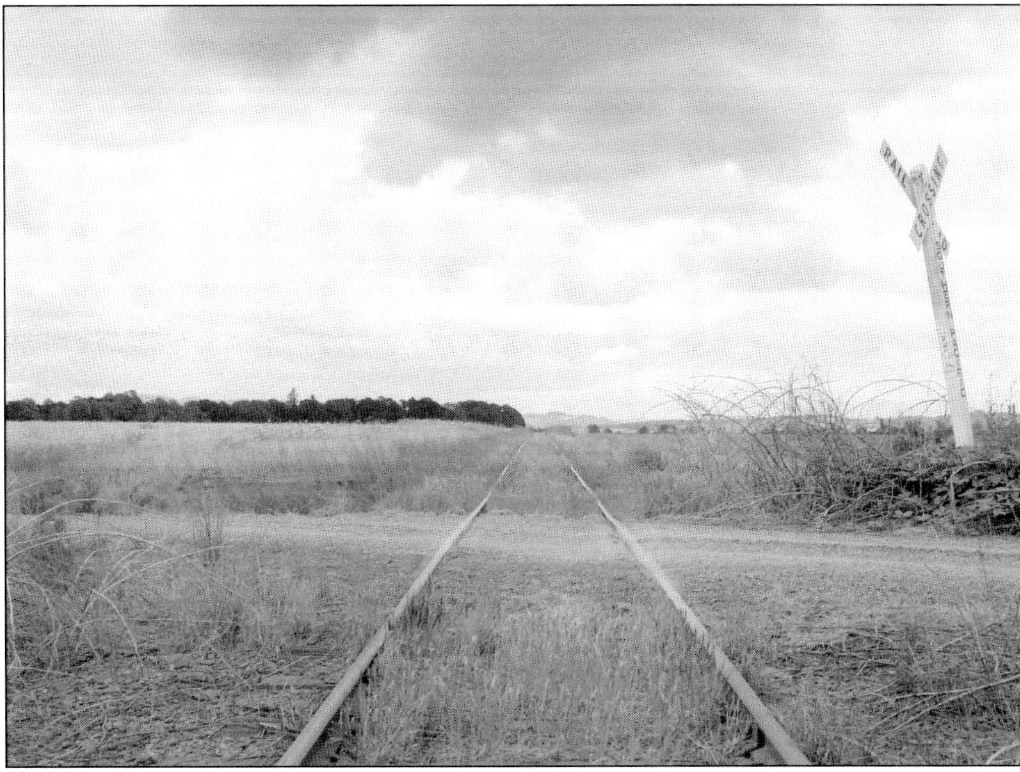

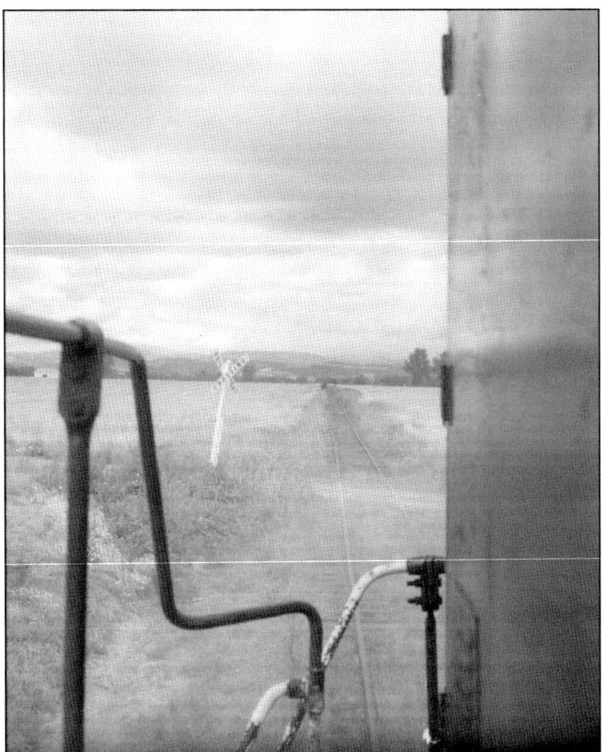

The rails are now standard gauge, meaning they are spaced four feet, eight-and-a-half inches apart, and the country roads are now graveled or at least mostly graveled. Aside from those visible clues, little appears changed from the days when the rails were spaced three feet apart and the roads were mostly dirt, or mud depending on the weather. The date is in fact July 25, 1983, and SP No. 4326 is making a rare trip over the remaining track to Perrydale.

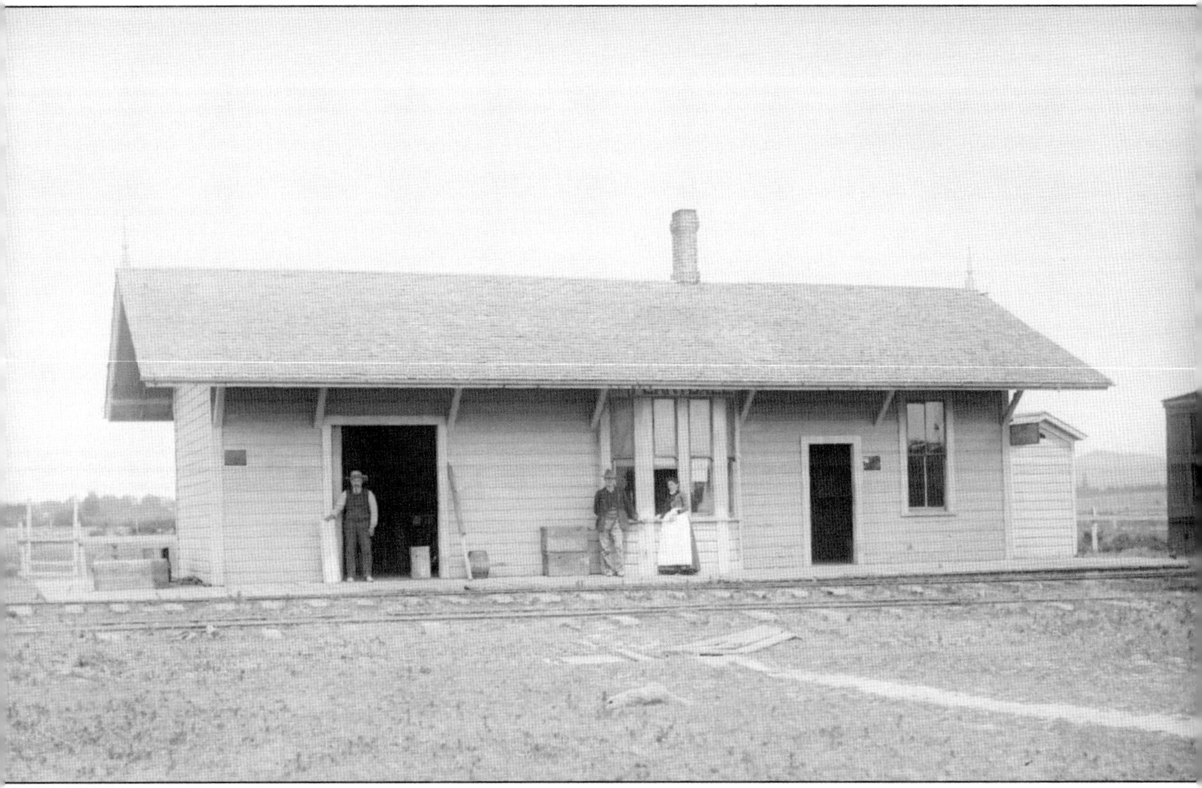

The recently completed Perrydale depot appears rather pristine in this c. 1880 view. Note the original decorative finials at either end of the roof. Also note the extremely light rail on both the main track and siding in the foreground. While indicative of narrow-gauge railroads, this light rail would not withstand the loads later carried on the line. Also interesting is the end of a boxcar barely visible at the extreme right. Careful observation reveals a link and pin coupler. Although very dangerous, these early "finger clippers" were still in use when the narrow-gauge line was built. In those days one could sometimes tell how experienced a brakeman was by how many fingers he had remaining.

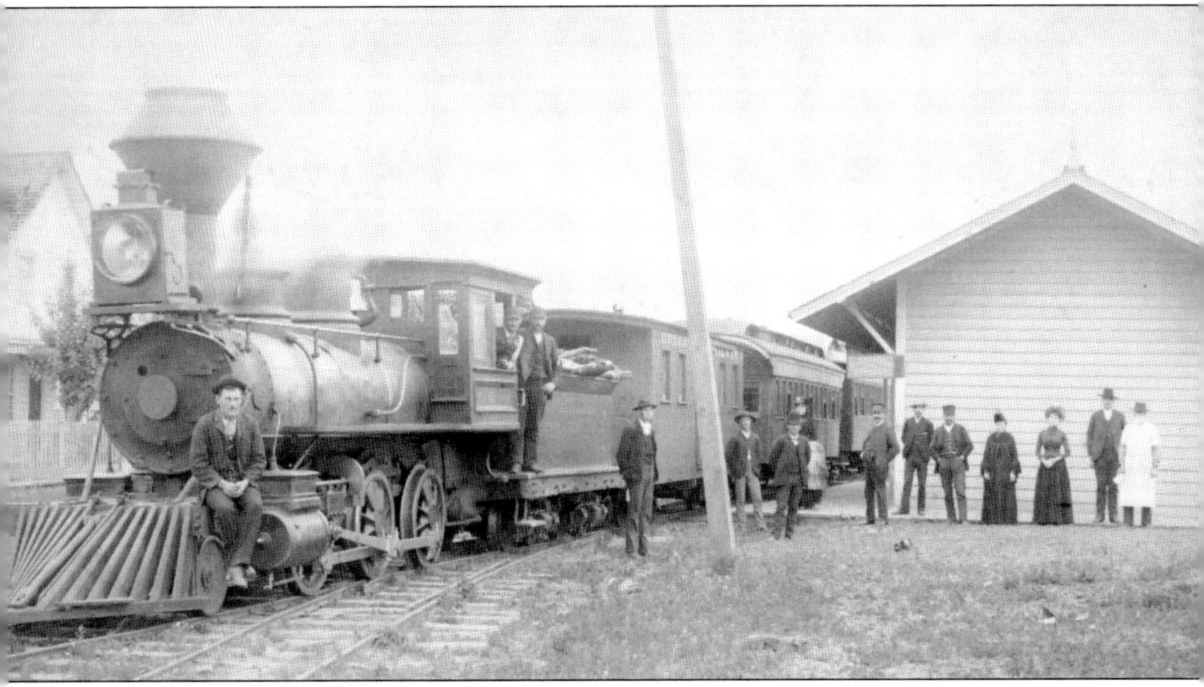

This later view finds the southbound train pausing at the Perrydale depot. If the train is on time today, it is 4:30 p.m. and the train is still two hours and 20 minutes away from Airlie. The straight boiler confirms the locomotive to be No. 4, the *Brownsville*. She was built by the Pittsburgh Locomotive Works under construction No. 430 in July 1880 and sold to the Southern Pacific of California in February 1905, where she was renumbered 1025. She was resold to the McKenzie Shipyard in Oakland, California, in September 1906.

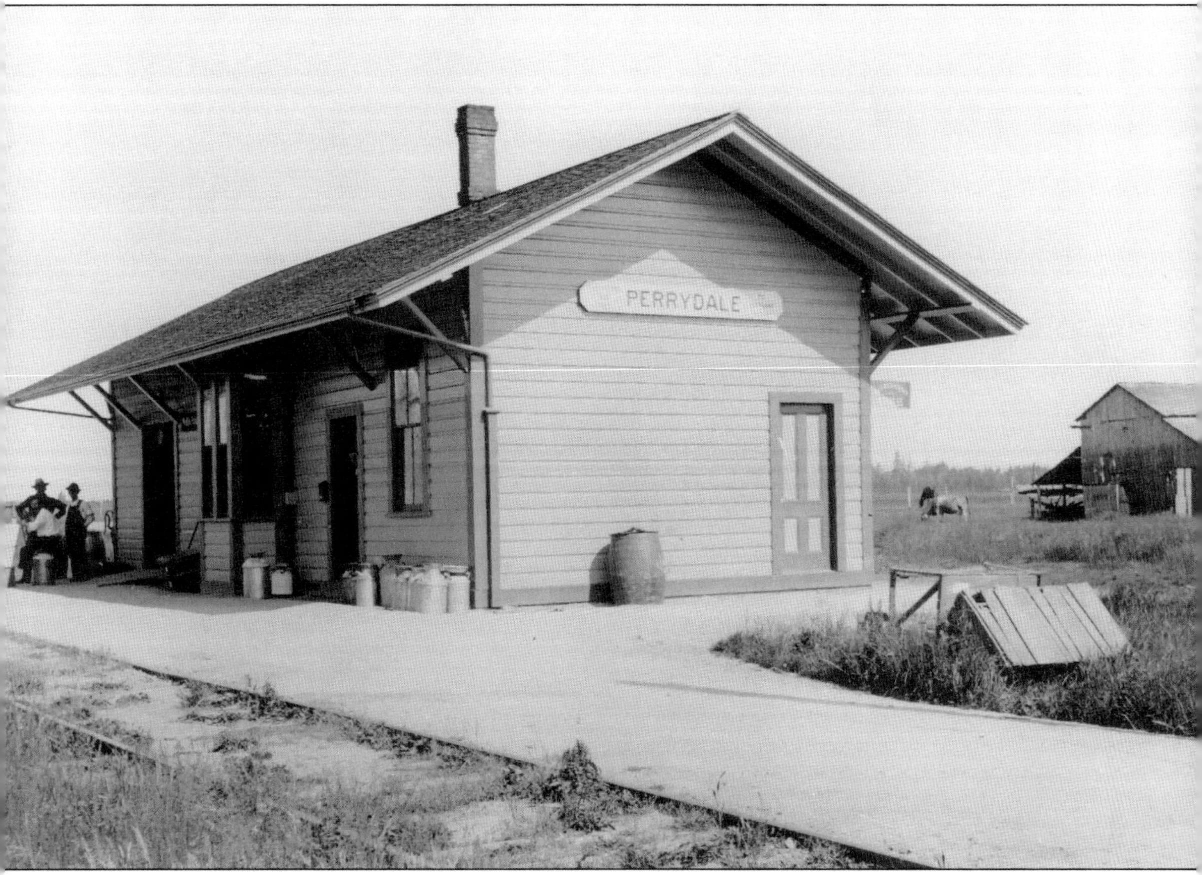

The Southern Pacific Railroad was firmly in control of the former Oregonian Railway when this photograph was taken around 1910. The track is now standard gauge, the rail slightly heavier, and the finials are gone. Otherwise, things appear little changed from previous decades. Although weeds are prevalent in the right-of-way, business still appears brisk judging by the milk cans and boxes waiting on the platform. Since the previous photograph was taken, a door has been added and the station sign has been moved to the end of the building per SP's standard practice. The Oregonian Railway seems to have preferred placing station signs above the operator's bay window. This practice would make identification of the location only possible from directly in front of the depot rather than while approaching the depot from either direction.

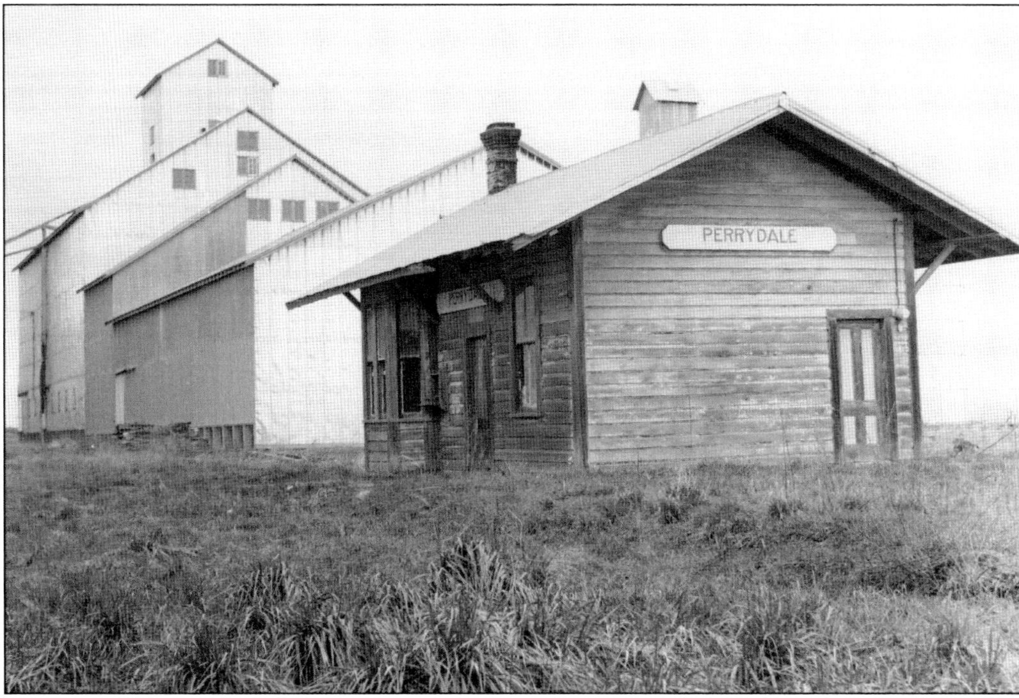

Abandoned in 1945, the Perrydale depot looked rather forlorn when these two views were recorded around 1960. The former freight section of the building is gone, but someone had the foresight to save the station sign from the old south end of the building and place it on the front wall to the right of the operator's bay window. Although by this time the track had been cut off just south of the depot, the rails are still in place in front of the depot waiting for a train that will never arrive.

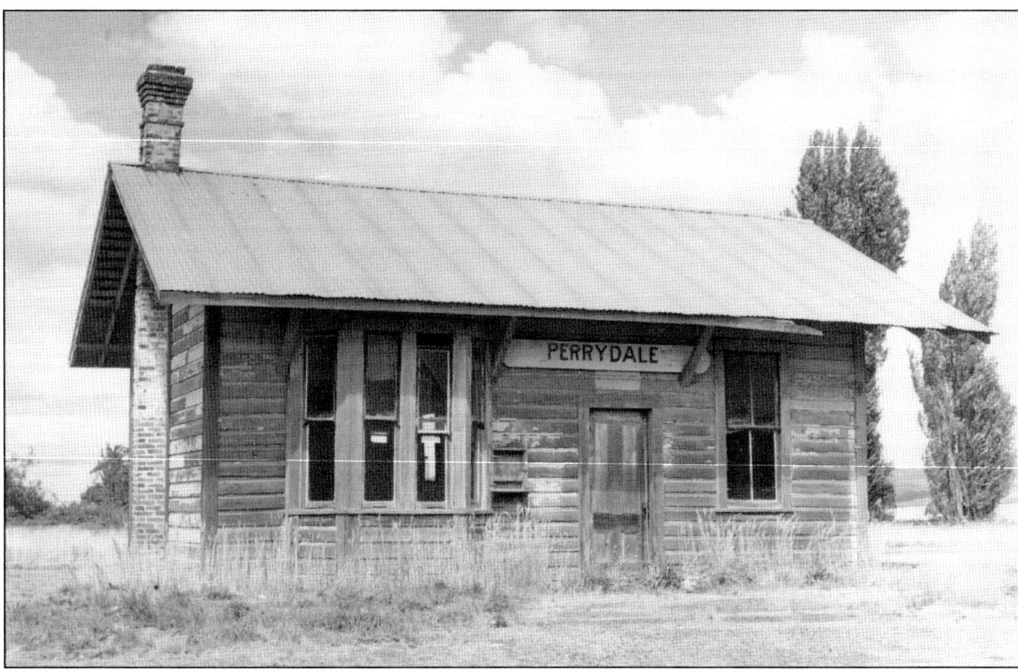

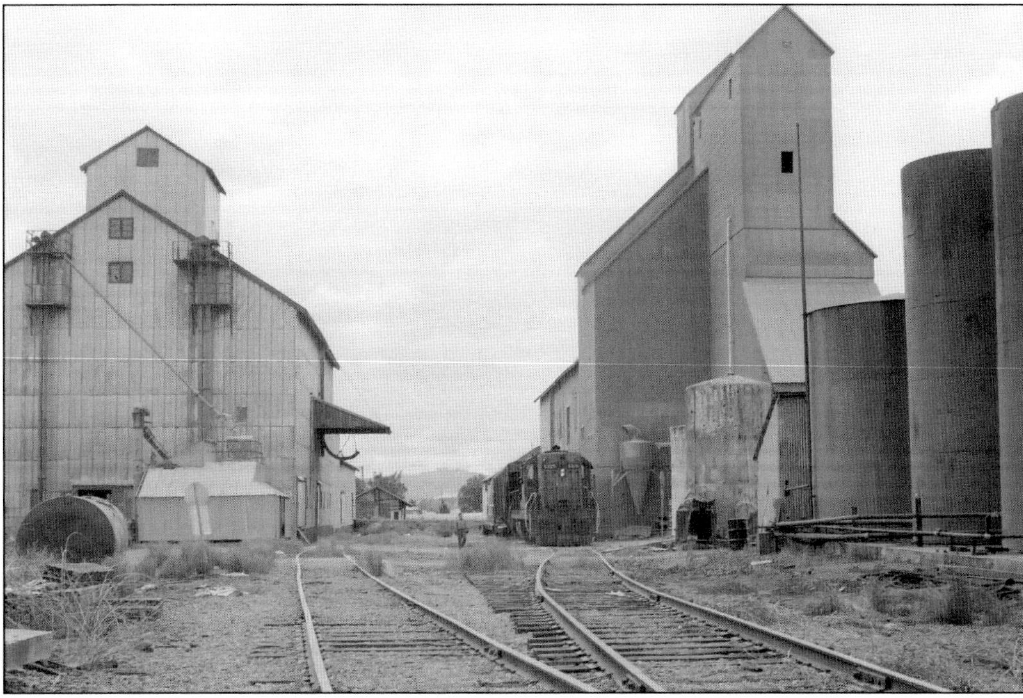

We are now back to July 25, 1983, and the SP local has arrived at Perrydale. The long abandoned depot is visible in the distance to the left of the track. However, an earthen embankment would now prevent No. 4326 from reaching the depot even if the crew had wanted to. After spotting the single covered hopper, No. 4326 will return to Broadmead light (without cars), where she would pick up the remainder of her train and continue her trip to Sheridan and Willamina.

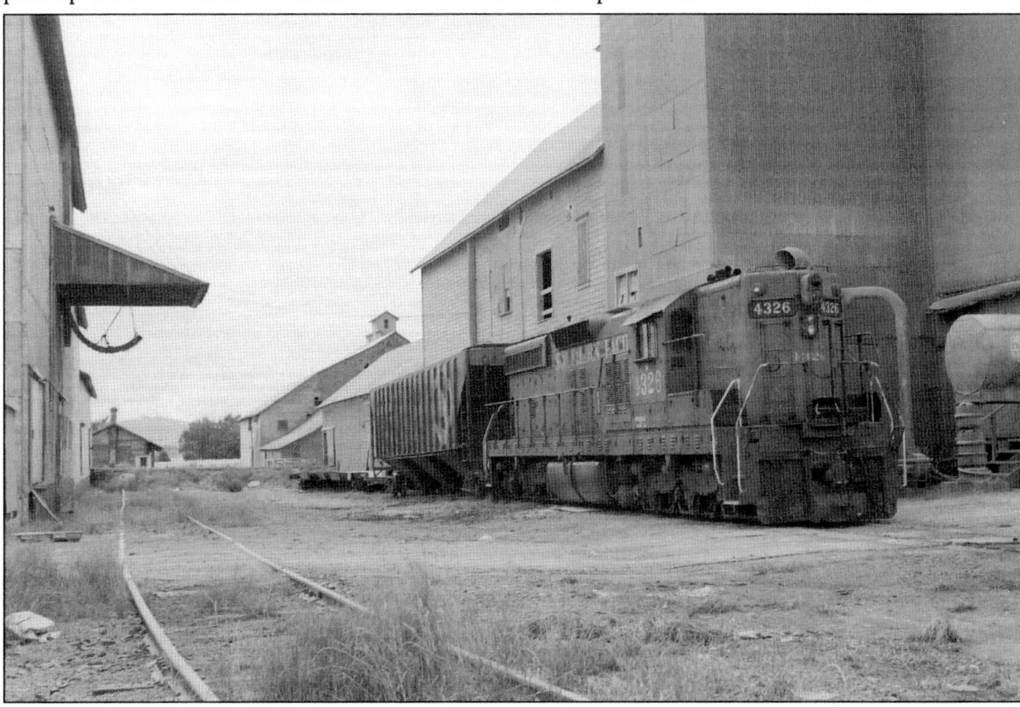

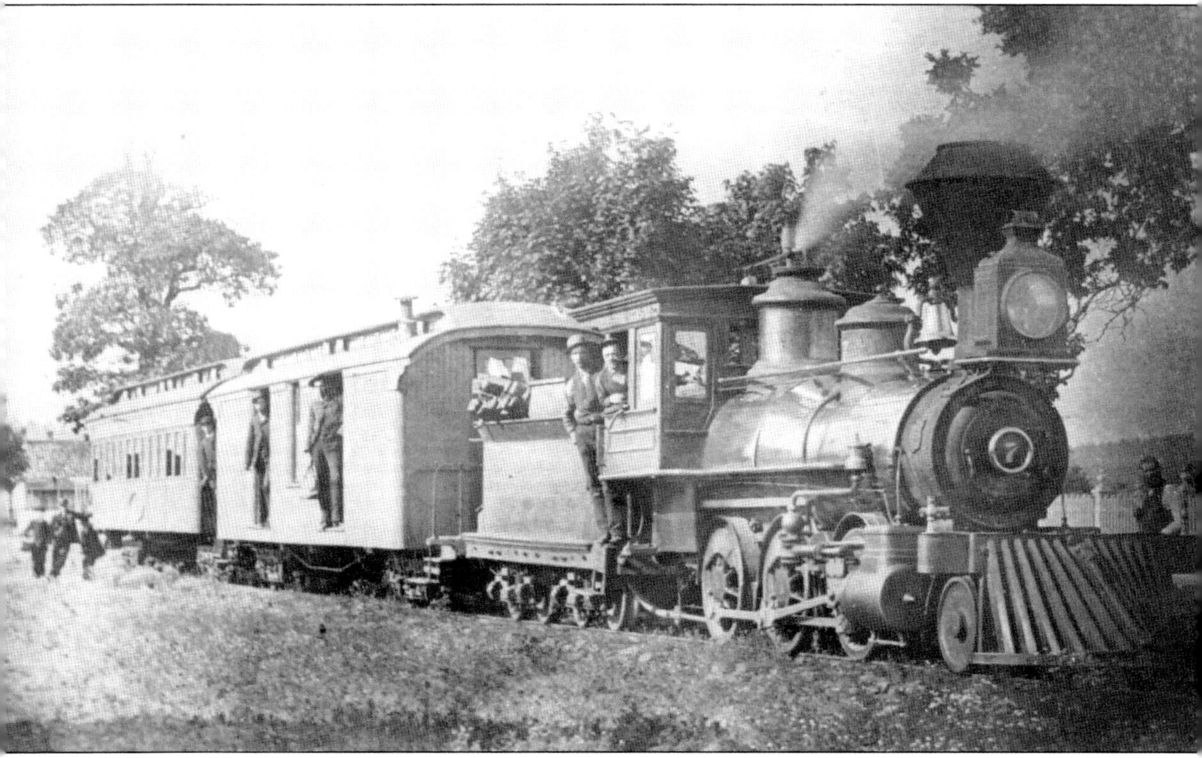

Oregonian Railway 2-6-0 No. 7, the *Scio*, has paused long enough for the photographer to record this view sometime in the early 1880s. Apparently the novelty of a photographer was enough to draw the attention of the crew as well as some passengers. "Mogul" was the name applied to locomotives with a 2-6-0 wheel arrangement, and No. 7 was the last of three Moguls acquired by the Oregonian Railway Company from H.K. Porter during June, July, and August 1880. She is seen here near Dallas lacking modern features such as air brakes or automatic couplers.

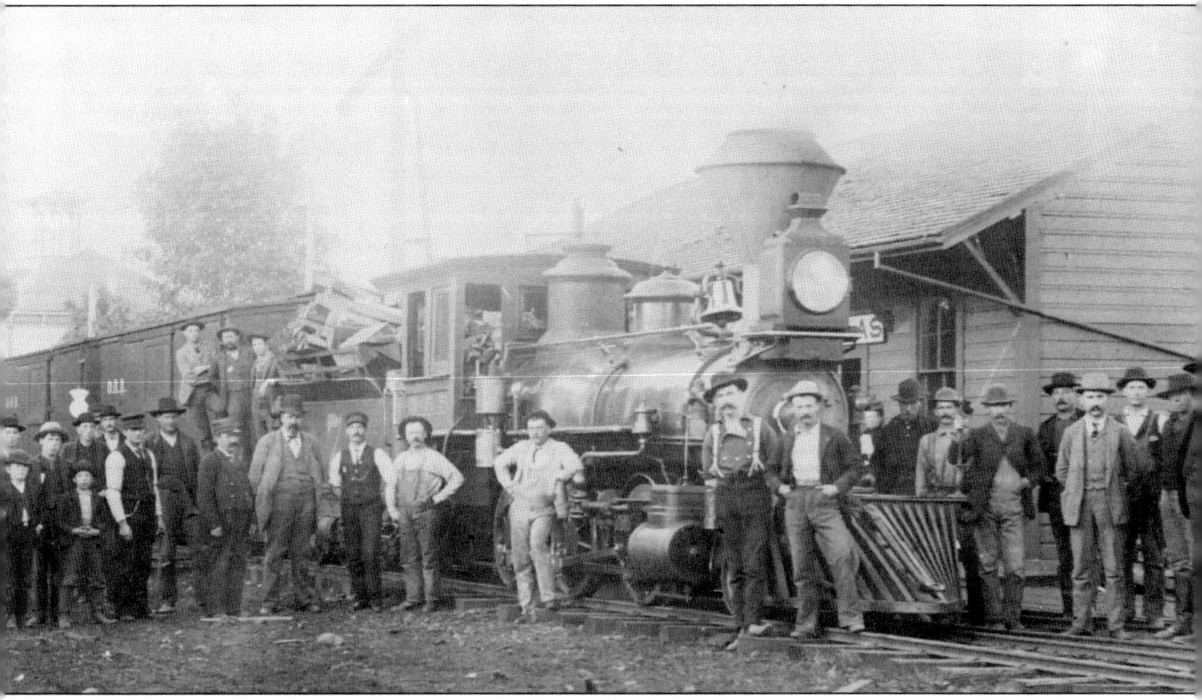

A decade has passed since the previous view, and Porter-built 2-6-0 No. 7 now works for the Oregonian Railroad, a subsidiary of the standard-gauge Southern Pacific Railroad. It appears narrow-gauge No. 7 is handling a rather typical freight train of the time, so the occasion for the large crowd is unknown. Steam locomotives had been a fixture in Dallas for well over 10 years, so perhaps a farm demonstration train or some other event has generated this seemingly large crowd. Note that No. 7 is now equipped with air brakes, as witnessed by the single phase air pump just ahead of the cab.

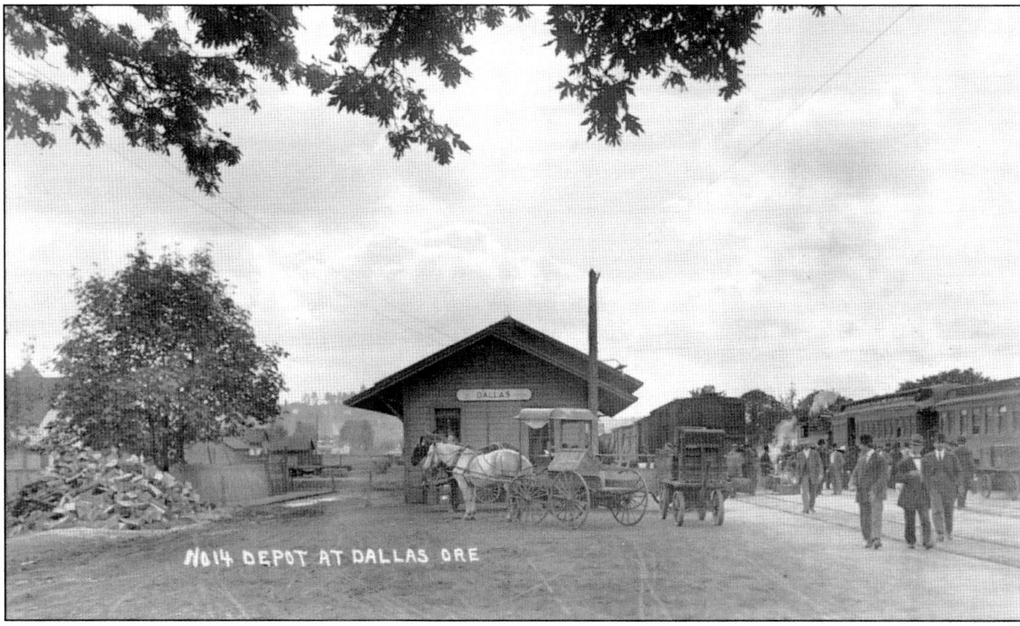

Another decade has passed since the previous view was recorded at Dallas, and the depot has been expanded by its new owner, the Southern Pacific Railroad. SP train No. 76 is at the depot preparing for its scheduled 2:00 p.m. departure for Portland via Broadmead and Whiteson. By this date, around the early 1920s, Dallas had become a thriving community served by two standard-gauge rail lines and narrow-gauge trains were a fading memory.

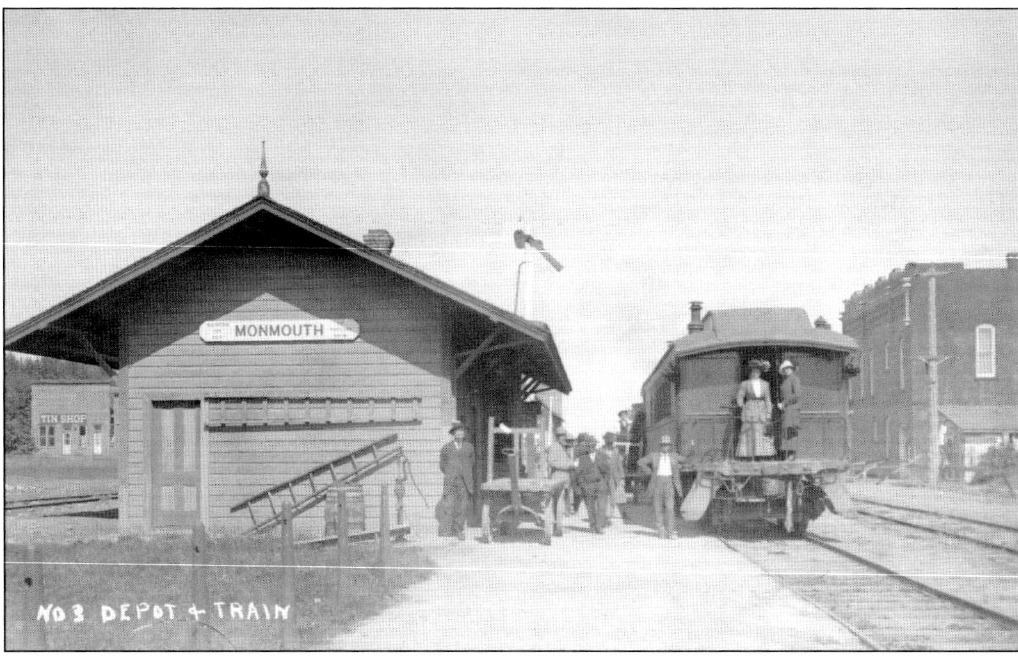

A slightly later view of the original Monmouth depot highlights similarities it shares with the Perrydale depot. Note the decorative finial seen more clearly here. Riding the train was an occasion to dress up, as witnessed by the men wearing ties and the women on the end platform who have dressed to be seen.

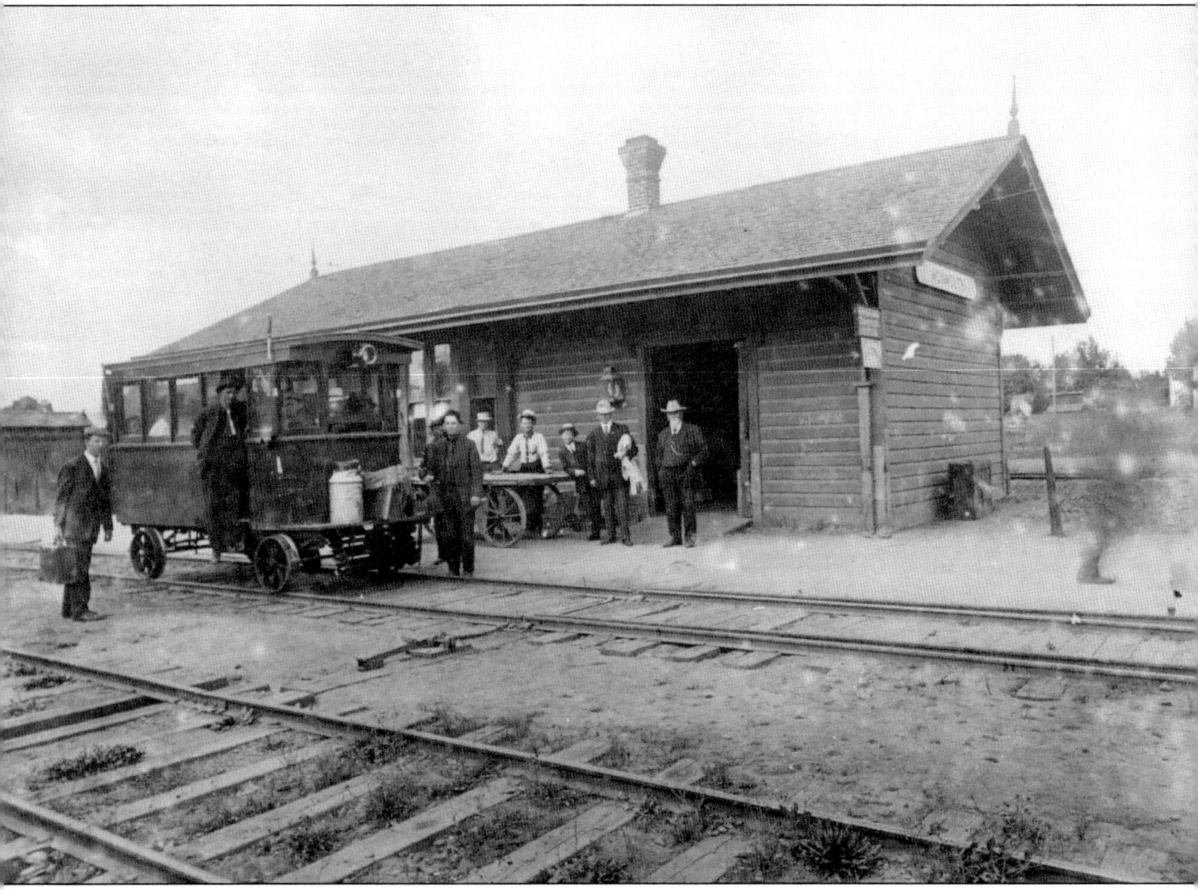

The original Oregonian Railway depot at Monmouth, seen around 1911, was basically the mirror image of the Perrydale depot. This structure served from 1882 until it was replaced by an SP "Harriman"–style depot around 1915. The small rail bus is from the Independence & Monmouth (I&M) Railroad, which constructed two-and-a-half miles of track connecting—predictably—Independence and Monmouth. The I&M opened for business on August 24, 1890, and after the Airlie Branch was converted to standard gauge it obtained trackage rights to operate over the SP line from Monmouth south to Airlie and north to Dalles, a distance of 16 miles.

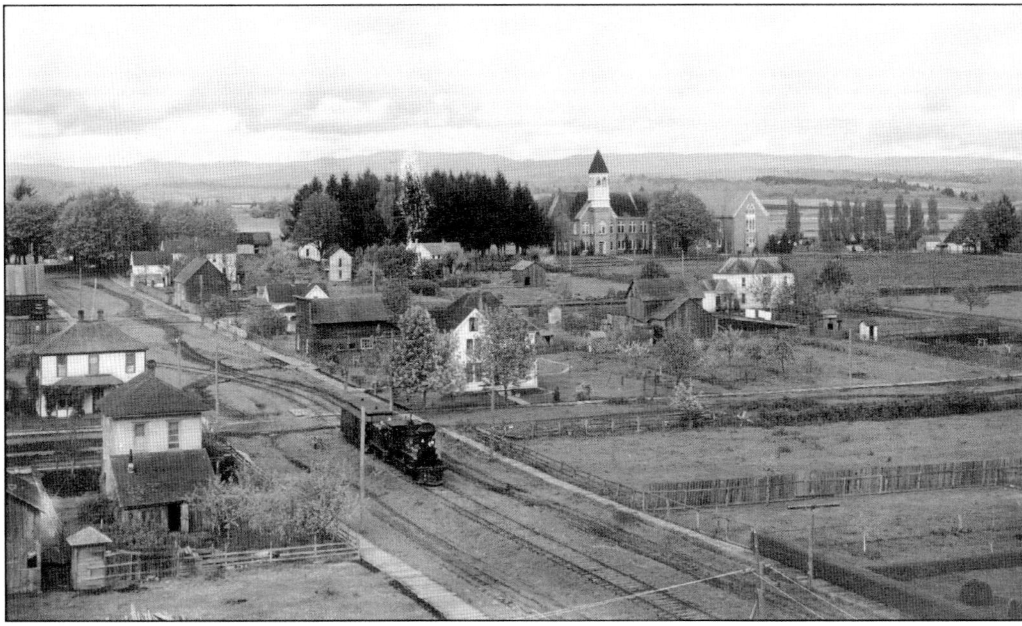

Independence & Monmouth Railroad 4-4-0 No. 1243 leads a single coach east along Jackson Street in Monmouth headed to Independence around 1907. The track behind the train can be seen curving to the south where it joins the SP Airlie Branch, which is just discernible along Warren Street. Note the SP boxcar visible at left. Later, a wye was located at this point to facilitate I&M trains operating north to Dallas and south to Airlie via the SP Airlie Branch.

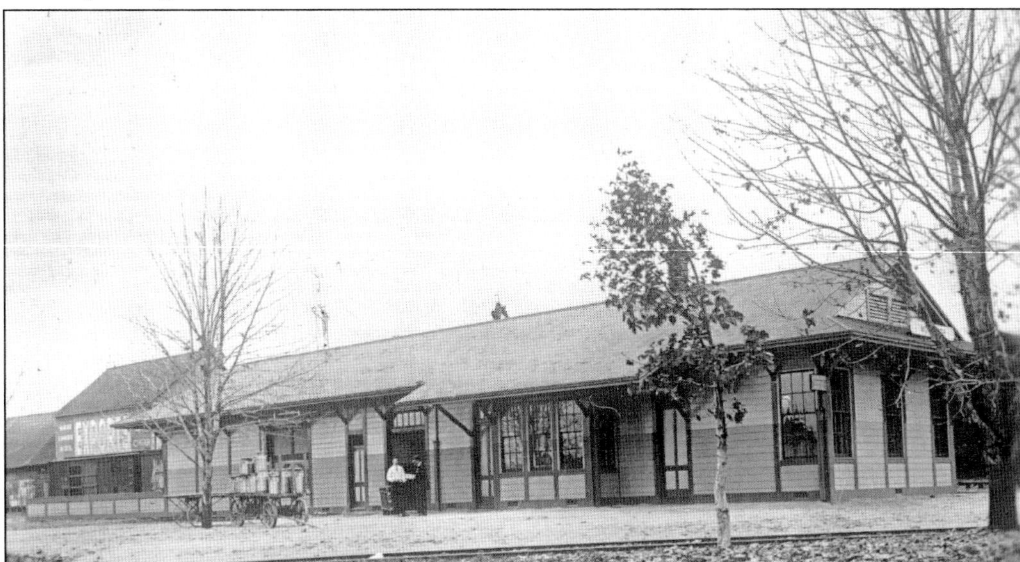

Even though the Airlie branch would be abandoned south of Monmouth in barely 10 years, the Southern Pacific constructed this new depot around 1915. The building was located within the wye at the intersection of Warren and Jackson Streets. Here, the SP's Airlie Branch passes on the far side of the depot while the north leg of the I&M wye is seen in the foreground. It is possible that this depot had two operator bay windows: one seen here, and another facing the Airlie Branch on the opposite side of the building where the train order board is visible above the roof.

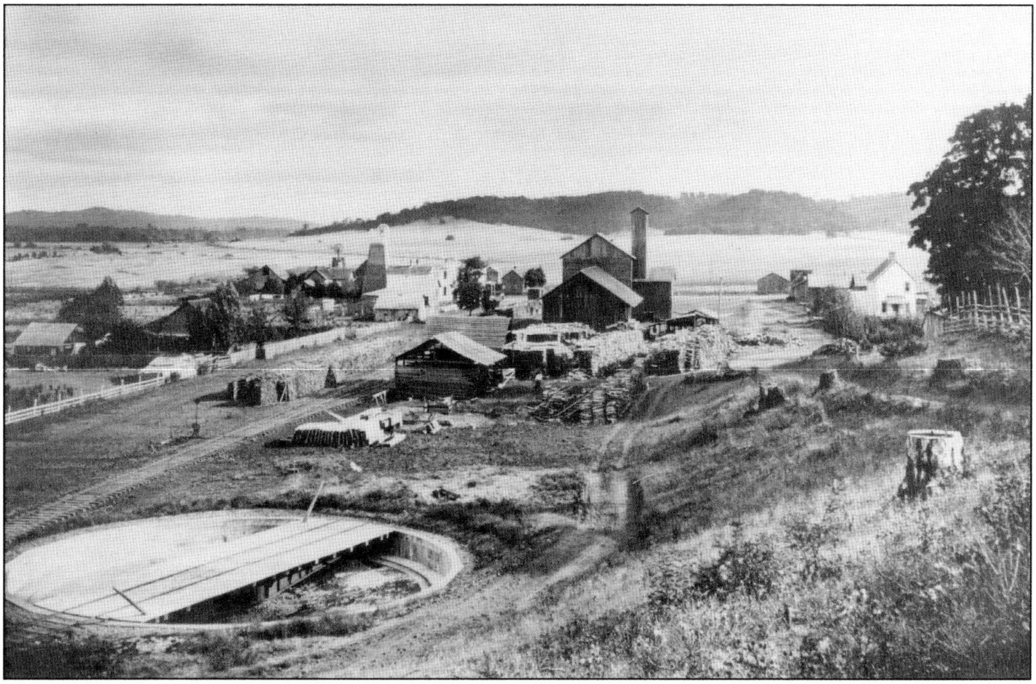

Airlie was the extreme southern end of the Airlie Branch and this photograph gives an excellent overview of the entire community around 1900. The depot would be out of sight behind the building with the tall shaft at center. The view looks to the south-southeast. (Courtesy Bob Lowry.)

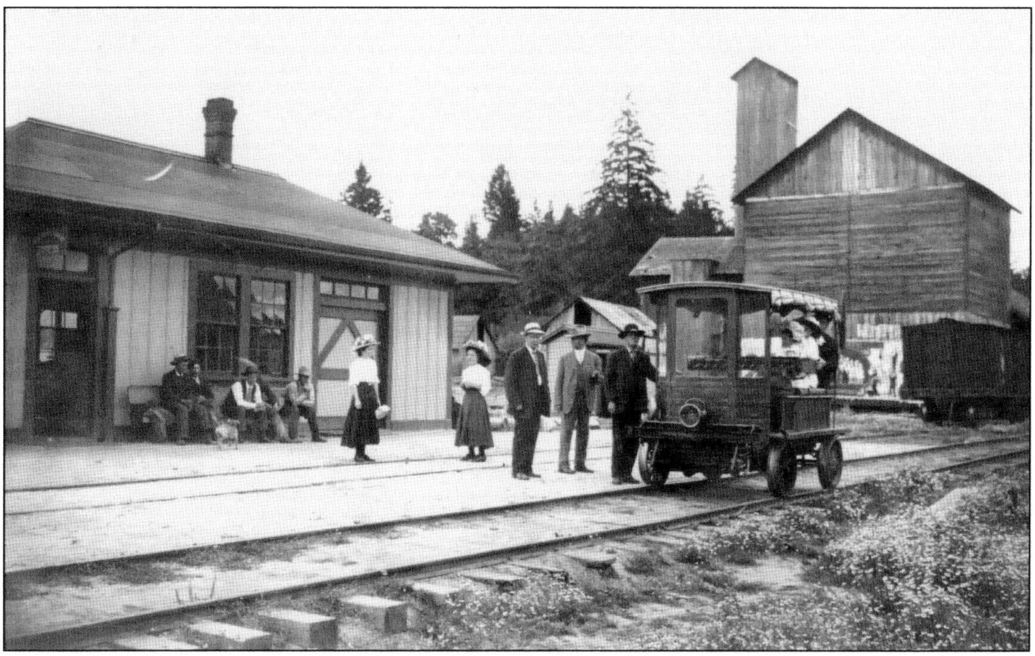

The original Airlie depot is pictured around 1909. By the looks of the primitive Independence & Monmouth speeder turned rail bus, there may be more passengers than there are seats today. One hopes the gentlemen relinquished their seats to the young ladies if necessary. The dog appears to be a depot regular and was presumably not scheduled to be a passenger on this trip.

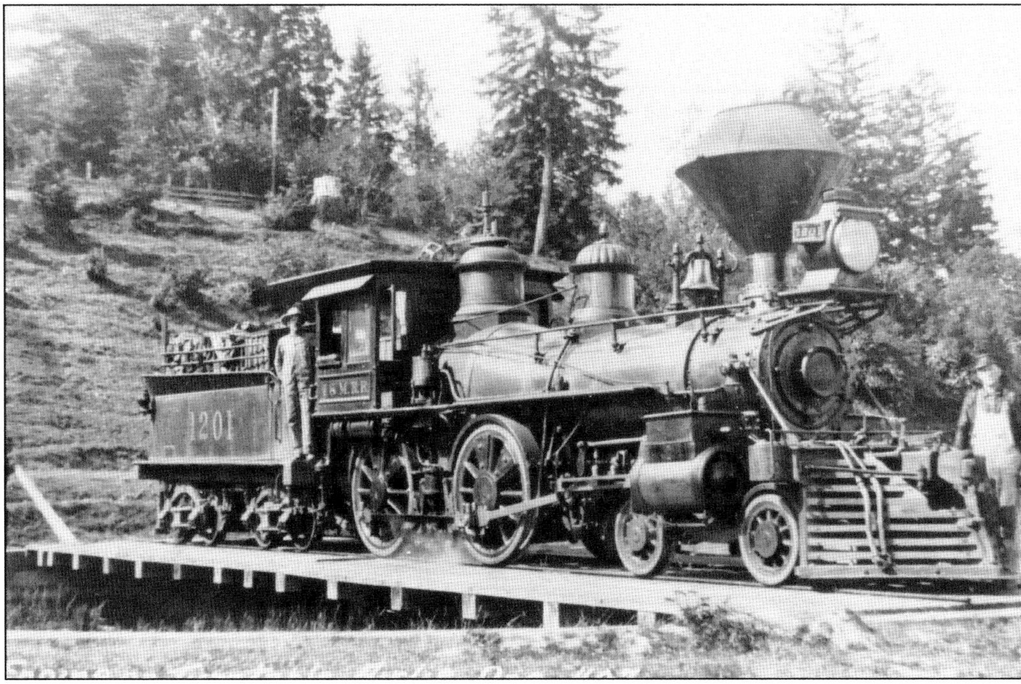

Independence & Monmouth Railroad 4-4-0 No. 1201 poses on the Airlie turntable at the end of a run south from Monmouth around 1905. The stately locomotive was purchased secondhand from the Southern Pacific on October 17, 1904. She was later renumbered I&M No. 1. (Courtesy Bob Lowry.)

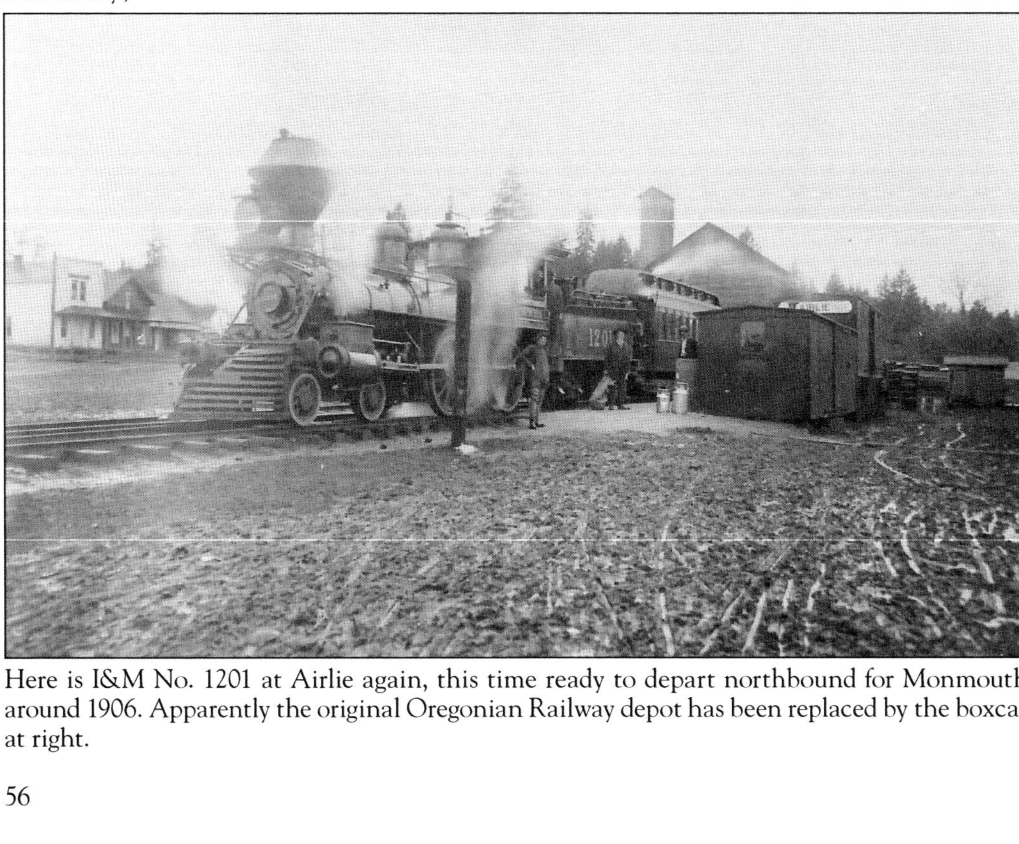

Here is I&M No. 1201 at Airlie again, this time ready to depart northbound for Monmouth around 1906. Apparently the original Oregonian Railway depot has been replaced by the boxcar at right.

Three

Ray's Landing to Coburg and Springfield

In 1879, William Reid's vision for the Dayton, Sheridan & Grand Ronde Railroad went beyond local communities. Barely two weeks after gaining control of the DS&GR, Reid broke ground at Silverton for an extension down the east side of the Willamette Valley.

During the fall of 1880, David Graham Drummond Ogilvy, Earl of Airlie, toured the Willamette Valley holdings on behalf of Scottish investors. Apparently impressed, the earl authorized construction of a bridge across the Willamette River connecting the Westside and Eastside Divisions. He also approved surveys extending the Eastside Division across the Cascade Mountains to Nevada. By October 1880, the narrow gauge was completed from Ray's Landing to Silverton via St. Paul, Woodburn, and Mount Angel, and in November, construction of the Willamette River Bridge began.

July 1881 saw completion of the narrow gauge to Brownsville, but here work stopped. Henry Villard's Oregon & California Railroad dominated rail transportation in Oregon and the expanding narrow-gauge system posed a threat that Villard needed to control. Henceforth, the narrow-gauge interloper would be operated solely for the benefit of the O&C. Villard stopped work on the Willamette River Bridge and suspended service between Ray's Landing and Woodburn. The Eastside Division was extended from Brownsville to Coburg in July 1882, but this would be the end of the narrow-gauge rails.

When Villard's empire collapsed in 1884, attempts to revitalize the narrow-gauge system were unsuccessful; by 1890, control had passed to the Southern Pacific. Work on the Willamette River Bridge was halted for the last time and the line from Ray's Landing to Woodburn was abandoned. The Eastside line from Woodburn to Coburg was converted to standard gauge in 1891 and construction south from Coburg resumed. By September 1891, standard-gauge track reached Natron, in the Cascade foothills.

Although the narrow gauge Oregonian Railway never achieved its goal of reaching Nevada, the route did eventually prosper as the SP's Woodburn-Springfield Branch. For many years secondary traffic, including logs destined for the huge Weyerhaeuser mill at Springfield, used the Woodburn-Springfield Branch as an alternative to the SP mainline.

Abandonment of the original Woodburn-Springfield branch began in 1976; by 1985, the track south of Tallman had been removed, as had the track between West Stayton and Shelburn. By the late 1980s, the Southern Pacific was looking to shed some of its branchlines in Oregon. Thus, shortline operators began assuming some operations. In February 1993, the Willamette Valley Railroad leased the original narrow-gauge route from Woodburn to West Stayton, and in 1996, purchased the line. Today, the track is still intact to Stayton, but trains seldom go past Mount Angle or Silverton.

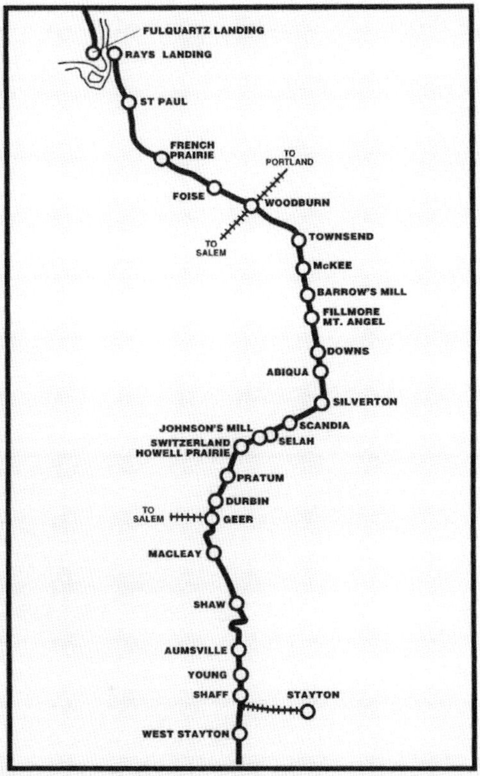

Railroad Ray's Landing to Coburg
With Southern Pacific Railroad lines shown for reference

These three maps give a simplified overview of the narrow-gauge railway from Ray's Landing to Coburg around 1881. Related Southern Pacific Railroad lines are shown as crosshatched lines for reference. Not all of these SP lines existed in 1881.

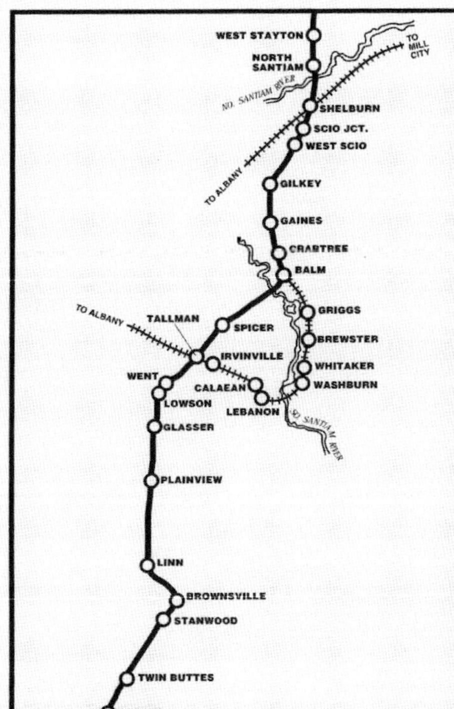

Railroad Ray's Landing to Coburg
With Southern Pacific Railroad lines shown for reference

No photograph has ever come to light that can be verified as showing the Oregonian Railway between Ray's Landing and Woodburn. This section of track was abandoned in 1892 without ever being converted to standard gauge. This 1891 plat map shows the route of the narrow-gauge passing through St. Paul to the north of the church properties. The map also suggests a spur perhaps serving a warehouse or agricultural facility.

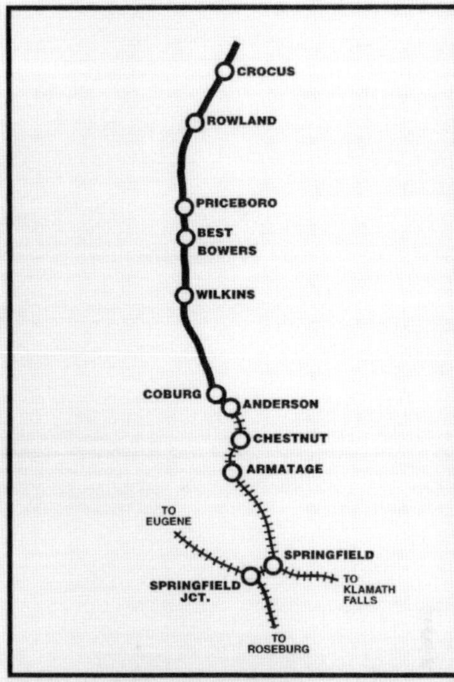

Railroad Ray's Landing to Coburg

With Southern Pacific Railroad lines shown for reference

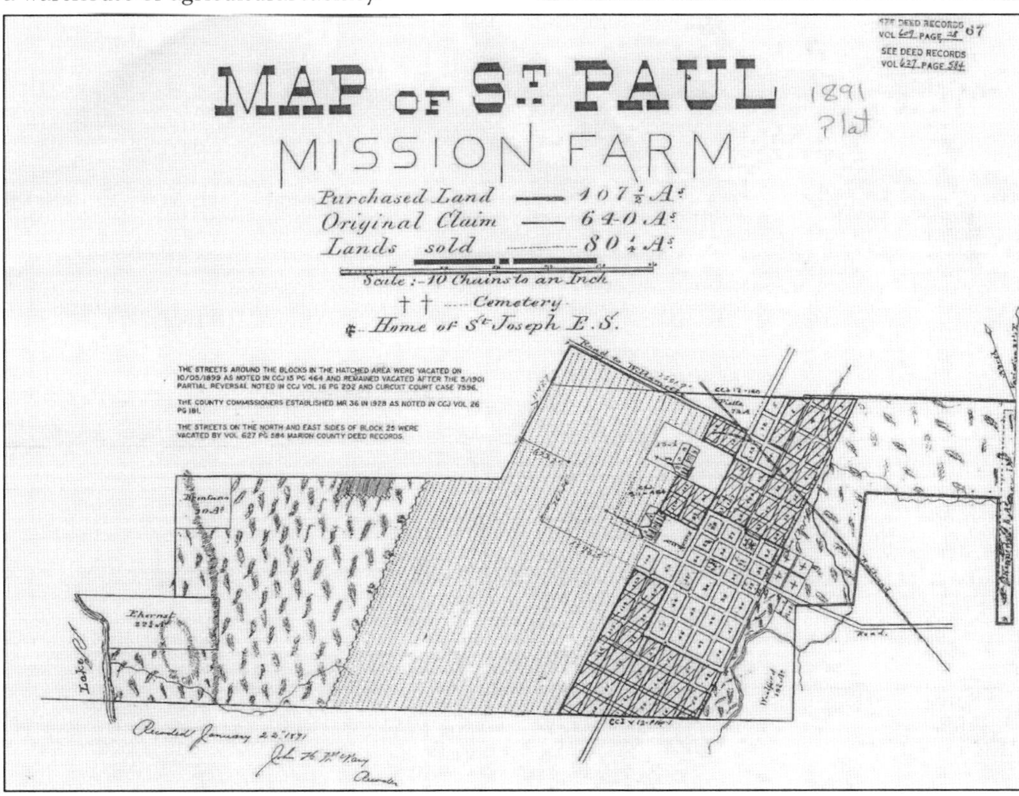

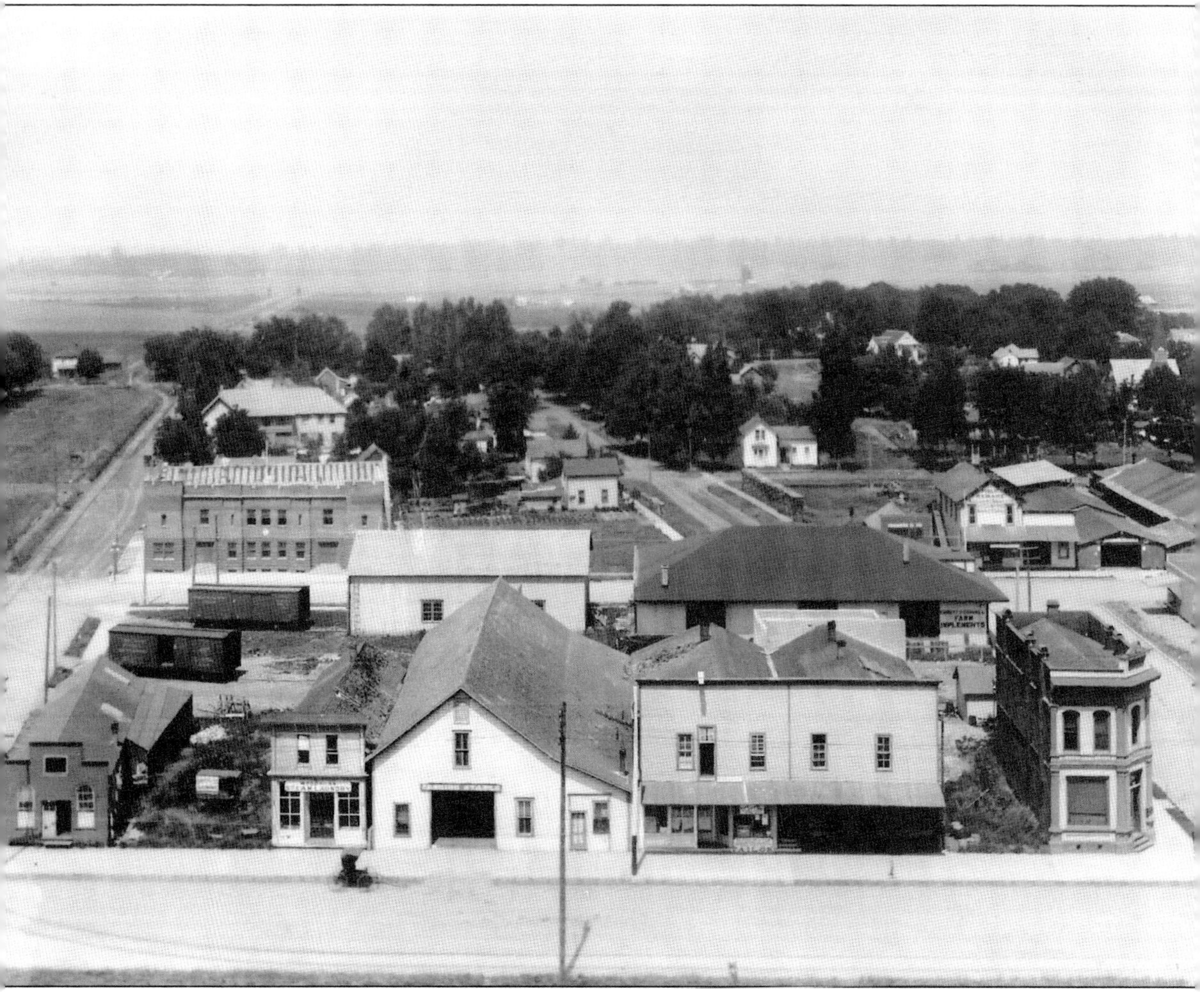

This is an image from Woodburn around 1912, looking east with Arthur Street to the right and Cleveland Street to the left. Front Street is in the foreground along the Southern Pacific Railroad, which is just out of sight. The Oregon Electric Railway is seen entering Woodburn along Cleveland Street. This is approximately the same alignment that was used by the Oregonian Railway 30 years earlier. However, unlike the Oregon Electric, which is seen curving onto Front Street, the Oregonian Railway continued east crossing Front Street and the SP mainline.

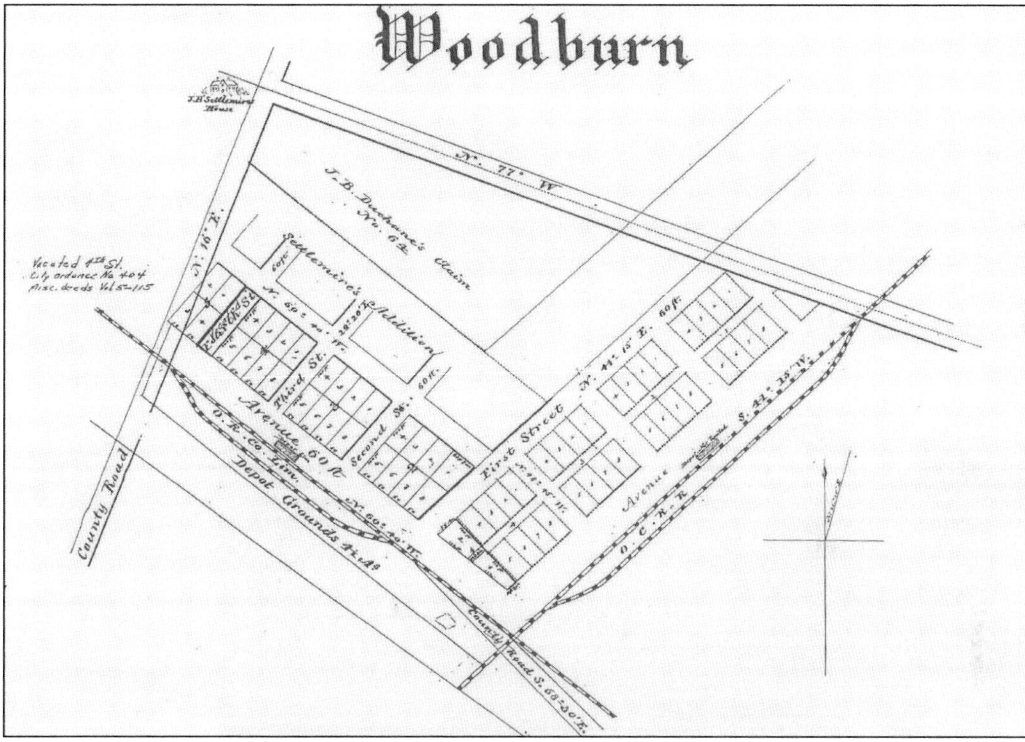

This c. 1890 plat of Woodburn shows the Oregonian Railway entering along the alignment of Cleveland Street and crossing the Oregon & California mainline. Note the Oregonian Railway depot indicated between Second and Third Streets. No photograph of this depot has come to light, if it was in fact actually built.

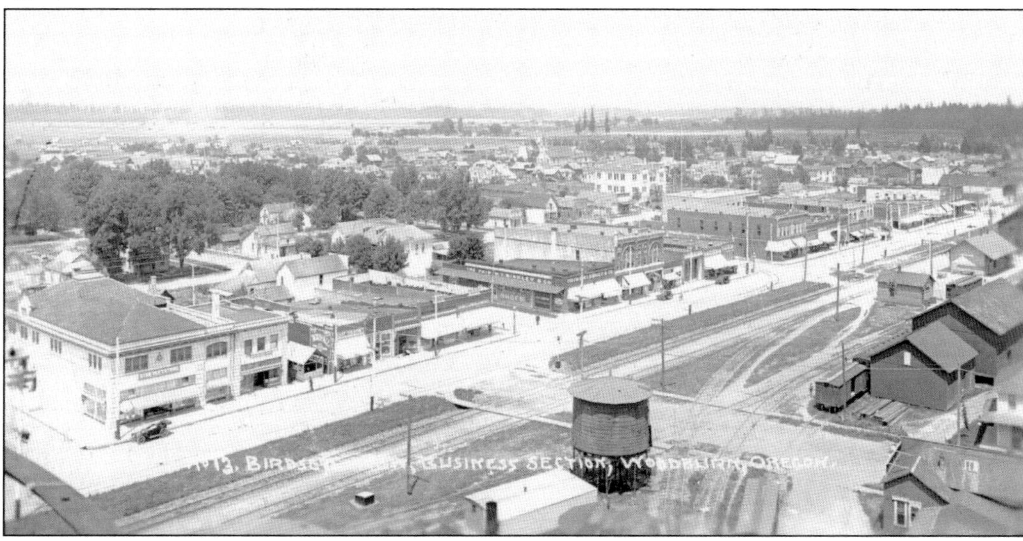

Woodburn had changed significantly by the time this photograph was taken around 1920. Looking north, the SP depot can be seen at the far right. Although it was long gone by this time, the Oregonian Railway would have been just to the left of this scene. The track curving into the lower foreground is the north leg of the wye connecting the SP mainline with the former narrow-gauge Eastside Division.

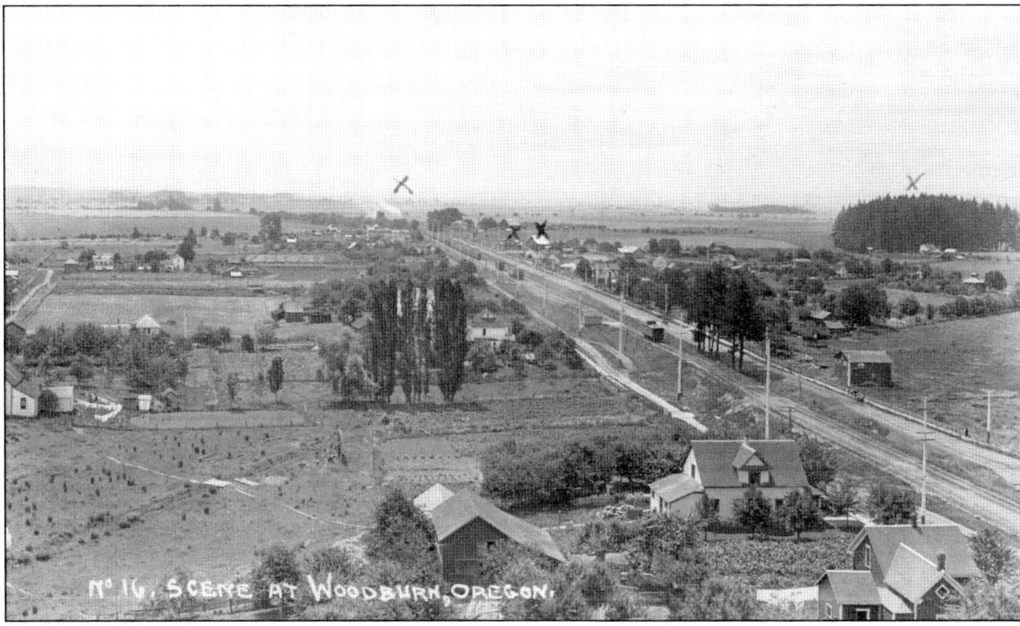

This view looks south from about the same location as the previous photograph. The SP mainline runs diagonally from the lower right to the center. Note the train apparently working in the distance with its caboose left standing on the mainline closer to the photographer. The original narrow-gauge alignment would be nearly under the photographer. The county road paralleling the SP mainline would become Highway 99E.

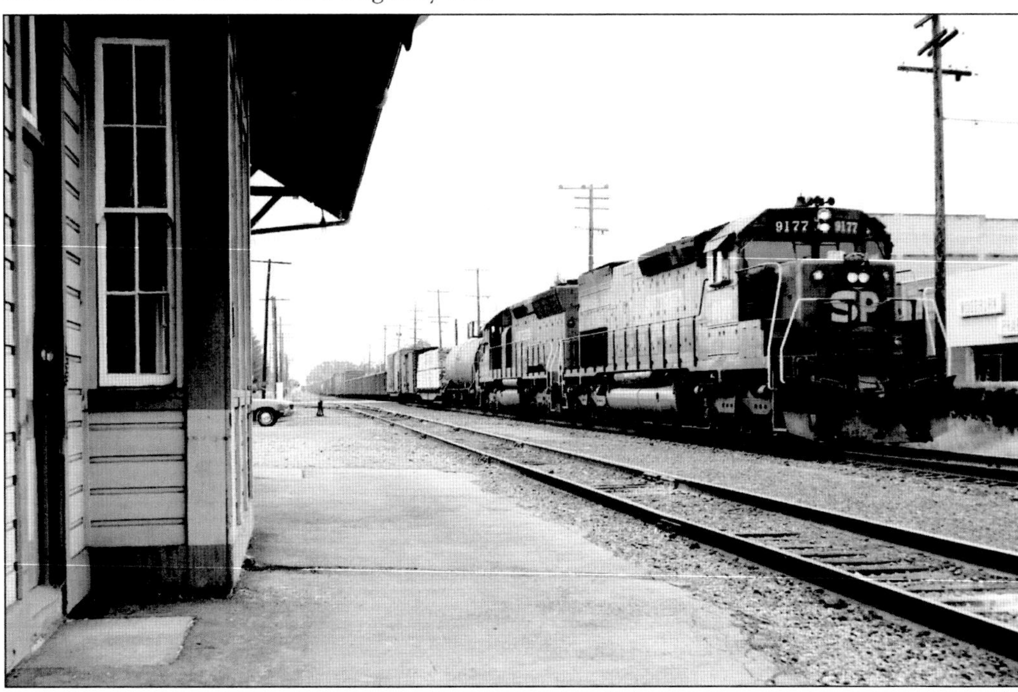

Here, SP Extra 9177 rumbles past the Woodburn depot on July 7, 1973. Eighty years earlier, the Oregonian Railway narrow-gauge line would have been crossing the SP line about where the low gondola cars are visible farther back in the train.

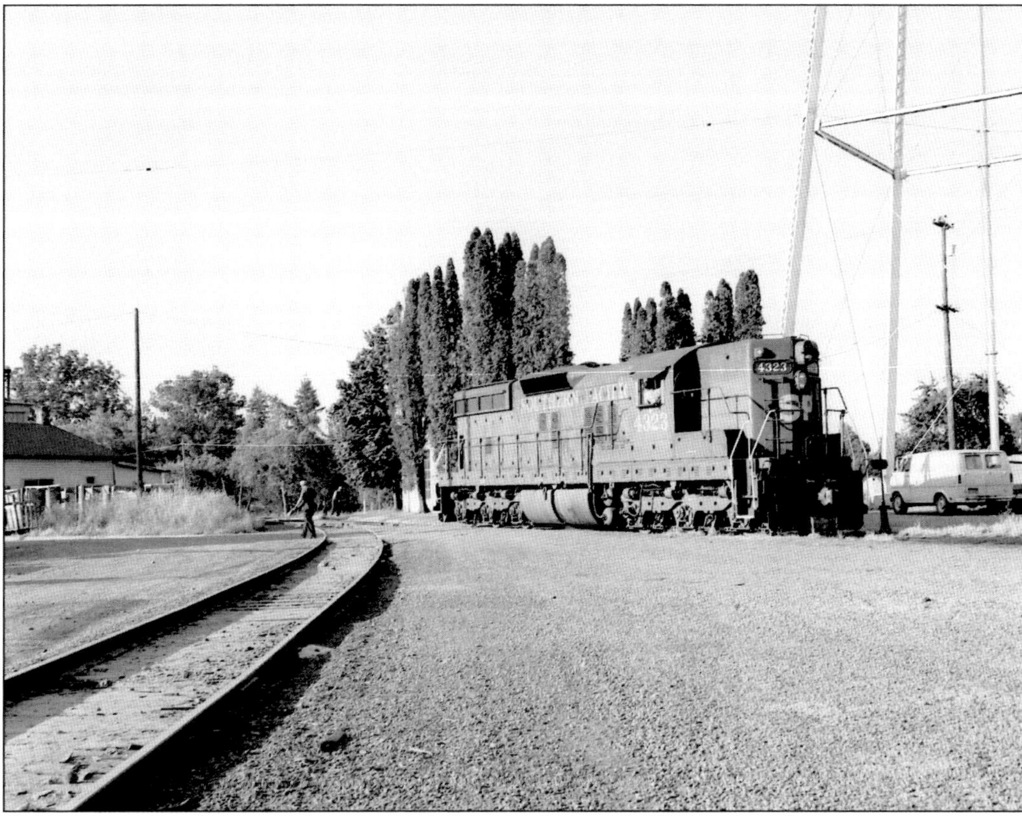

At 7:00 a.m., the SP's *West Stayton Turn* is preparing for another trip out of the old Oregonian Railway's Eastside Division. The date is June 28, 1978, and it is doubtful any thought is being given to the historic route today's run would travel.

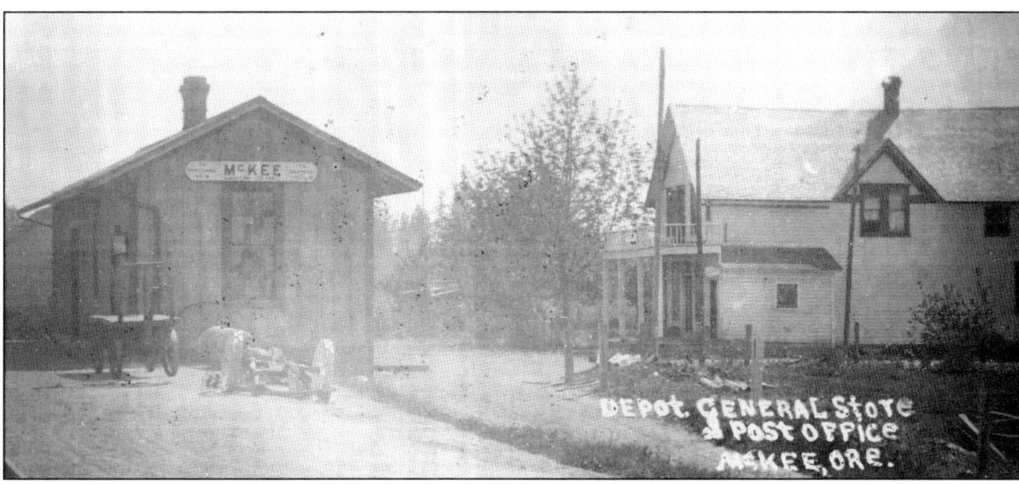

This extremely rare view shows the depot, general store, and post office at McKee around 1910. The McKee depot measured 14 feet by 45 feet and served as both the freight and passenger facility for the small community until being retired in September 1927.

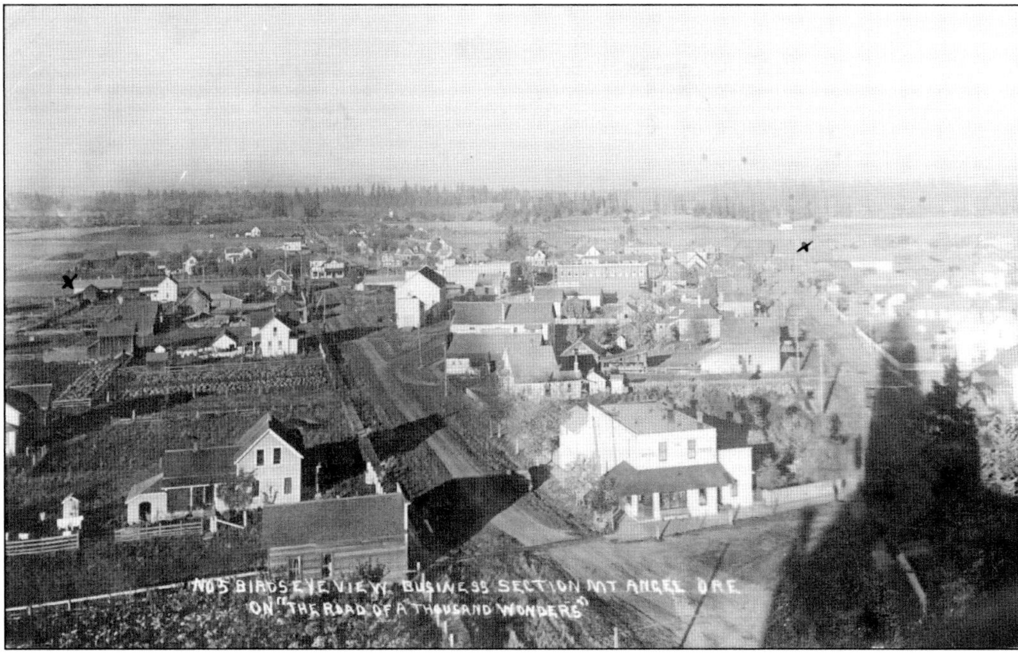

This is an image of Mount Angel looking west from Abbey Hill around 1915. The railroad runs across the upper center. The roof of the SP depot is discernible above the building with 12 closely spaced windows visible near the center.

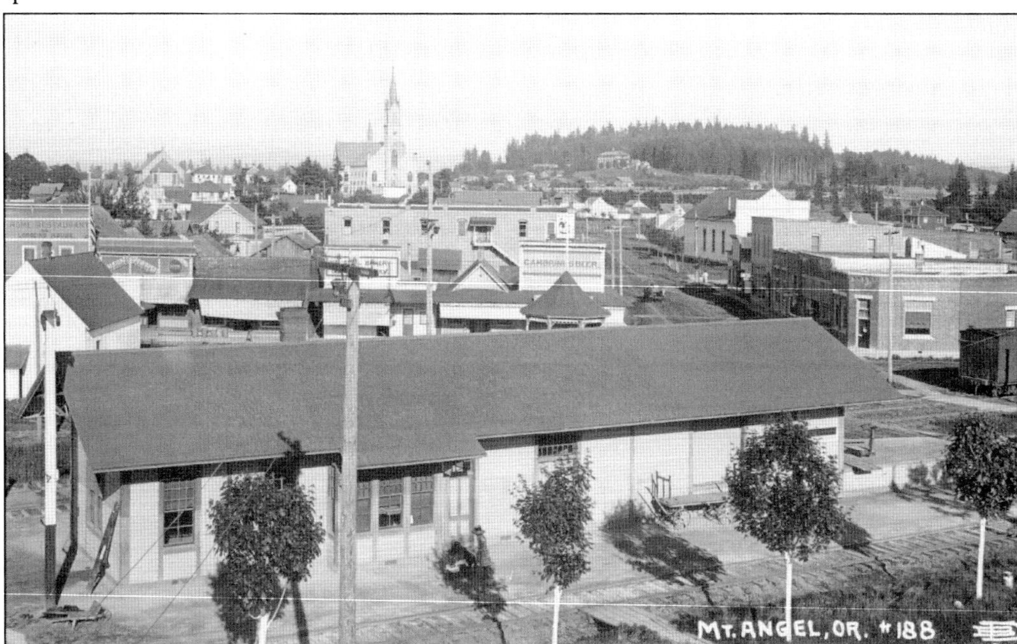

This view looks east toward Abbey Hill with the Mount Angel depot in the foreground. According to SP records, the building was constructed in 1906, but, unfortunately, the accuracy of this information is suspect. Mount Angel became a train order office for the SP in 1892 and it is likely the original structure was built at that time. It appears the freight section of the building was enlarged at some later date, with a second freight door being added to the right.

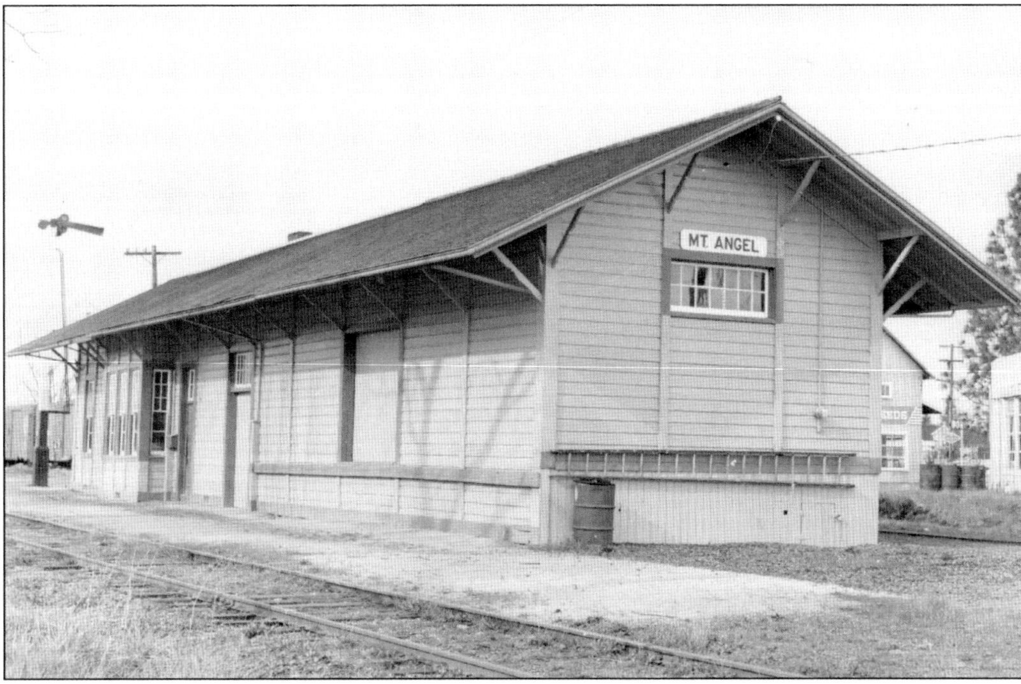

The Mount Angel depot is seen again around 1955. Note the train order board at the far end of the building. Mount Angel served as a train order office from 1892 until 1958. The depot was retired in August 1961, but the building still remains in this location in 2014 in private ownership.

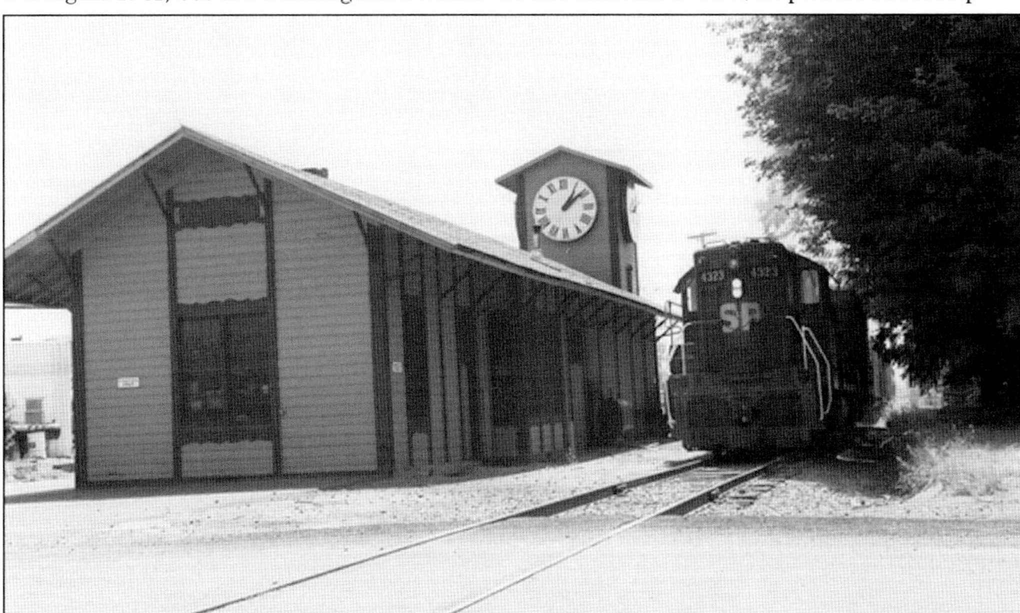

By 1978, the old Mount Angel depot had been converted to an antique shop with a few owner modifications including a rather ludicrous clock tower. Interestingly, the building remains in its original location along the still-active track in 2014. Generally, railroads frown upon keeping retired railroad buildings along active tracks due to safety concerns, but apparently Mount Angel was an exception.

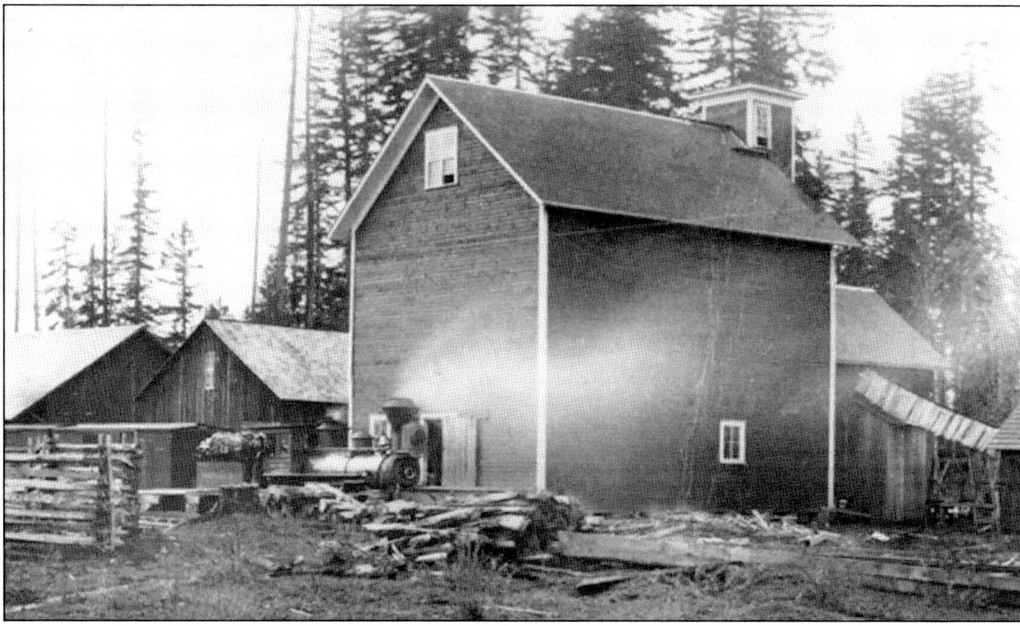

Action views from the narrow-gauge era are extremely rare, but fortunately an unknown photographer captured this image of one of the Oregonian Railway's Porter-built 2-6-0s with a freight train at Downs Station between Mount Angel and Silverton around the early 1880s. Downs never rated a formal depot, but the SP did maintain a 10-foot-by-14-foot passenger shelter here between 1916 and 1927.

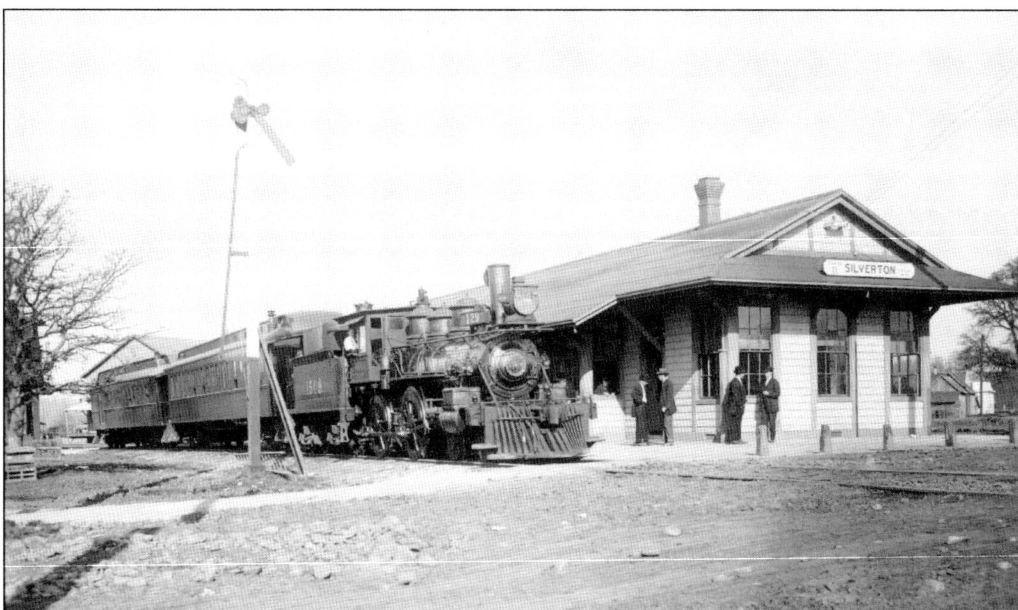

SP 4-4-0 No. 1509 strikes a classic pose at the Silverton depot around 1913. Train No. 129 appears ready for its 3:00 p.m. departure. At Geer, the train diverged from the old Oregonian Railway Eastside Division, taking the Geer Branch to Salem, where it was due to arrive at 4:00 p.m. After the Silverton depot was retired in August 1969, it was moved to a new location where it now serves as a visitor center and museum.

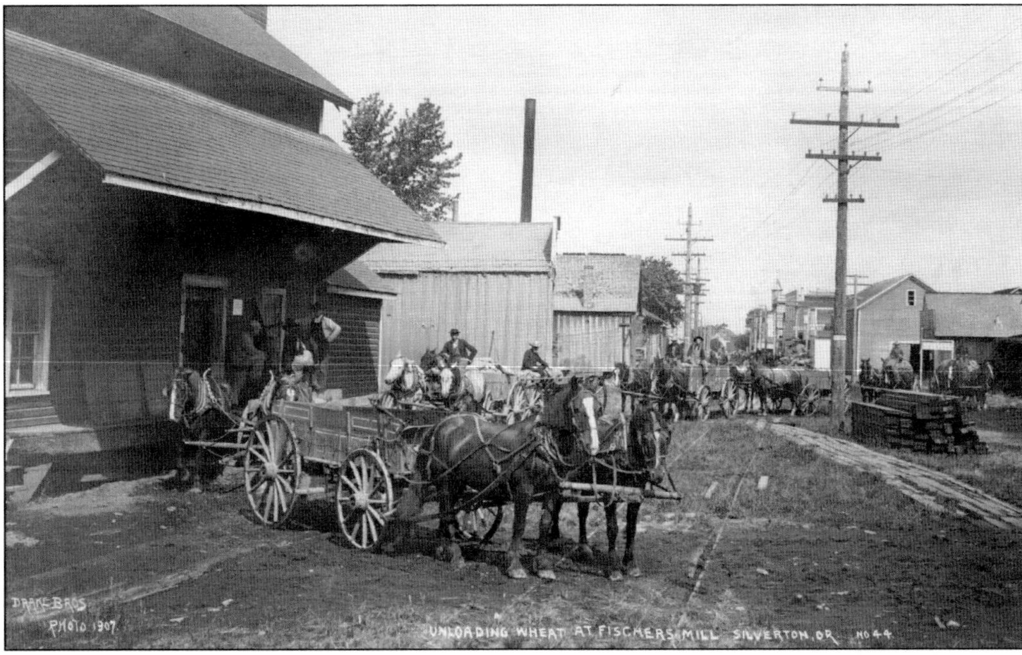

Wagons loaded with wheat line up waiting a turn to unload at Fischer's Mill in Silverton in 1907. At its peak, this mill processed more than 90,000 bushels per month and shipped oatmeal and cereals worldwide. Wagons are reported to have lined up for several blocks in either direction during harvest time. Finished products were shipped out by rail to Portland and beyond.

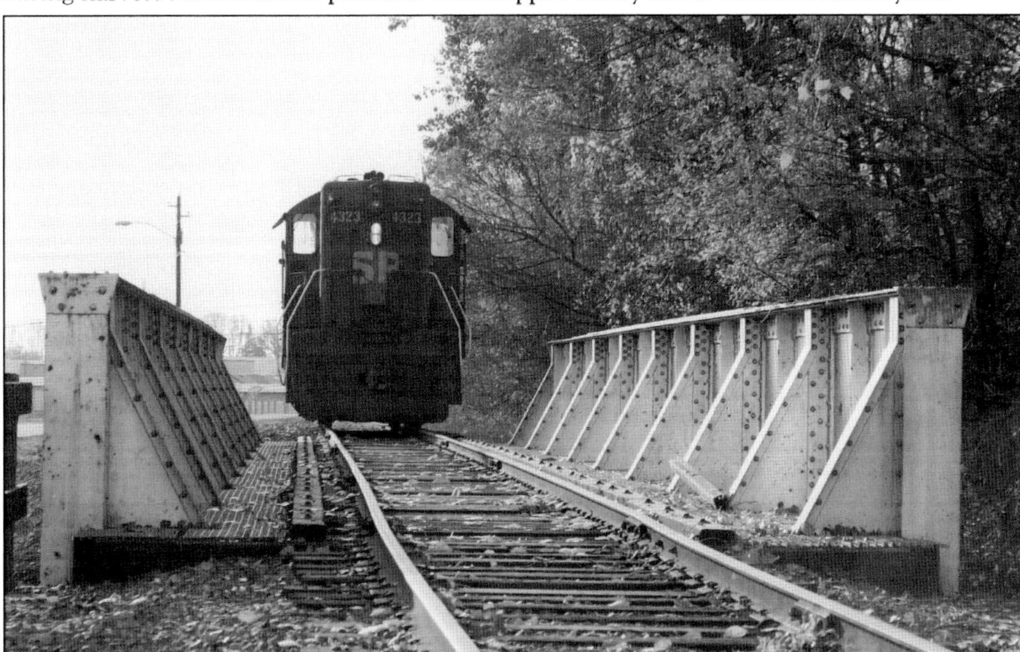

The SP *West Stayton Turn* has paused long enough for the crew to make a quick trip to a nearby market for lunch. After a few minutes, the train continued south, crossing Silver Creek via the through-plate girder span in the foreground.

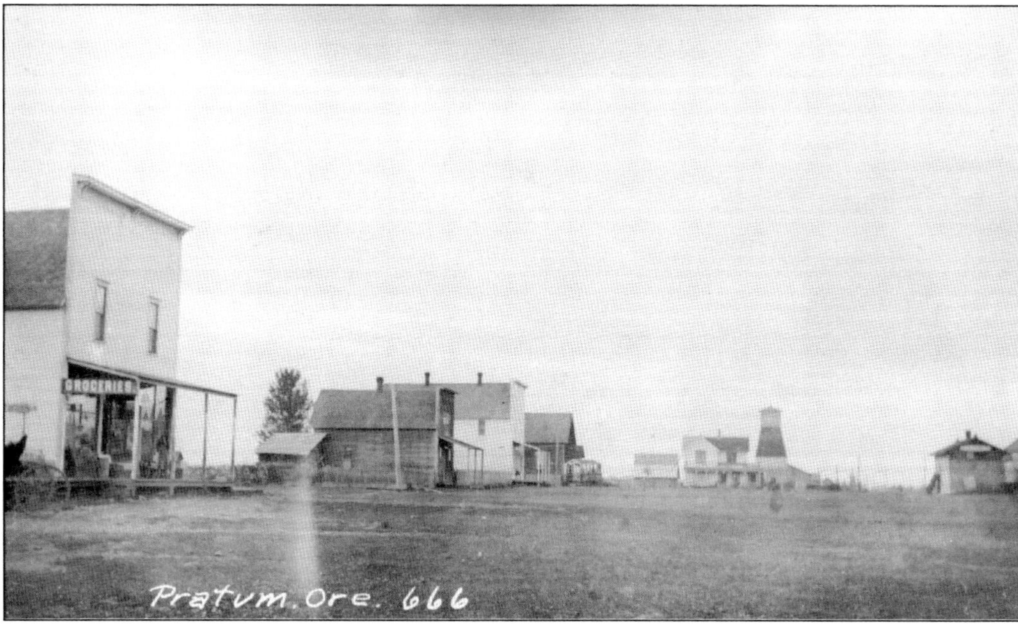

Pratum, seen here around 1909, was originally called East Side Junction when the Oregonian Railway built through the area in late 1880. The name was changed to Enger, but this was easily confused with Eugene, and it was changed to Pratum in 1898. The SP maintained a depot at Pratum until September 1938.

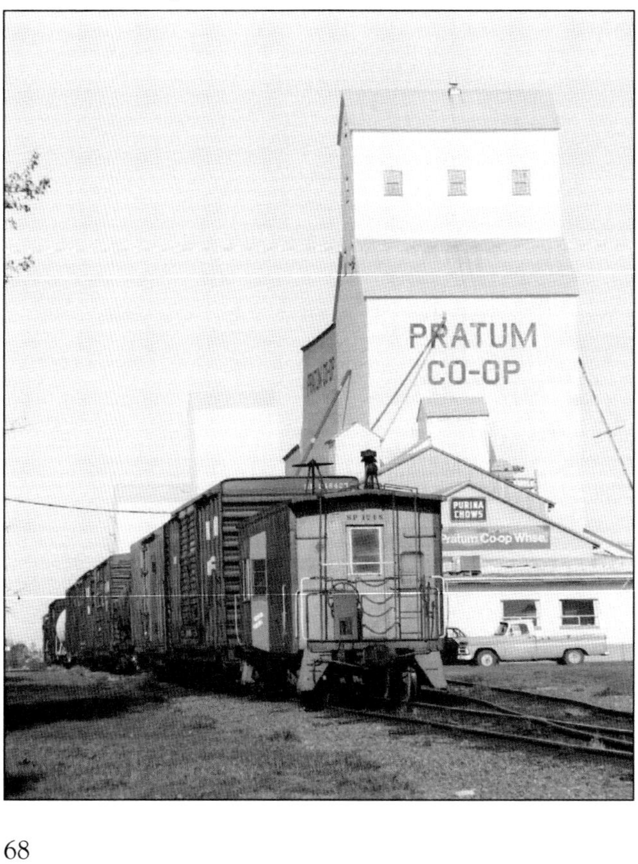

The SP continued to provide sporadic service to Pratum, as seen here, until February 1993 when operation of the line was taken over by the Willamette Valley Railroad. Today, Pratum is most recognized for the Pratum Co-Op, which is visible from some distance. Although the track was still in service to Pratum in 2013, trains seldom venture this far out the old narrow-gauge route.

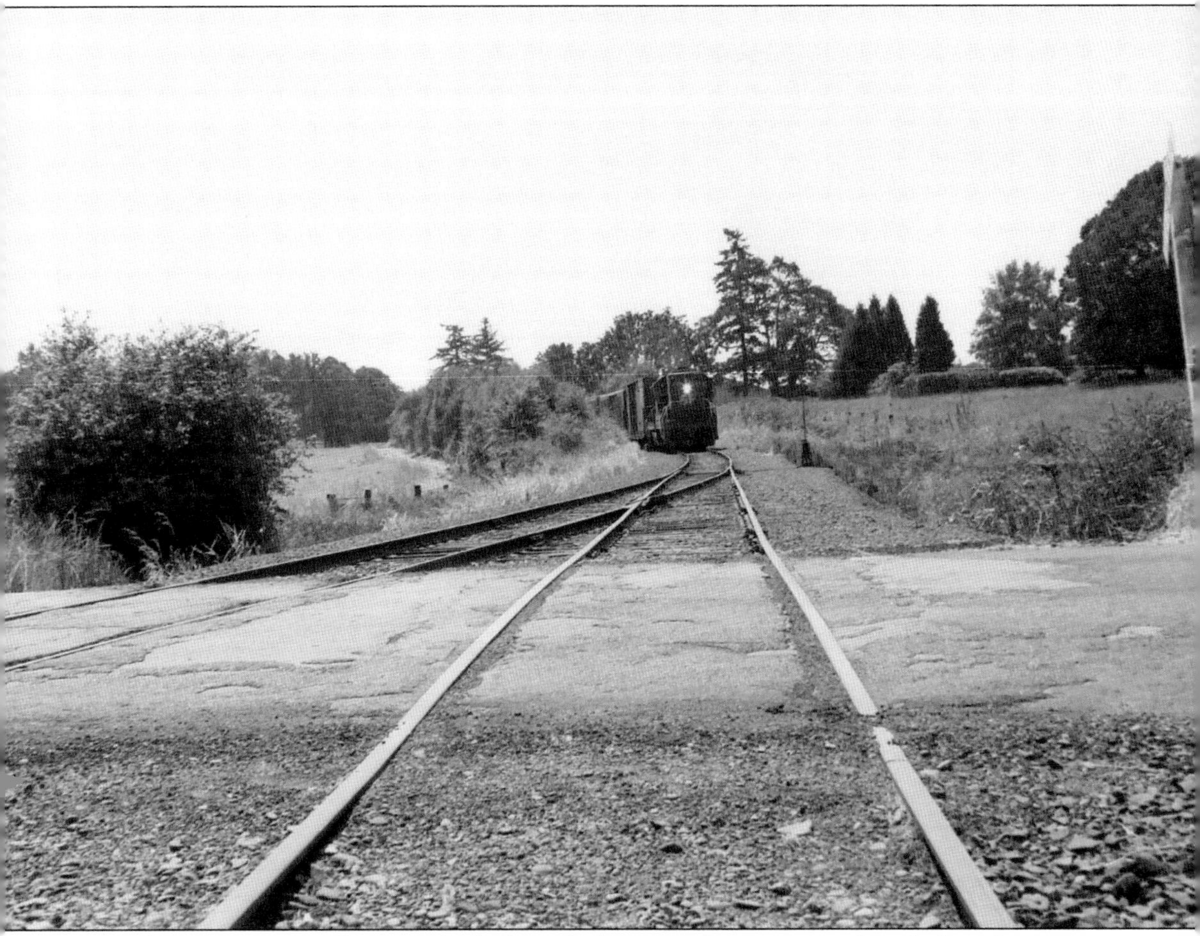

When the Oregonian Railway was built through this area, Geer was not identified as a location. However, in 1912, Geer was created when the SP extended a line from Salem east to this junction with the old narrow-gauge route as part of a projected electric interurban system. A wye was built to allow train movements to and from the Geer Branch in either direction onto the Eastside line. Here, the *West Stayton Turn* is approaching Geer from the south. The track to the left follows the original narrow-gauge route north toward Pratum. The photographer is standing on the south leg of the Geer wye with State Street crossing both lines in the foreground.

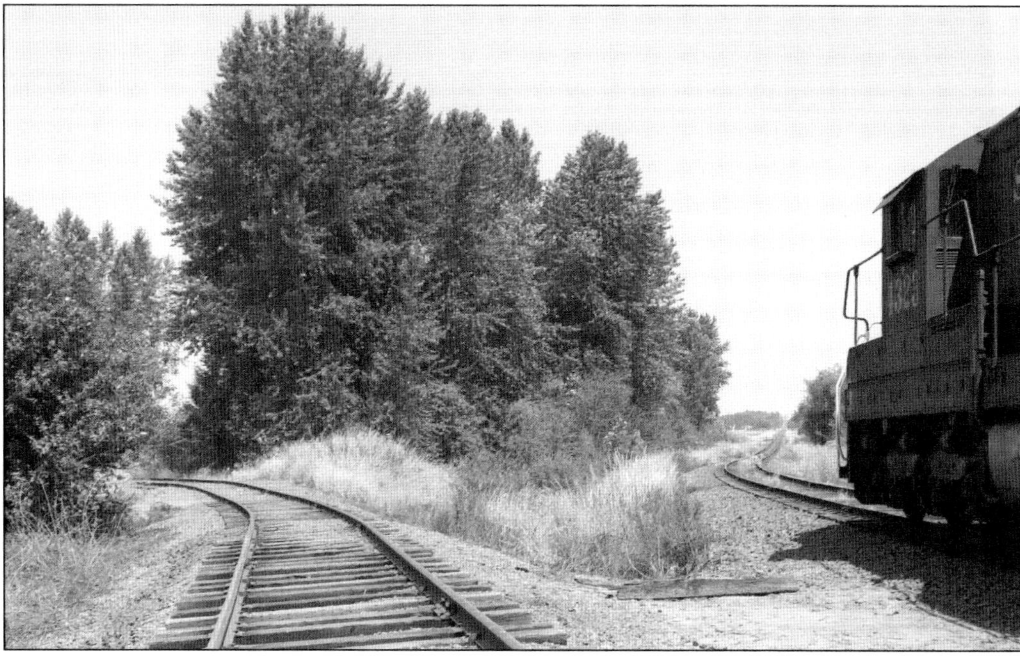

Turning to the north, the local is seen continuing toward Pratum with the south leg of the Geer wye turning to the west toward Salem. Geer never rated a depot, but a 10-foot-by-20-foot shelter was provided for passengers until October 1929. The wye track was still in place in 2014, but it is seldom used. The line between Geer and Salem has been abandoned and the rails removed.

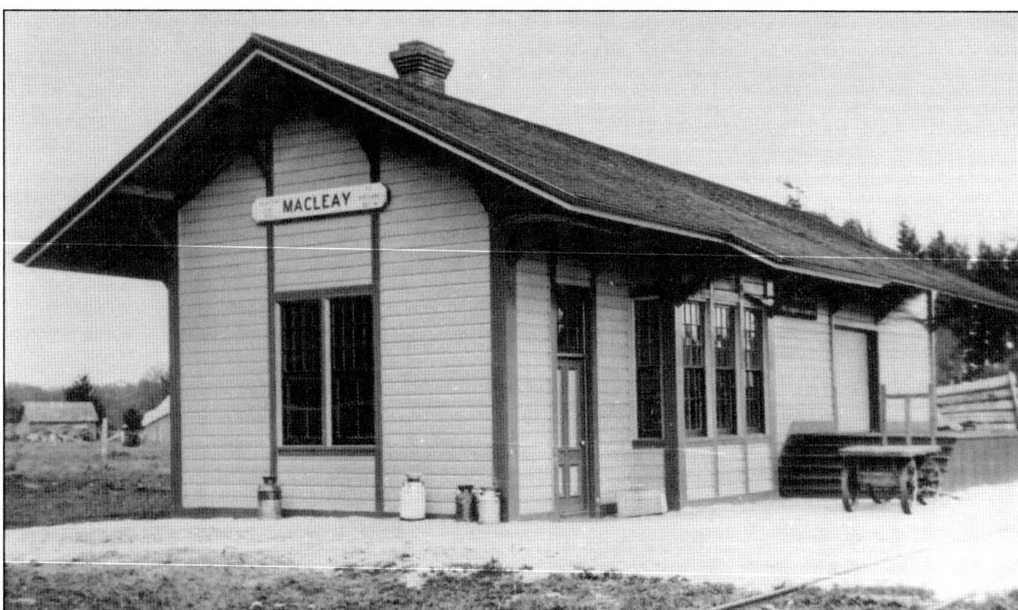

Narrow-gauge rails reached Macleay around Christmas 1880, with train service through the area beginning on January 10, 1881. The 20-foot-by-60-foot depot seen here remained in use until December 1934. Although this section of the old narrow-gauge route now belongs to the Willamette Valley Railroad and the track was still in service in 2014, trains very seldom travel this far out the line.

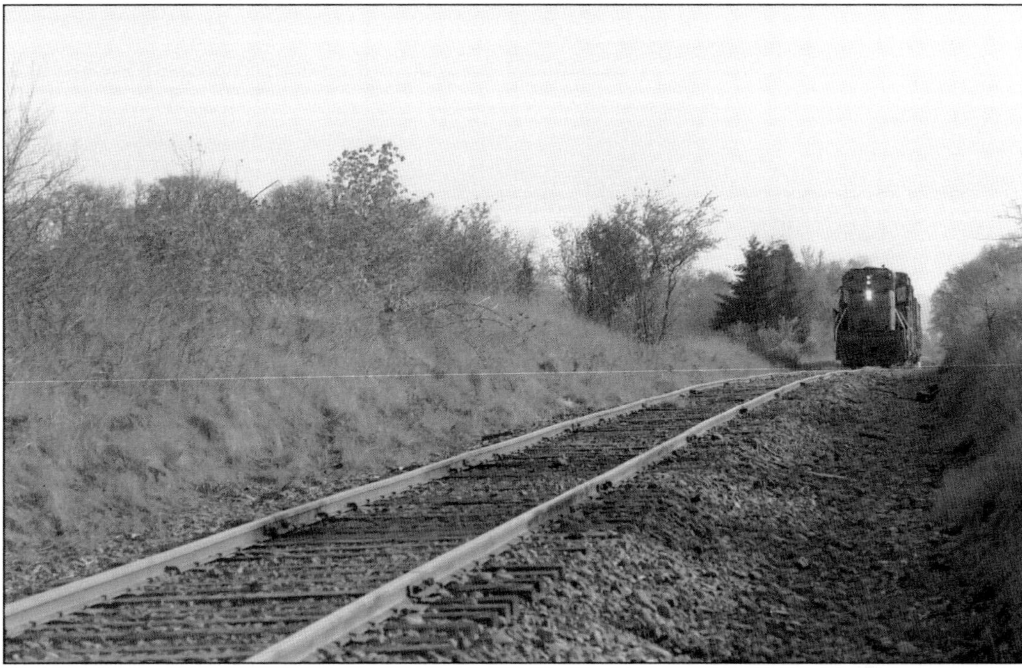

The rich farmland of the Willamette Valley extends into the foothills of the Cascade Range and it was these farmlands that the Oregonian Railway was built to serve. Thus, the narrow gauge was confronted with numerous hills and swales that required accommodation. Given its status as a secondary branchline under SP control, little or no attempt was made to improve the route. Here, a northbound SP local is cresting Macleay Hill between Geer and Stayton. Were this a mainline, such a minor hill would simply be leveled in the interest of more efficient operation.

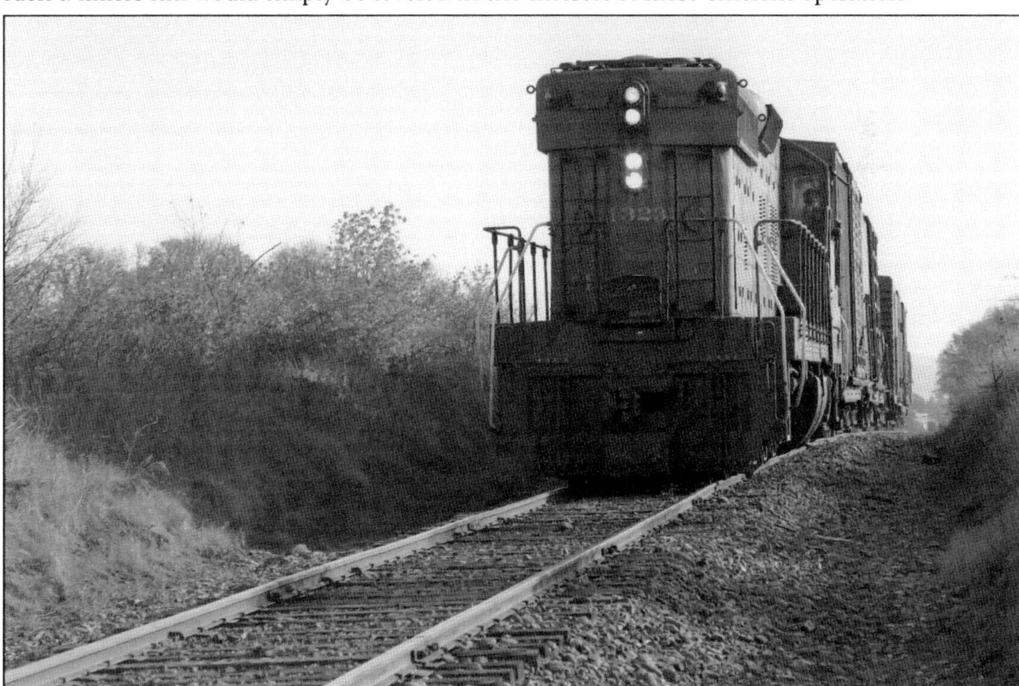

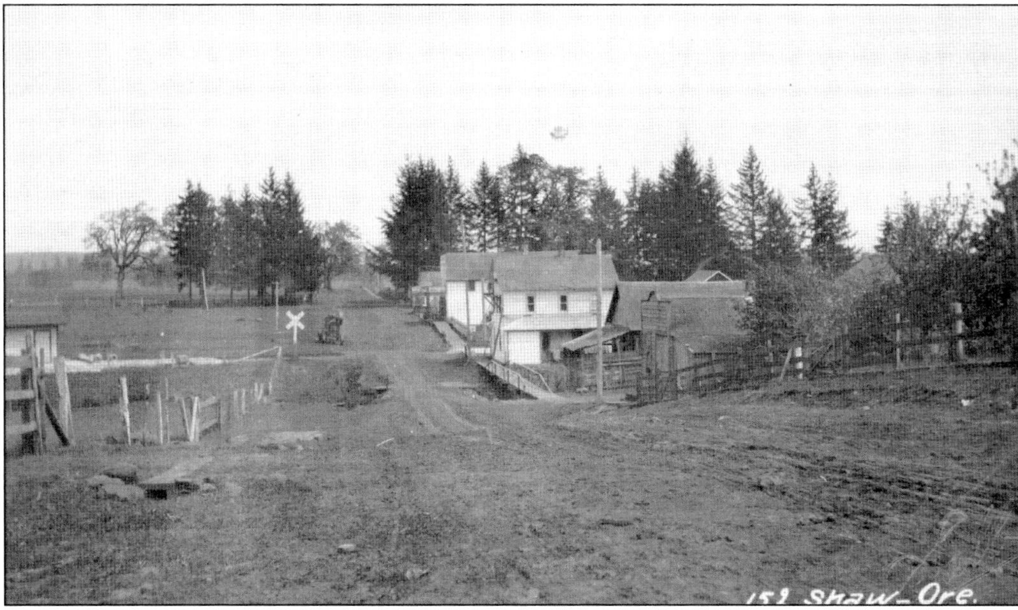

The condition of the county road through Shaw in 1909 leaves little doubt as to the advantage rail service offered to Oregon's rural communities prior to the advent of improved roads. The passenger shelter seen at the far left was moved five miles south to Shaft in 1916 and Shaw received an actual depot.

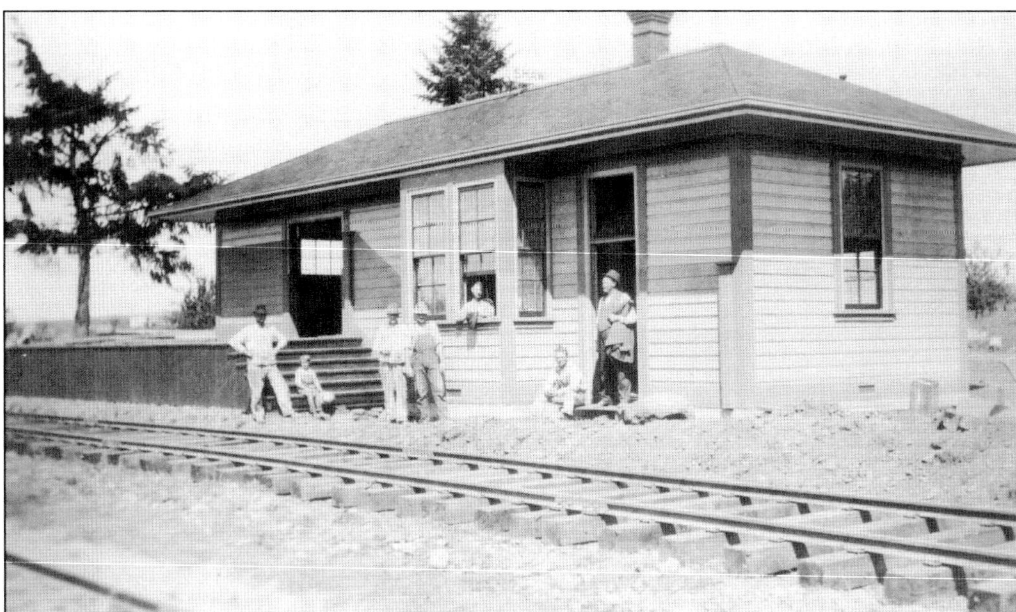

The new Shaw depot measured 16 feet by 46 feet and was a significant upgrade from the simple passenger shelter the SP originally provided here. The building was constructed in October 1916 and retired in September 1938. Note the lack of ballast and the seemingly new ties, suggesting some track replacement is in progress, perhaps in conjunction with construction of the new depot. Also note the extremely light rail typical on secondary branchlines of the period in Oregon.

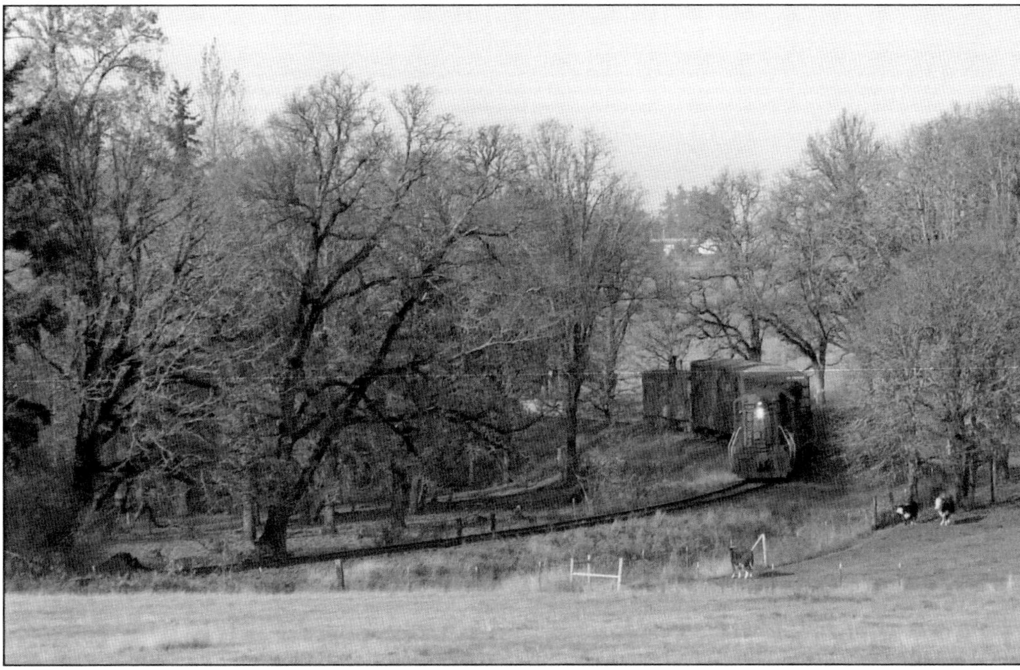

Between Shaw and Aumsville, the line encounters a series of sharp curves as it descends from the foothills to the flatland near Aumsville. The passing of today's train seems to garner only minor interest from the nearby bovines.

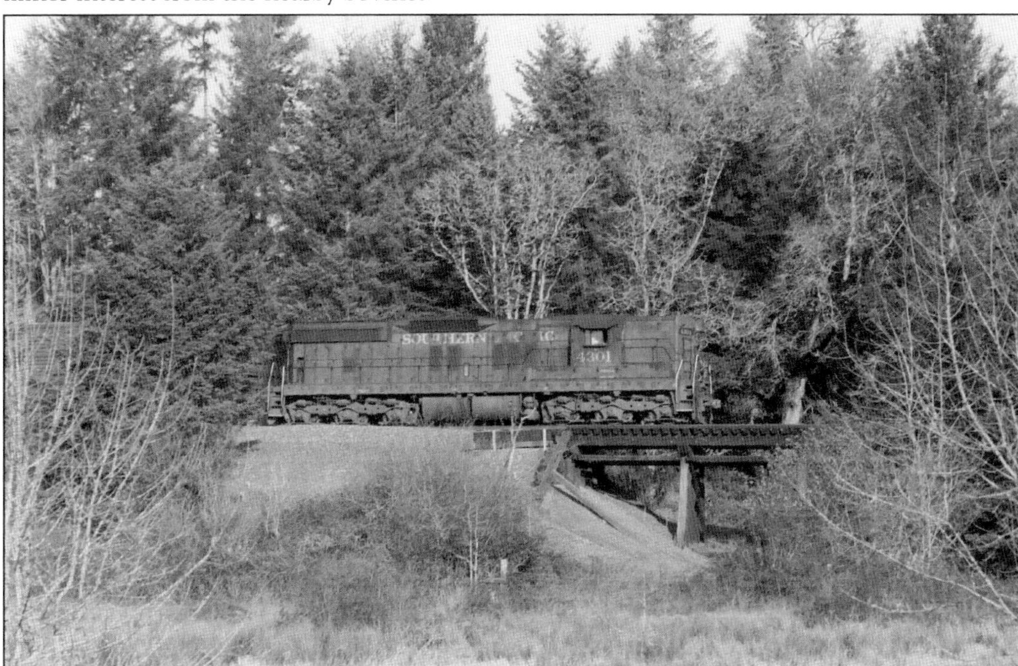

A few minutes later, the cows have turned their attention back to the grass at hand and the SP local is emerging from the woods now headed east. In a few moments, the train will cross Highway 22 and turn south again with Aumsville in sight.

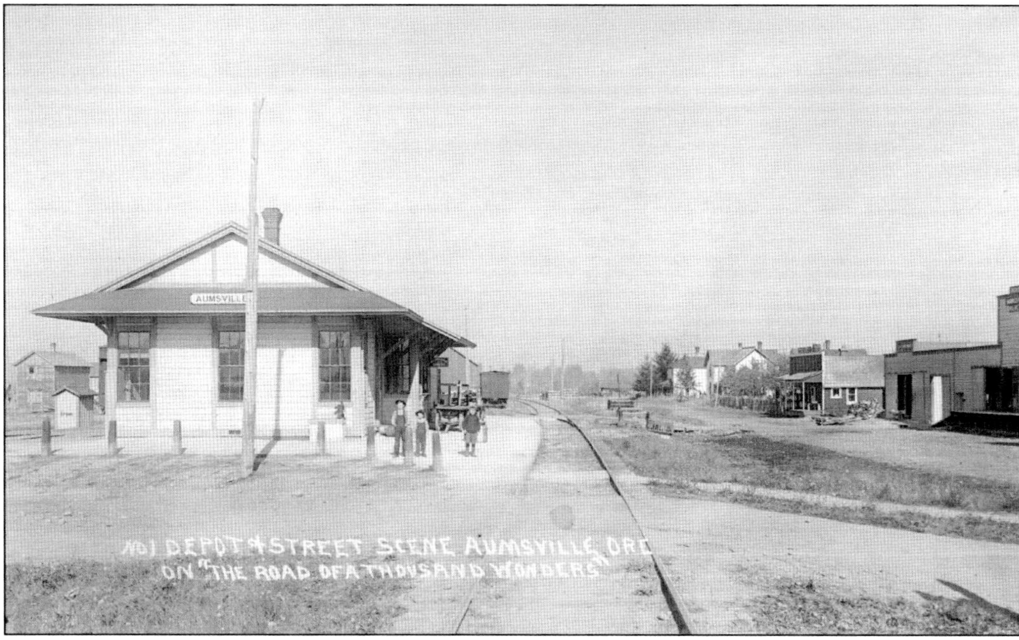

This view is looking north at the Aumsville depot around 1915. This location had served as a train order station from 1892 until 1899. The depot seen here was built around 1895 and retired in August 1938. At 25 feet by 80 feet, it was one of the larger depots between Woodburn and Coburg. The photographer seems, at least temporarily, to have gained the interest of the three young fellows on the depot platform. Were they waiting for a train or just hanging out looking for some action at the depot?

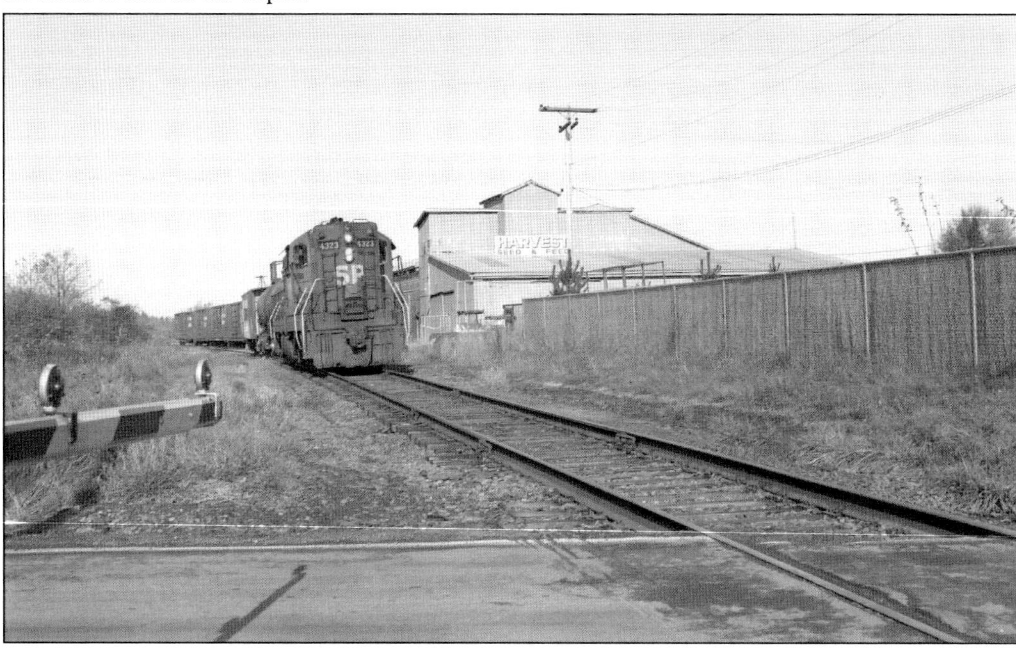

In the 40 years since the depot was abandoned, a lot has changed at Aumsville. However, the track still follows the same gentle curve of the original narrow-gauge alignment built here in 1880. The depot would have sat to the left of the locomotive.

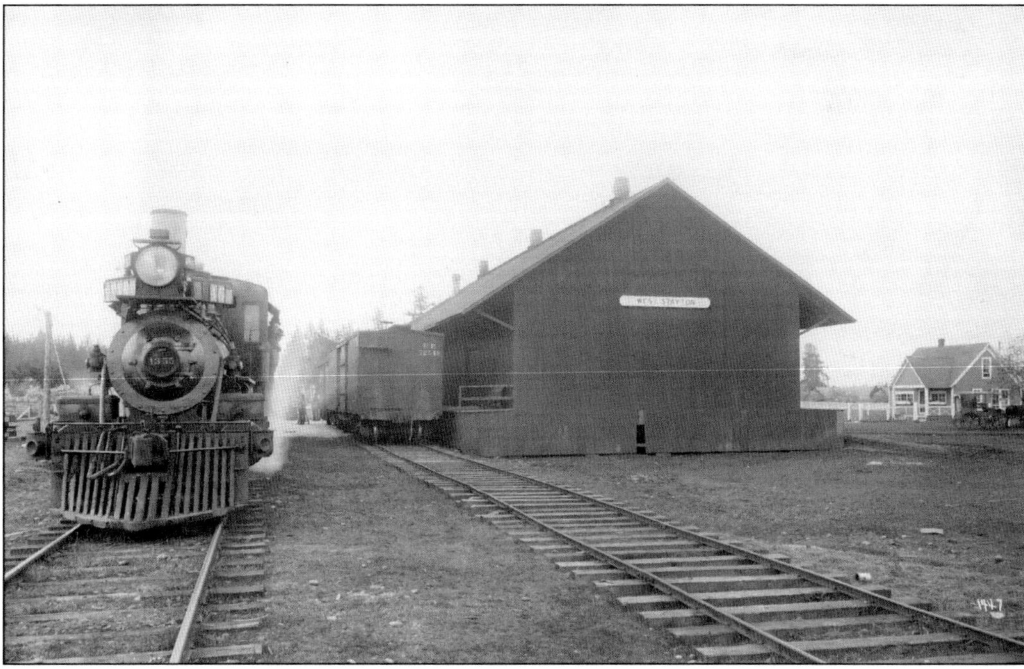

The year is 1913 and northbound train No. 46 is making its scheduled 7:54 a.m. stop at West Stayton. This train left Springfield at 5:00 a.m. and is due to arrive at Woodburn at 9:36 a.m., taking a little over four and a half hours to travel the 93 miles, a respectable pace for the time. The original narrow-gauge alignment did not go through Stayton, instead passing through West Stayton.

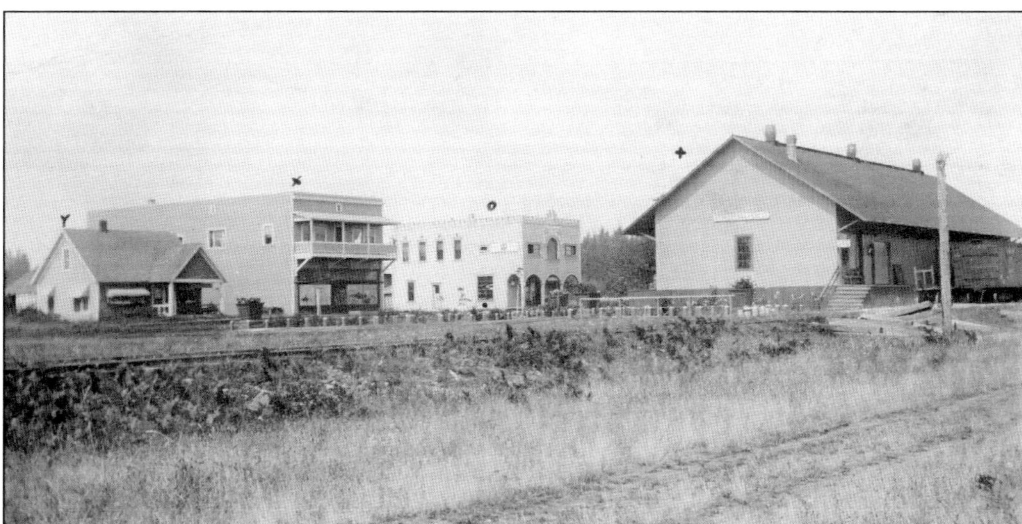

In its day, West Stayton could boast a small but attractive business district, as seen here around 1920. However, it was Stayton that emerged as the more substantial city, causing the SP to build a three-and-a-quarter-mile spur connecting Stayton with the Eastside line at Shaft one and a half miles north of West Stayton. The section of railroad south from Shaft through West Stayton to Shelburn was abandoned in 1963, after which West Stayton faded into obscurity.

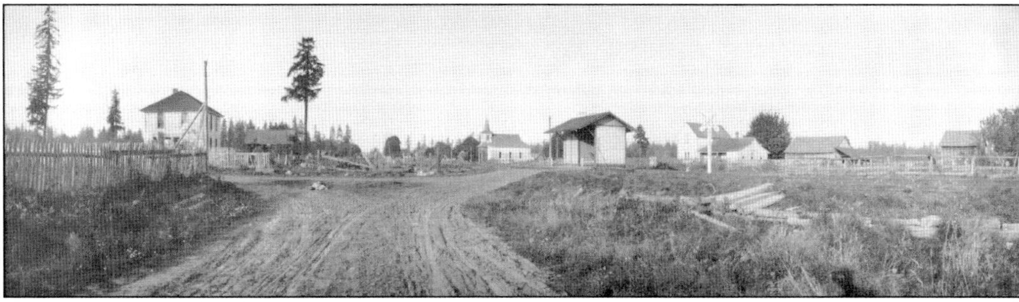

The small community of North Santiam never rated a depot, but the SP did provide the passenger shelter seen here. North Santiam was located approximately one and a half miles south of West Stayton near the point where the Oregonian Railway crossed the North Santiam River. The passenger shelter was removed in 1927 and when this section of railroad was abandoned in 1963, remaining signs of North Santiam vanished along with the track.

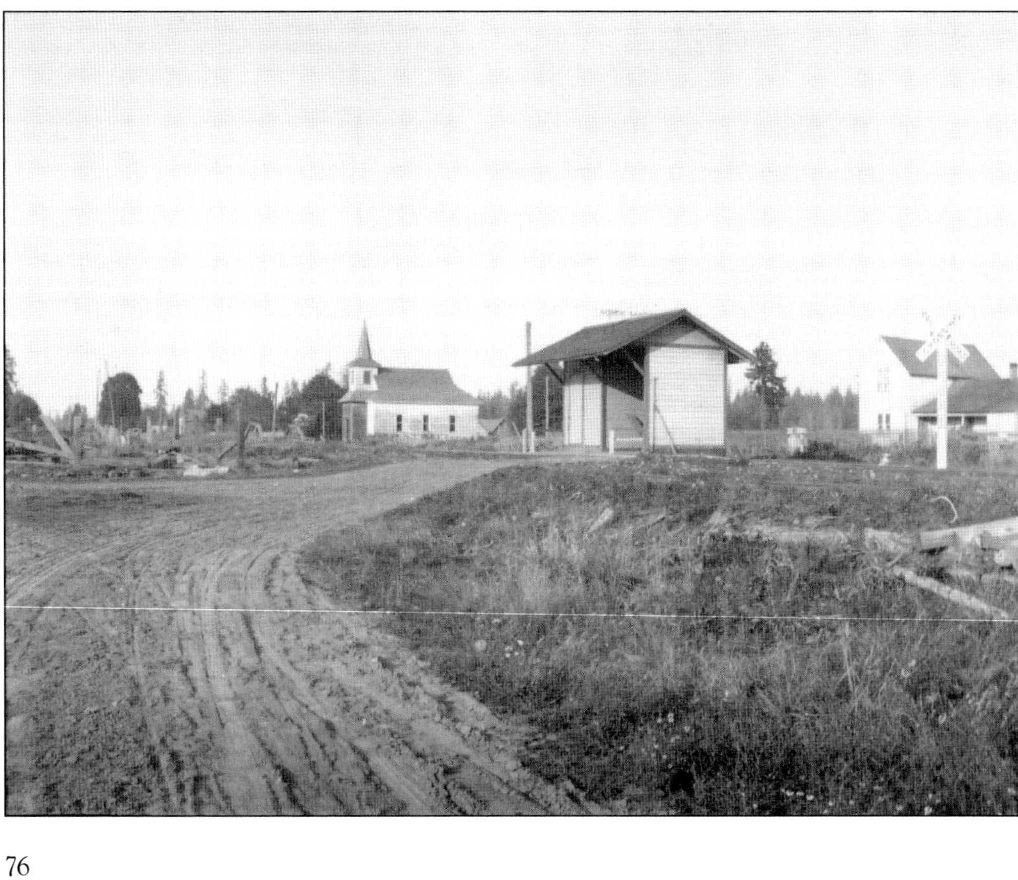

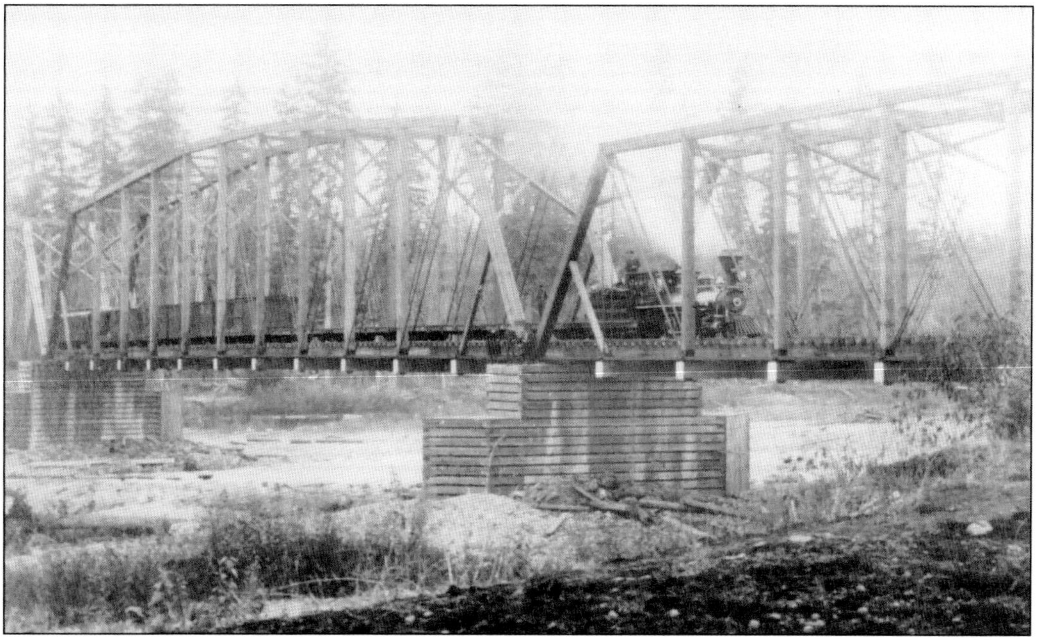

This is another rare view showing the Oregonian Railway in action around 1881. One of three narrow-gauge 2-6-0s built by H.K. Porter for the Oregonian Railway is crossing the North Santiam River between North Santiam and Shelburn. The SP replaced the wooden through-truss bridge seen here with an iron through-truss bridge set on concrete and rock-filled iron caissons. The second bridge was abandoned in 1963 along with this section of track, although the caissons remained in place in 1980.

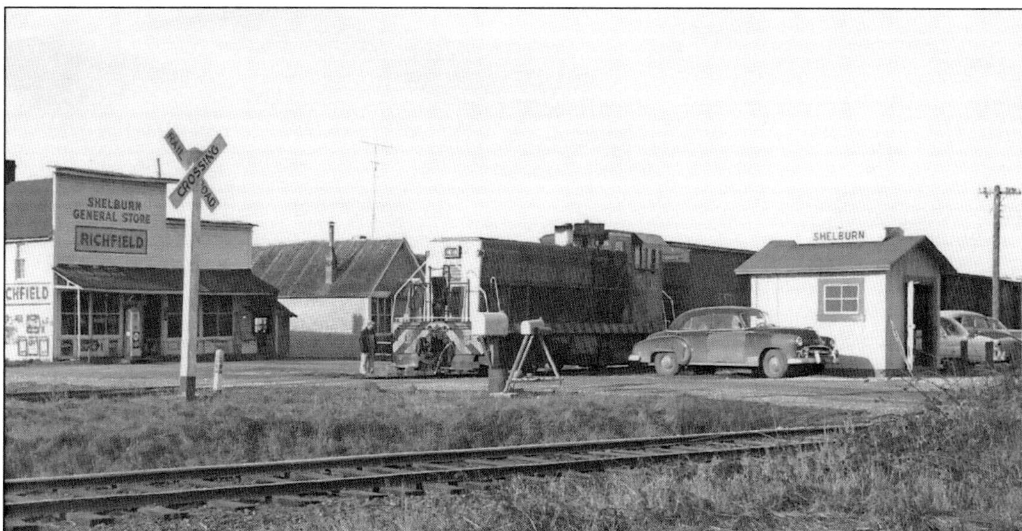

When the Oregonian Railway built through this location in 1880, Shelburn did not exist. However, when the Oregon Pacific Railroad extended its standard-gauge line east from Albany to Mill City in 1887, it crossed the narrow-gauge line at this point called Shelburn, seen in 1956. The Oregon Pacific track from Shelburn to Albany was abandoned in 1930 and the line north from Shelburn to West Stayton was abandoned in 1963. Hence, Shelburn ceased to be a junction between two lines and, today, only a few structures and a single track mark the location.

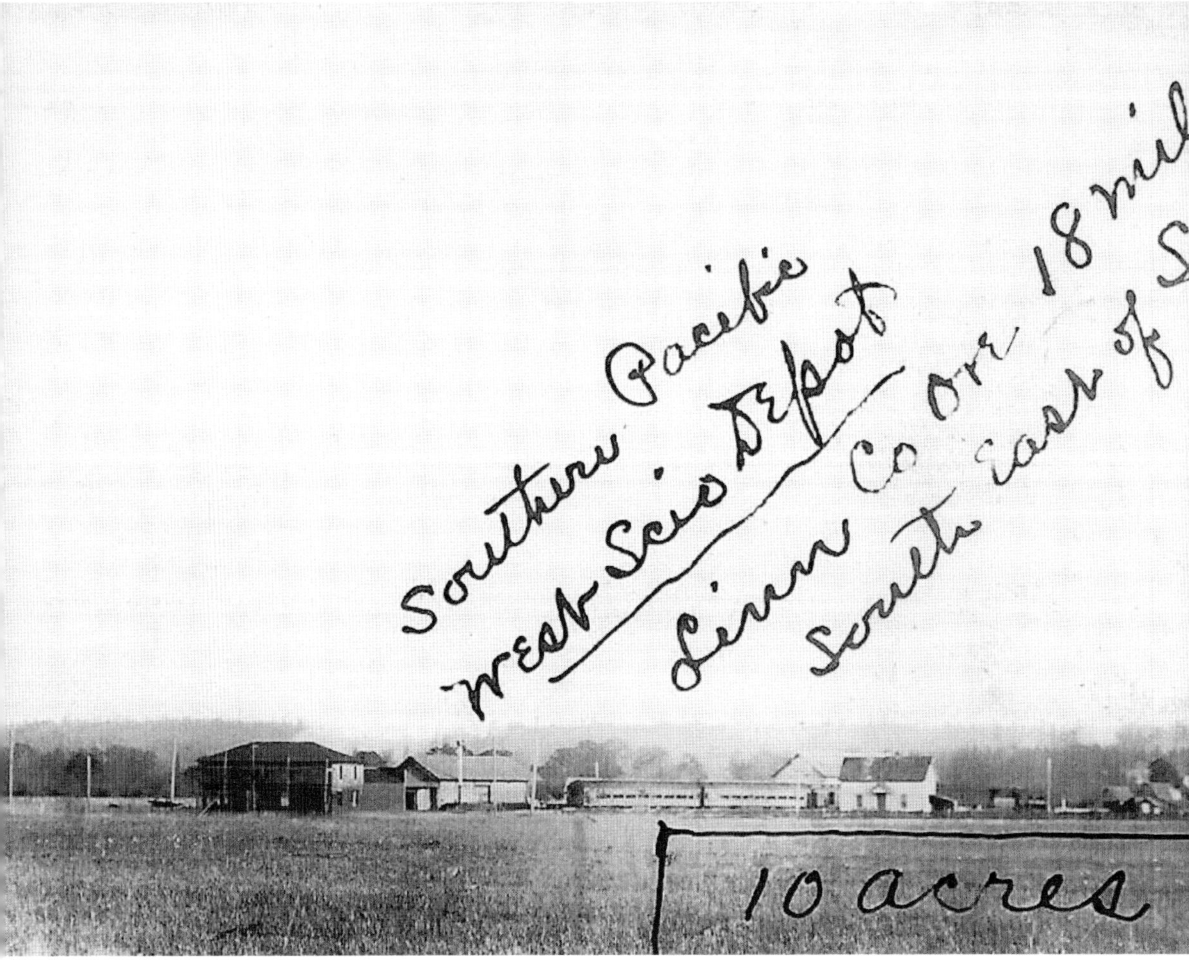

Scio was another community bypassed by the Oregonian Railway in 1880. Instead, the narrow gauge was built through West Scio, one and a half miles west of Scio. The SP depot at West Scio is visible in this view looking east in the direction of Scio c. 1920.

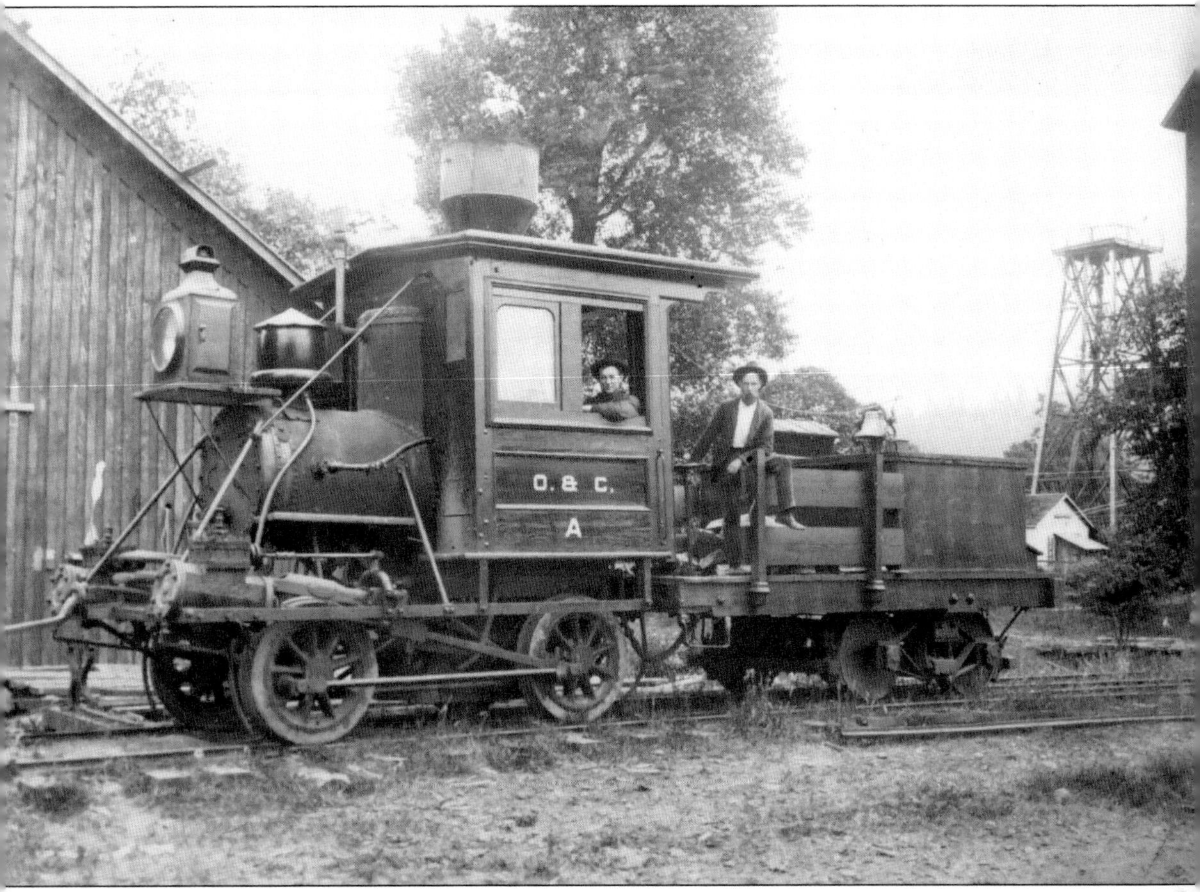

Unlike some other communities, Scio was not to be left off the railroad map. Having been bypassed by the Oregonian Railway and unwilling to wait for the SP to get around to building a standard-gauge branch to their town, the citizens elected to build their own railroad. Motive power for Scio's railroad was this well-worn little teakettle purchased third-hand from the Oregon & California Railroad. The little locomotive, along with the one-and-a-half-mile railroad it served, faded from the scene in the early part of the 20th century. Today, trains still occasionally roll through West Scio, but Scio remains off the railroad map.

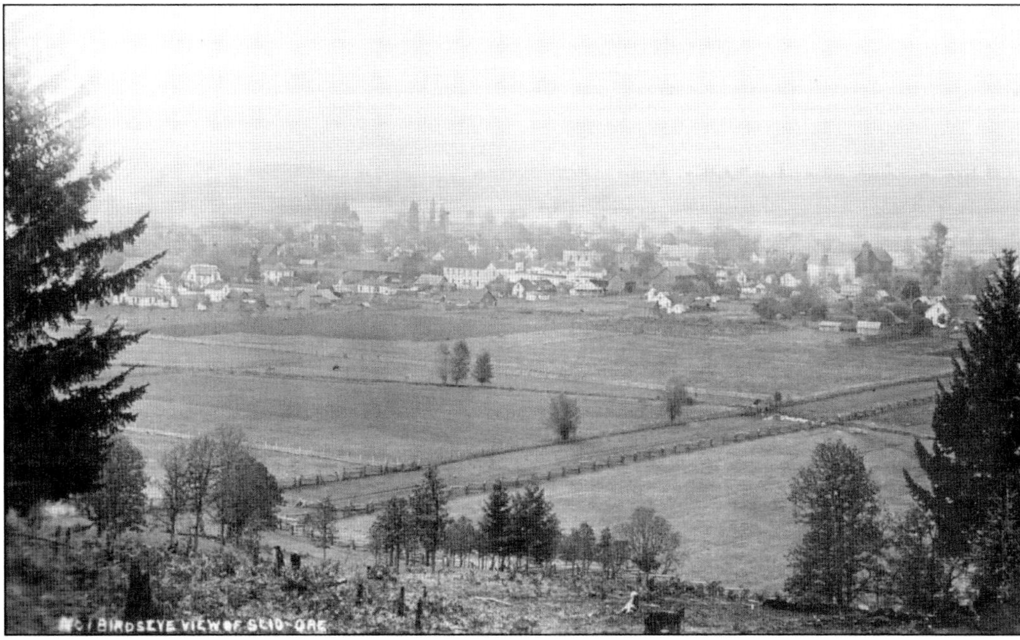

This is Scio as it looked around 1916. The white building at right center was the Scio Roller Mill, which was served by Scio's independent railroad.

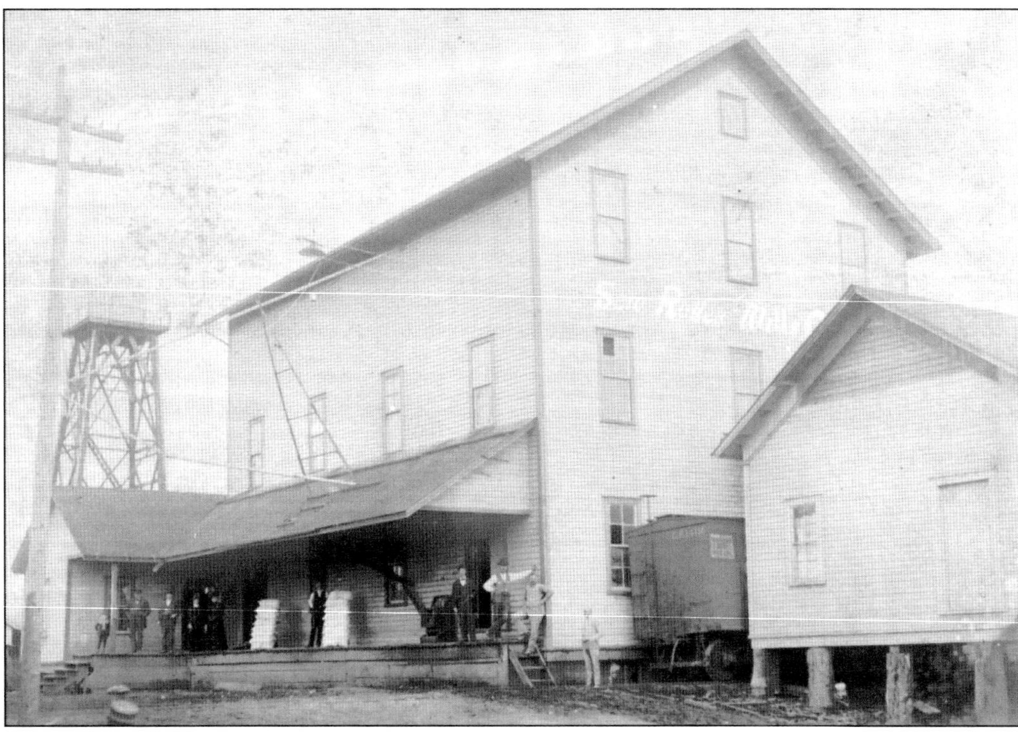

Lest there be any doubt that Scio was once served by rail, note the boxcar alongside the Scio Roller Mill. The car has been equipped with air brakes but still uses link and pin couplers, which were banned by the Rail Safety Act of 1893, thus giving an approximate date for this photograph.

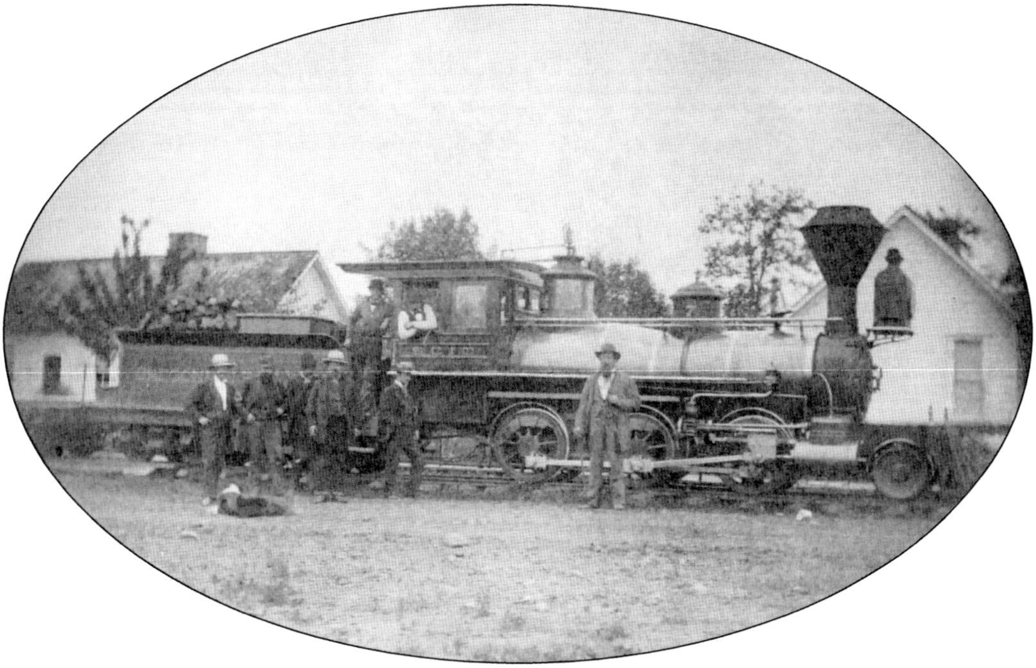

Although the Oregonian Railway didn't build its line through Scio, it at least named a locomotive for the community. The H.K. Porter–built narrow-gauge 2-6-0 No. 7 was named *Scio*, as seen in this view from around 1881.

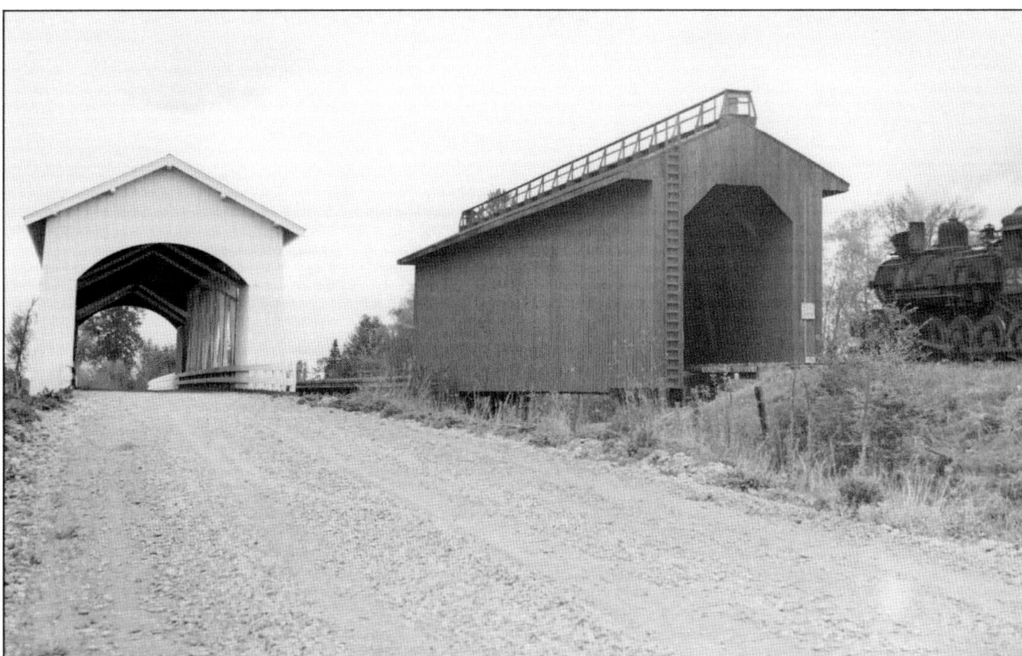

Oregon's reputation for rain is well deserved, and when bridges were primarily made of wood, covering them proved useful in extending their serviceable lives. Here, the county road and railroad bridges cross Thomas Creek near Gilkey. Although lacking a depot, Gilkey did rate a standard 10-foot-by-20-foot passenger shelter until 1929.

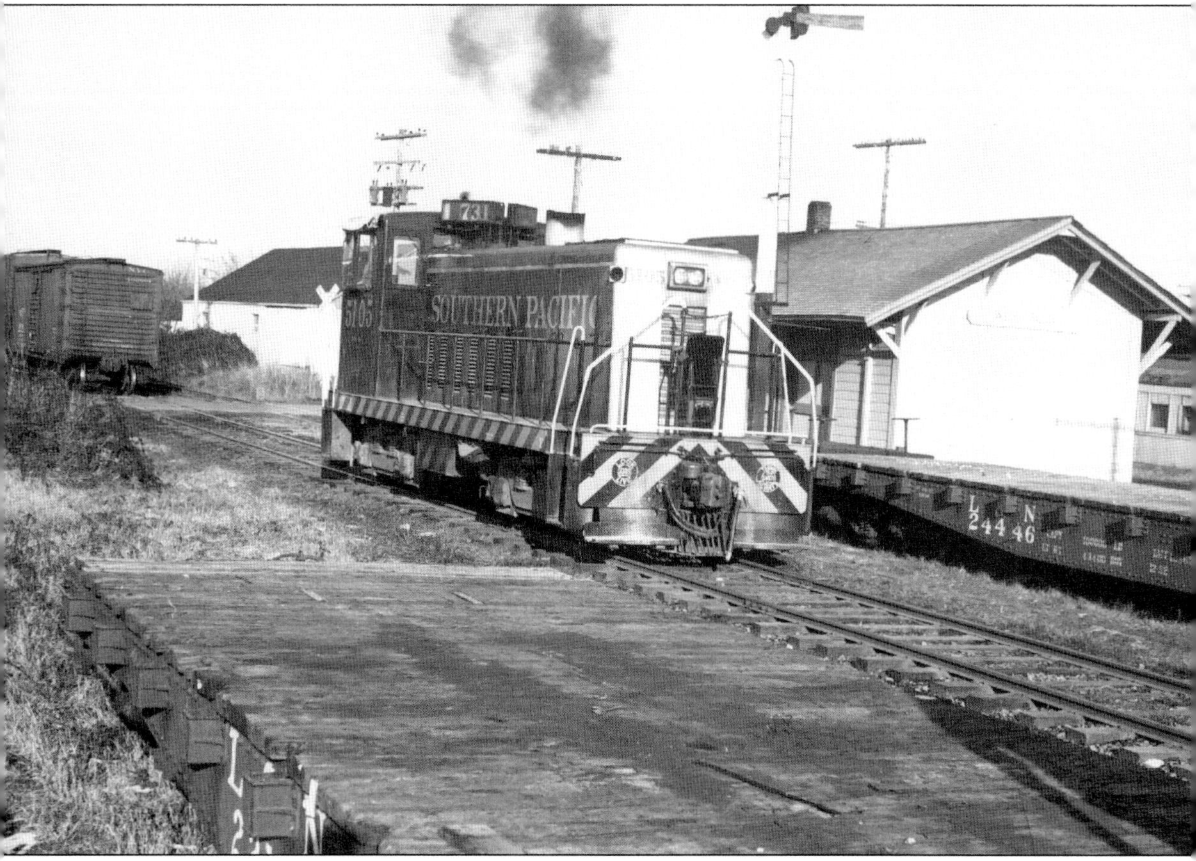

Back at West Scio in 1956, SP 70-tonner No. 5105 is switching some cars. Under SP control, the original narrow-gauge line was converted to standard gauge and bridges and other infrastructure were improved. However, the route was always relegated to secondary branchline status and weight restrictions limited the equipment that the line could safely handle. As a result, train crews referred to the line as the "wooden axle route." Little General Electric diesels like No. 5105 only weighted 70 tons and were kept in Oregon long after they otherwise might have been scrapped because their light weight allowed them unrestricted use on the line.

Between Crabtree and Tallman, the Oregonian Railway encountered its second major river crossing on the Eastside Division. This was at the South Santiam River, where wooden through-truss spans crossed the generally mild-mannered South Santiam. However, during the winter of 1907, the South Santiam lost its temper and in the process washed out the railroad bridge. These two photographs are believed to show the aftermath of the flood. As a result, this line was never rebuilt. Instead, a new line was built from Balm to Lebanon where it connected with the Albany & Lebanon Railroad, which crossed the original narrow-gauge route at Tallman. Thus, traffic formerly routed from Balm directly to Tallman now took a circuitous route through Griggs and Lebanon in order to get to its original route at Tallman.

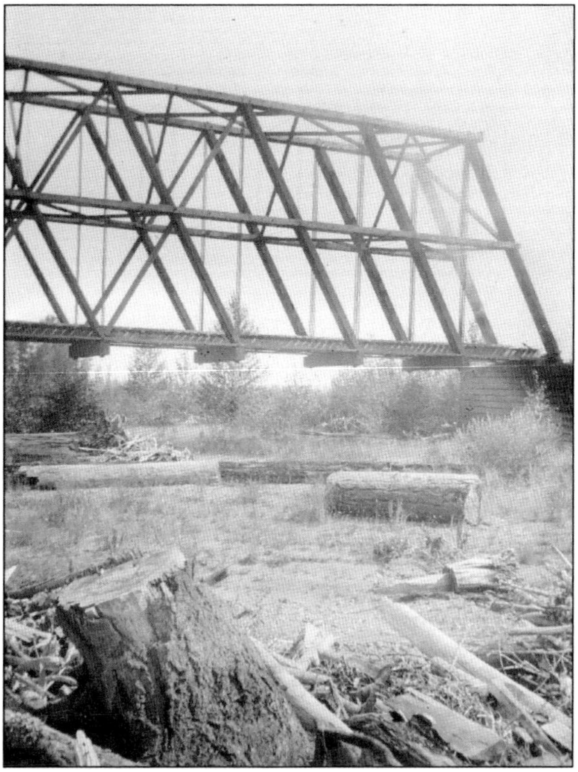

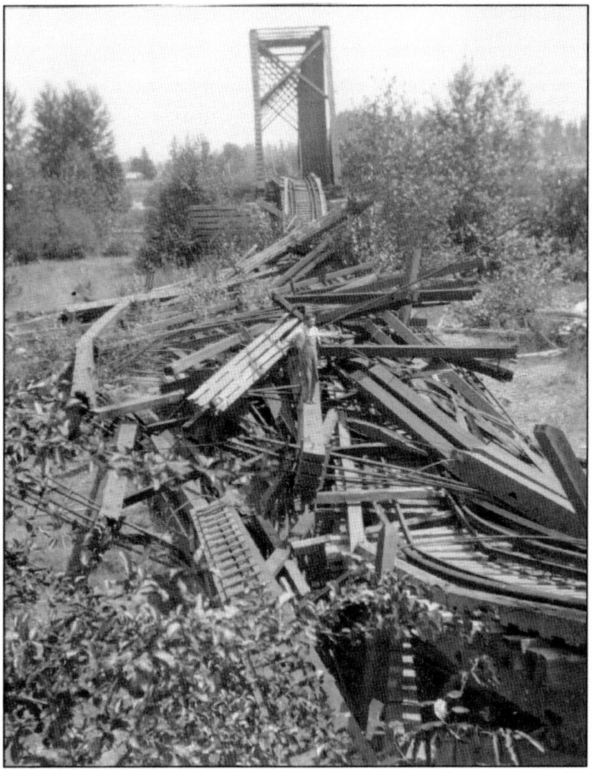

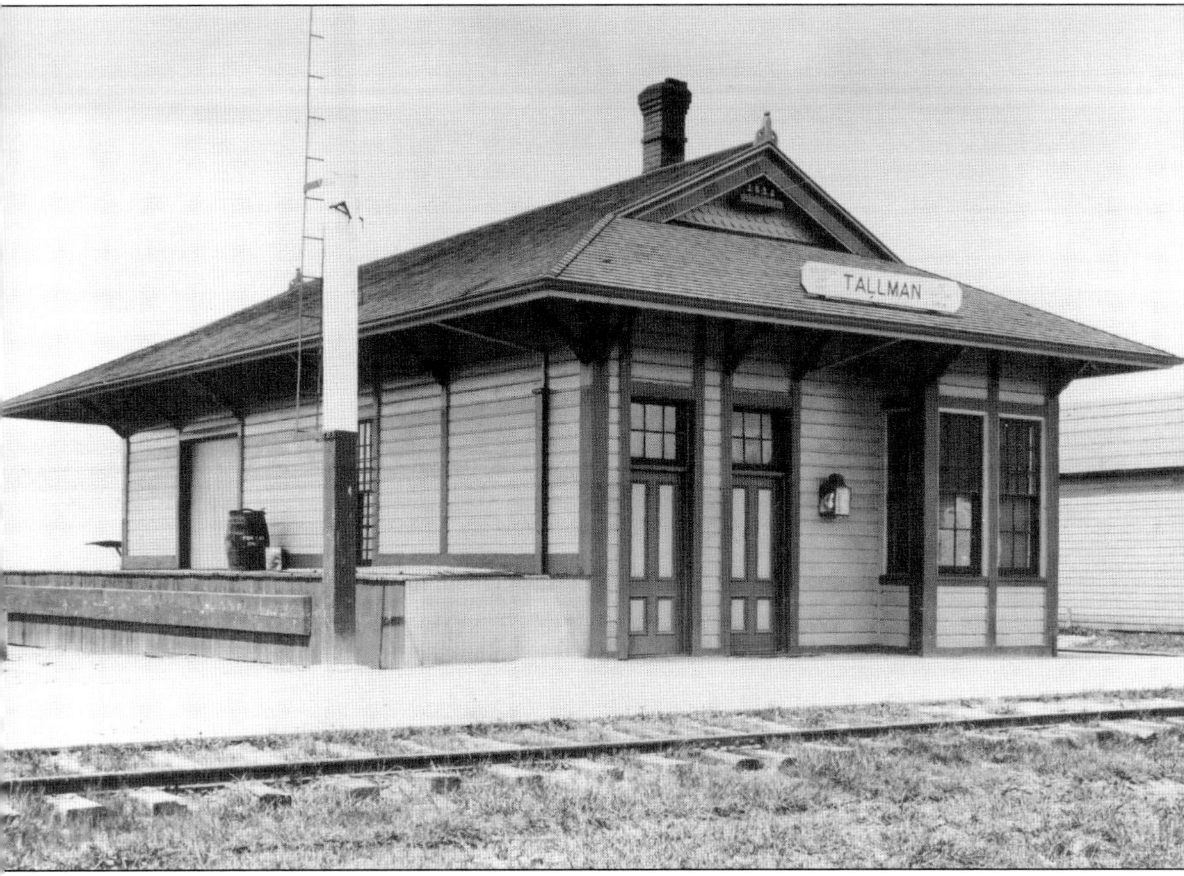

The north-to-south Oregonian Railway and the west-to-east Albany & Lebanon Railroad met at Tallman. The Albany & Lebanon Railroad was a halfhearted attempt by Henry Villard's Oregon & California Railroad to discourage the narrow-gauge system from expanding farther south in the Willamette Valley. At the time, Lebanon offered significant potential rail traffic and apparently Villard reasoned that by building a line to Lebanon he would deprive the narrow gauge of that business, which was effectively true. Undeterred however, the narrow gauge simply crossed the O&C at grade and continued south, bypassing Lebanon. The Tallman depot, seen here around 1900, served as a train order office from 1895 until 1909.

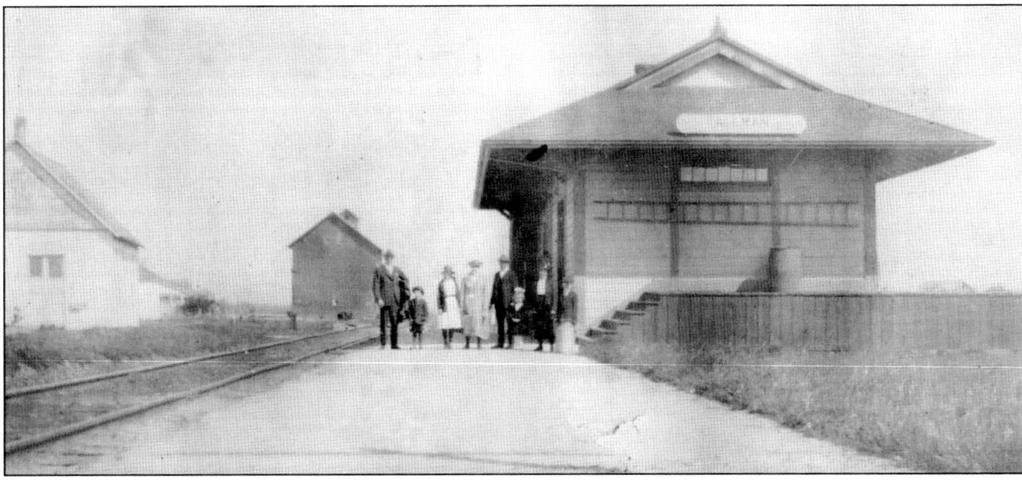

Another view of Tallman seen from the other end finds a family apparently ready to go to town as soon as the local passenger train arrives.

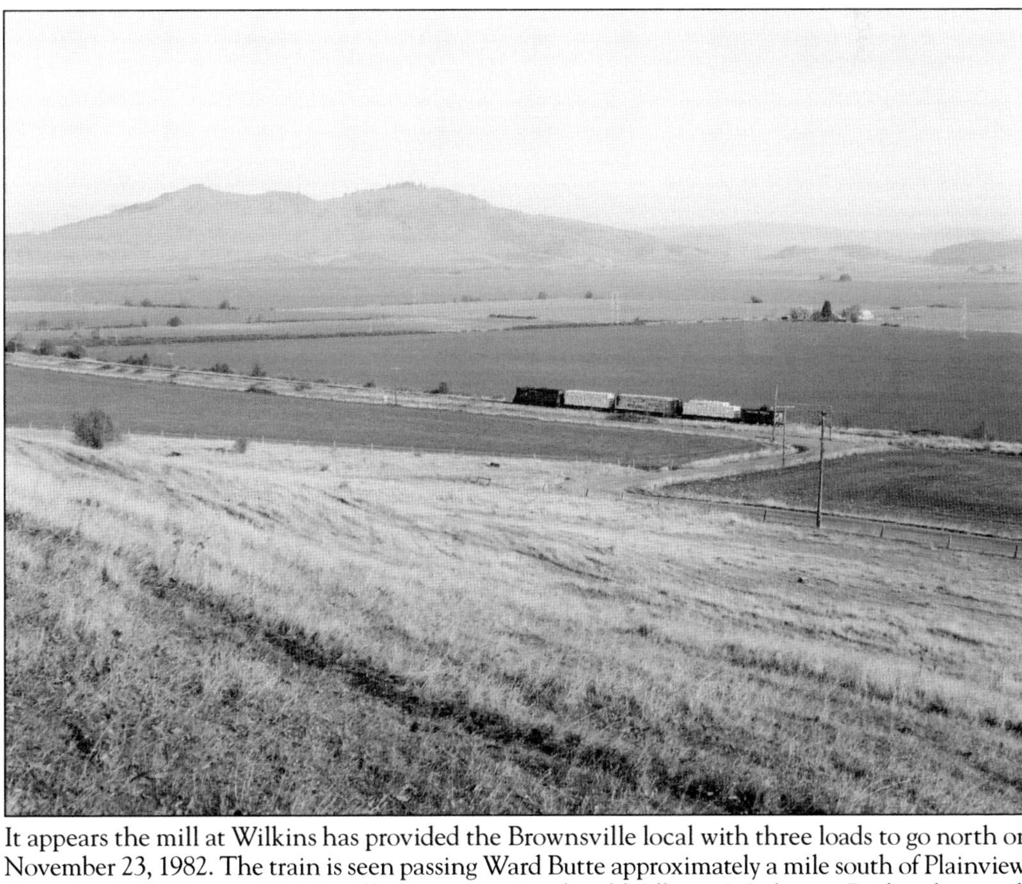

It appears the mill at Wilkins has provided the Brownsville local with three loads to go north on November 23, 1982. The train is seen passing Ward Butte approximately a mile south of Plainview. On arrival at Tallman, this job will turn west using the old Albany & Lebanon Railroad to reach Albany on the SP mainline.

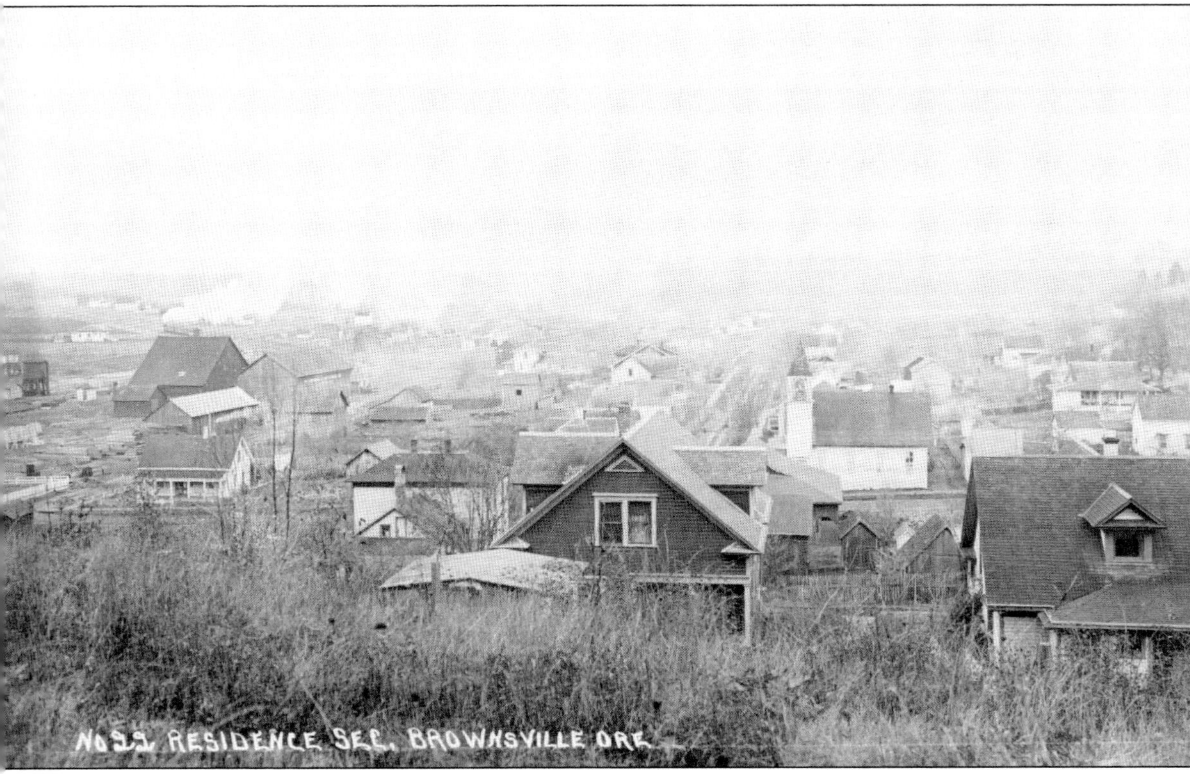

Prior to Henry Villard's takeover of the Oregonian Railway, Brownsville was the south end of the narrow gauge in the Willamette Valley. At the time, the farming community of Brownsville was the most significant city between Albany and Eugene. Apparently, a post office was established at the site in 1850, called Calapooya. The name was changed to Brownsville in 1859, and by 1880, it was a thriving community in need of a railroad. Looking carefully, a train can be seen departing Brownsville at upper left.

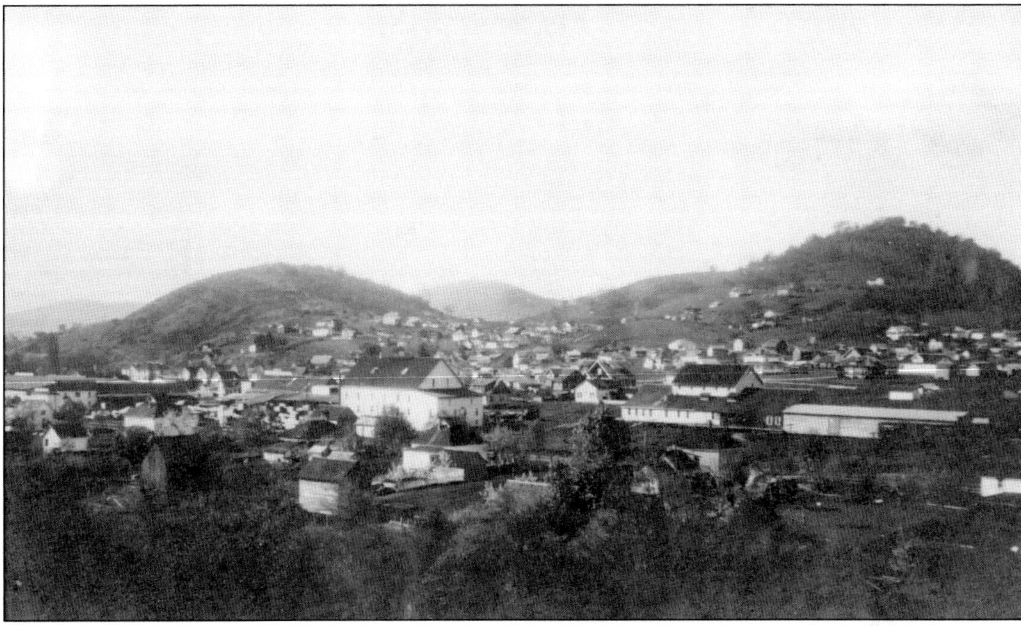

Another view of Brownsville looks east toward the Cascade foothills. The two small buttes are typical of the south end of the Willamette Valley. In the early years, this area was also well known for its population of rattlesnakes.

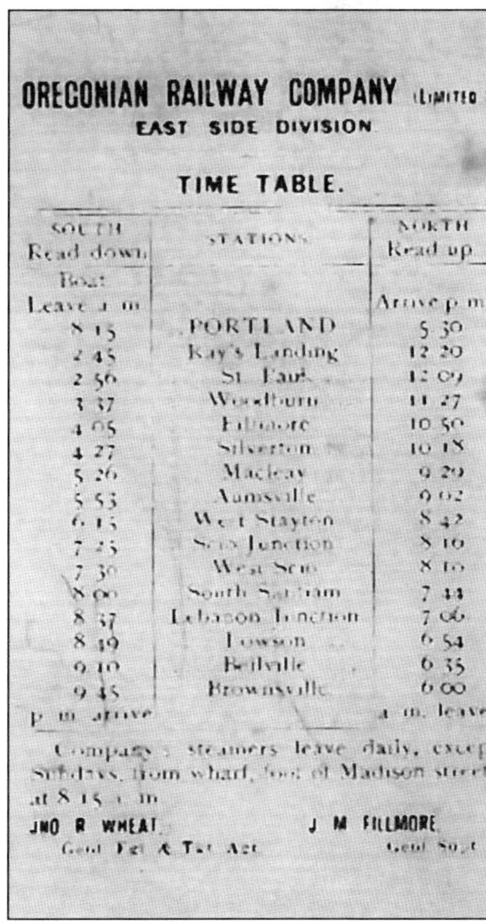

OREGONIAN RAILWAY COMPANY (LIMITED)

EAST SIDE DIVISION

TIME TABLE.

SOUTH Read down	STATIONS	NORTH Read up
Boat Leave a m		Arrive p m
8 15	PORTLAND	5 30
2 45	Ray's Landing	12 20
2 56	St Paul	12 09
3 37	Woodburn	11 27
4 05	Fillmore	10 50
4 27	Silverton	10 18
5 26	Macleay	9 29
5 53	Aumsville	9 02
6 15	West Stayton	8 42
7 25	Scio Junction	8 10
7 30	West Scio	8 10
8 00	South Santiam	7 44
8 37	Lebanon Junction	7 06
8 49	Lowson	6 54
9 10	Bellville	6 35
9 45	Brownsville	6 00
p m arrive		a m leave

Company's steamers leave daily, except Sundays, from wharf, foot of Madison street, at 8 15 a m

JNO R WHEAT, Gen'l Frt & Tkt Agt — J M FILLMORE, Gen'l Supt

This c. 1881 Oregonian Railway Eastside Division timetable indicates that by leaving Portland via steamboat at 8:15 in the morning and transferring to the narrow-gauge railway at Ray's Landing at 2:45 p.m., one could expect to be in Brownsville by 9:45 p.m. the same day, assuming everything went as planned. Prior to the arrival of the railroad, the idea of making a trip from Brownsville to Portland in a single day would have seemed inconceivable.

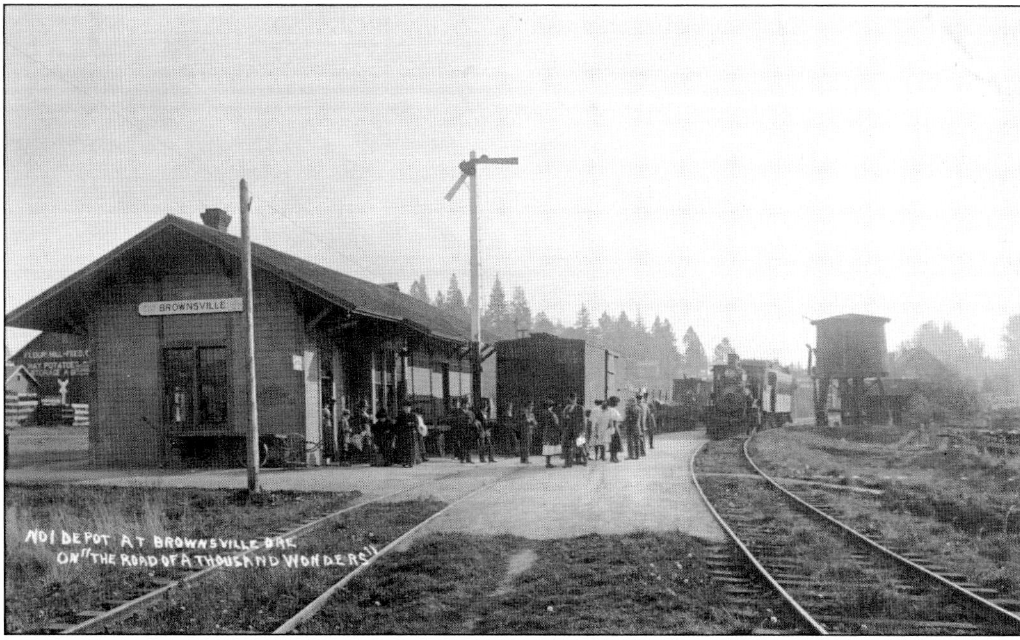

Speaking of making a trip from Brownsville to Portland, it appears a good-sized group plans to board the northbound SP local passenger train at Brownsville on this day around 1911. The train has come from Springfield and after stopping at Brownsville will continue to Woodburn. Note the Brownsville Flour Mill and Storage building visible behind and to the left of the depot.

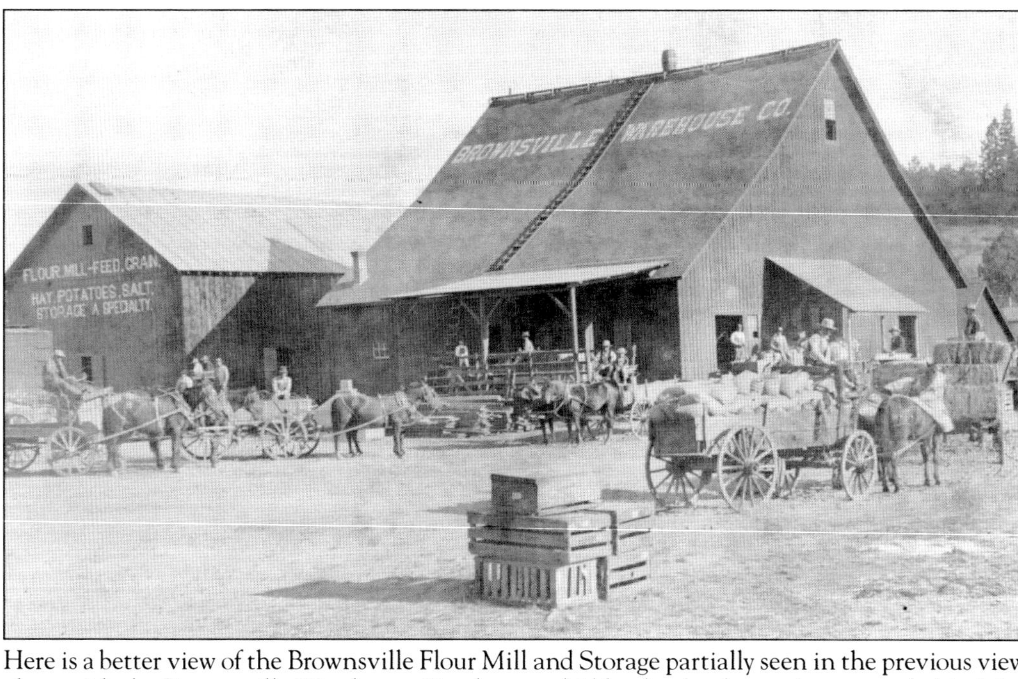

Here is a better view of the Brownsville Flour Mill and Storage partially seen in the previous view along with the Brownsville Warehouse Co. that was hidden by the depot. A spur ran behind the depot to serve these businesses.

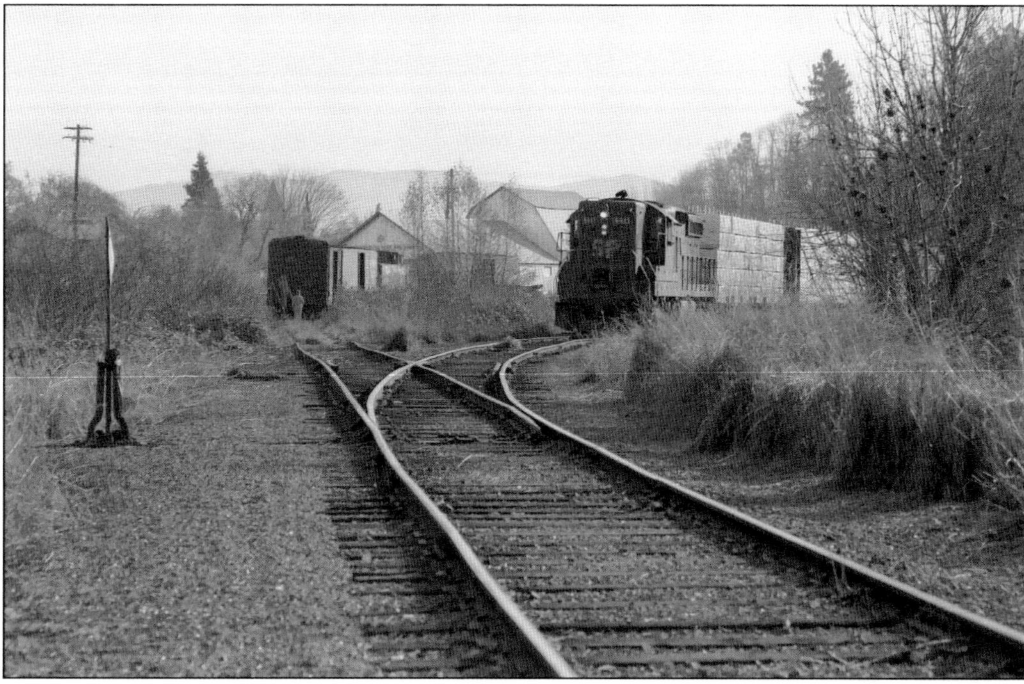

Fast forward to November 1982, and the SP Brownsville local is passing the long-vacant site of the depot. Amazingly, the old Brownsville Flour Mill still stands in the form of Brownsville Feed and Supply, seen behind the boxcars and caboose at left center.

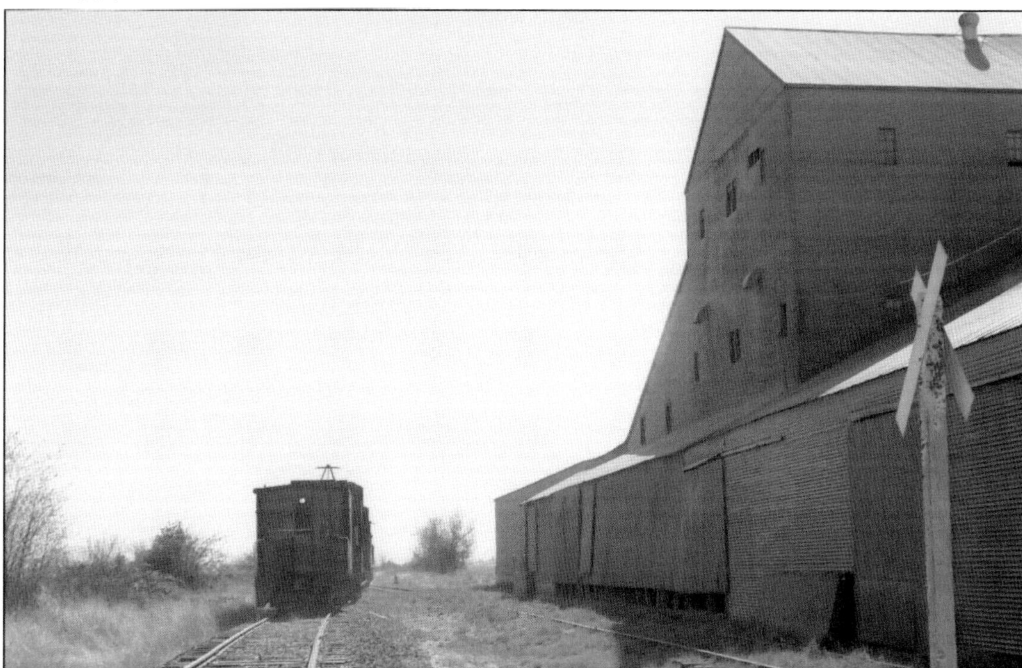

By September 1984 when the Brownsville local was photographed passing Bowers, trips this far out the Eastside line were becoming infrequent. Today's run is being made with a single empty flatcar that will be loaded at Wilkins.

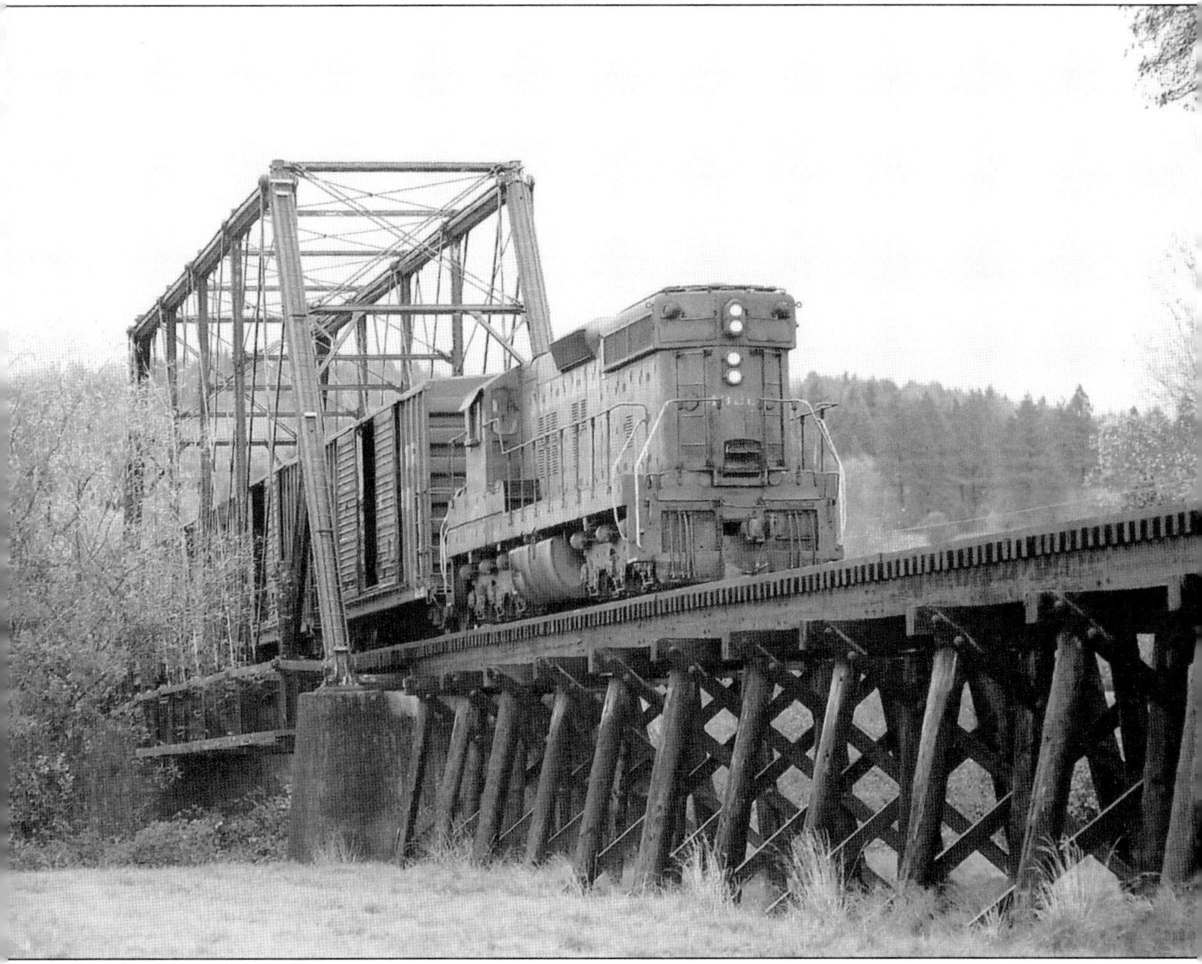

Under O&C control, the Oregonian Railway narrow-gauge line was extended south from Brownsville to Coburg. Immediately south of Brownsville, the line encountered the Calapooya River. The original wooden narrow-gauge bridge was replaced by this iron bridge manufactured by the Phoenix Bridge Company. Weighing 329,000 pounds, SP No. 4326 is one of the heaviest locomotives allowed to cross this fragile-looking structure. Despite being an artifact itself, this bridge remained in use until the line was abandoned in 1985. Two other examples of Phoenix Bridge Co. bridges remain in Oregon, both as historic attractions now limited to pedestrian traffic.

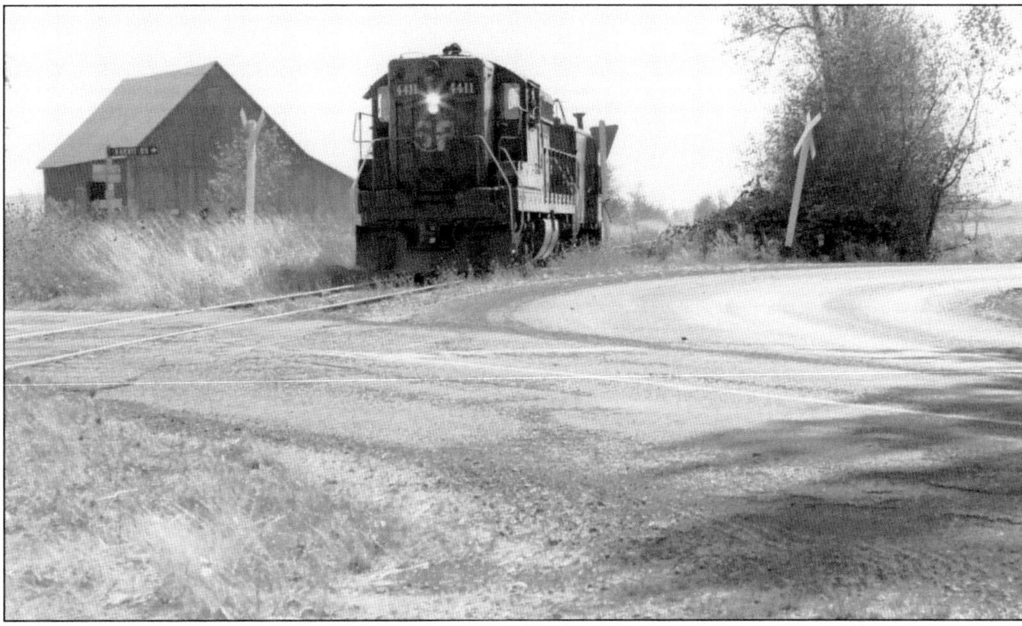

By the 1980s, the days of the old Eastside line south from Tallman were clearly numbered. A mill at Wilkins still required occasional service, and a small amount of business remained at Brownsville, but the economics of maintaining a long secondary branchline for so little traffic weren't working. Here, the Brownsville local is running with only a caboose in tow at Rowland on November 23, 1982. The empty siding to the right tells the story.

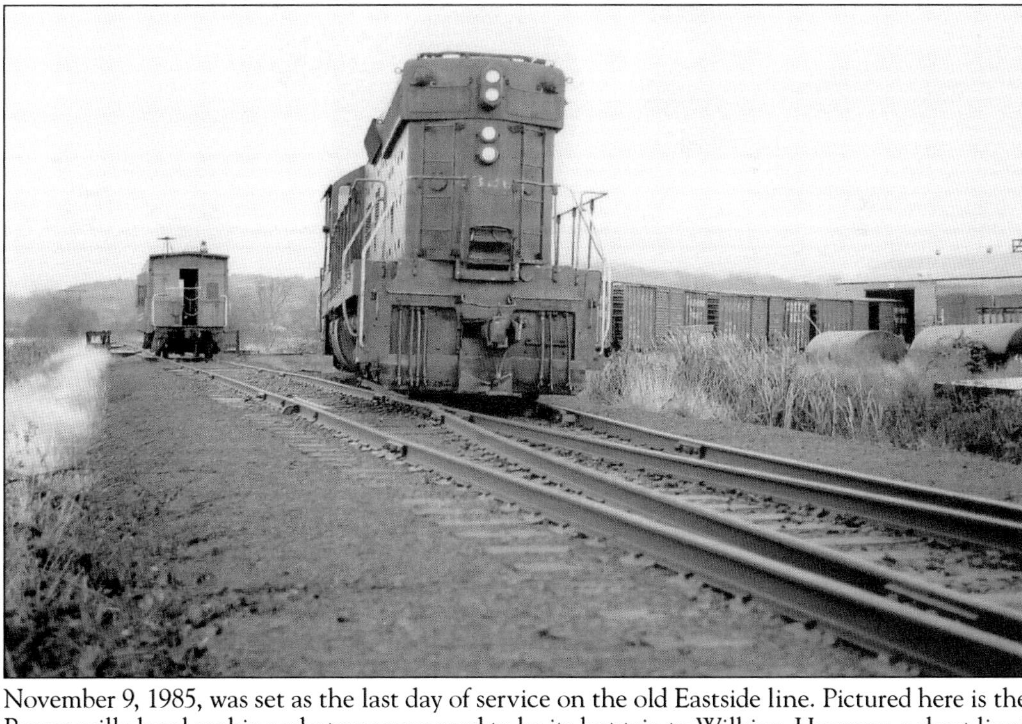

November 9, 1985, was set as the last day of service on the old Eastside line. Pictured here is the Brownsville local making what was supposed to be its last trip to Wilkins. However, a short-lived extension was granted and the last trip was actually made on December 15.

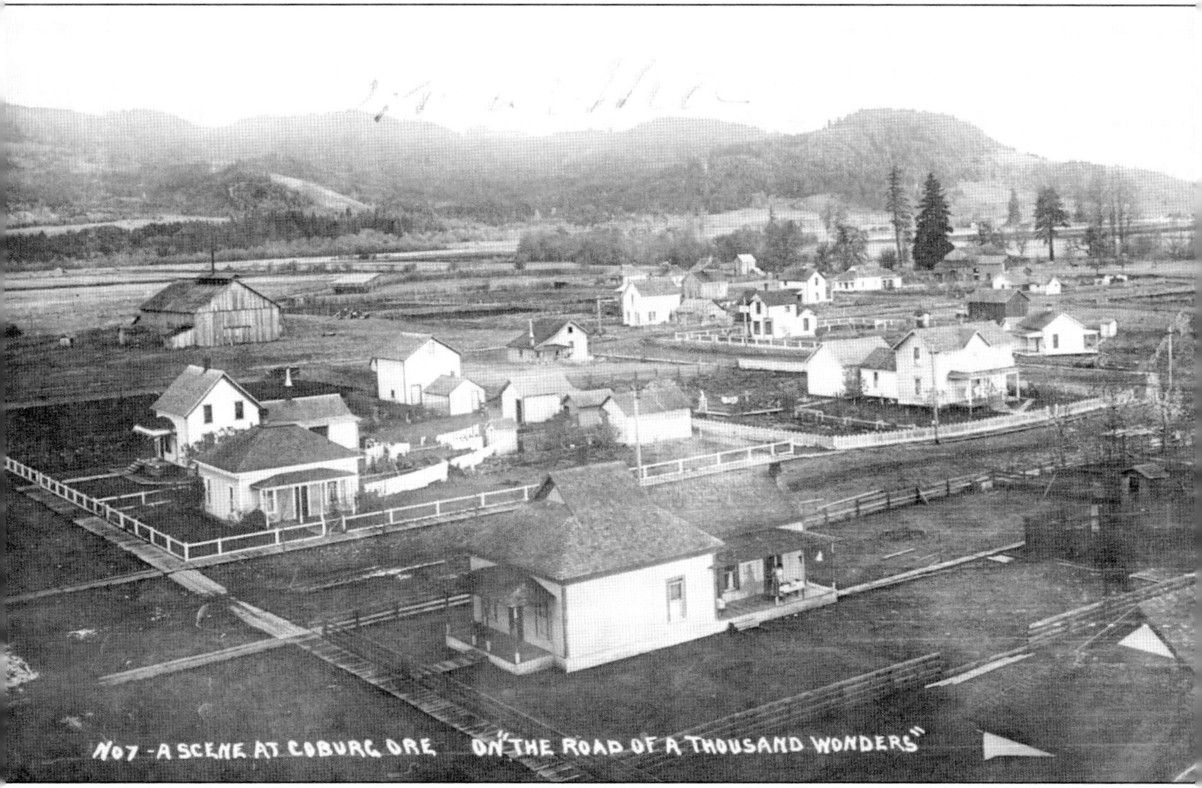

Coburg, seen around 1912, was the southernmost point reached by the narrow-gauge Oregonian Railway. Earlier visions of crossing the Cascades and connecting with the Central Pacific at Winnemucca, Nevada, faded while under the control of Henry Villard. Under Villard's direction the narrow gauge was completed to Coburg in July 1882, but only to serve as a feeder to his Oregon & California Railroad. It would fall to the Southern Pacific Railroad to resume construction nearly a decade later, by which time the track had been widened to standard gauge. Ironically, crossing the Cascades remained a goal and eventually a Southern Pacific route did reach Winnemucca, much as was envisioned many years earlier by William Reid and his Scottish investors . . . but that's another story.

Four

Portland to Dundee

As conceived, the Dayton, Sheridan & Grand Ronde Railroad was a relatively conservative venture. The narrow-gauge railroad was only to extend from Sheridan approximately 20 miles to a landing on the Yamhill River at Dayton. Here, adequate transportation to Portland and markets beyond was available via steamboat. To the local promoters of the venture, building a 20-mile railroad across relatively flat terrain was probably challenge enough. Simply gaining access to markets for their farm products and manufactured goods was the motivation driving the enterprise. Visions of creating a railroad empire would be left to others.

William Reid was one of those others. Reid had a grander vision for the fledgling narrow-gauge railroad. After gaining control of the DS&GR in 1879, he ordered significant new construction under the name Oregonian Railway Company Ltd. Among the new projects was a line from Dundee to Portland, which would eliminate dependence on steamboat operators. Grading for this extension was begun in 1881 but was promptly stopped after Henry Villard gained control of the Oregonian Railway.

However, Villard's railroad empire collapsed in 1884 and control of the Oregonian Railway returned to Scottish investors. As a result, William Reid incorporated the Portland & Willamette Valley Railroad on January 19, 1885, to take over construction of the line from Dundee to Portland that had been begun by the Oregonian Railway in 1881. Work began at Dundee Junction (near Dundee) in January 1886, and the line was completed via Newberg and Rex Hill to Oswego by year's end. Service to Jefferson Street Station in West Portland began on July 14, 1888.

Despite their efforts, returning the Oregonian Railway to profitability proved impossible, and by April 1890 much of the narrow-gauge system had come under the control of the Southern Pacific. By August 1892, the SP had acquired control of the properties of the Portland & Willamette Valley Railroad, thus completing acquisition of the entire narrow-gauge system. The remaining narrow-gauge lines were converted to standard gauge by the end of 1893, although the third rail remained in place from Dundee to Portland until 1895, allowing for dual-gauge operation over Rex Hill.

As part of its Red Electric operation, the SP extended overhead wire from Jefferson Street through Dundee in 1914. Electric interurban service continued until 1929, shortly after which all passenger service out of the Jefferson Street depot was discontinued. Subsequently, sections of the route were abandoned until by 1984 only the section between Wilsonia to Dundee remained. In 1993, the Willamette & Pacific Railroad took over operation of this remaining section of the original narrow-gauge route. As of 2013, this line is being operated by the Portland & Western Railroad. Both the Willamette & Pacific and the Portland & Western are controlled by parent Genesse & Wyoming.

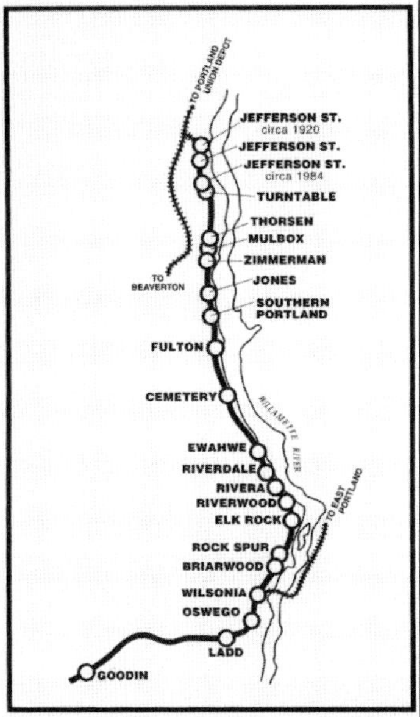

Railroad Portland to Dundee
With Southern Pacific Railroad lines shown for reference

These maps give a simplified overview of narrow-gauge railways between Jefferson Street and Dundee in the Willamette Valley around 1881. Related Southern Pacific Railroad routes are shown as crosshatched lines for reference. Note that not all of these SP lines existed in 1881.

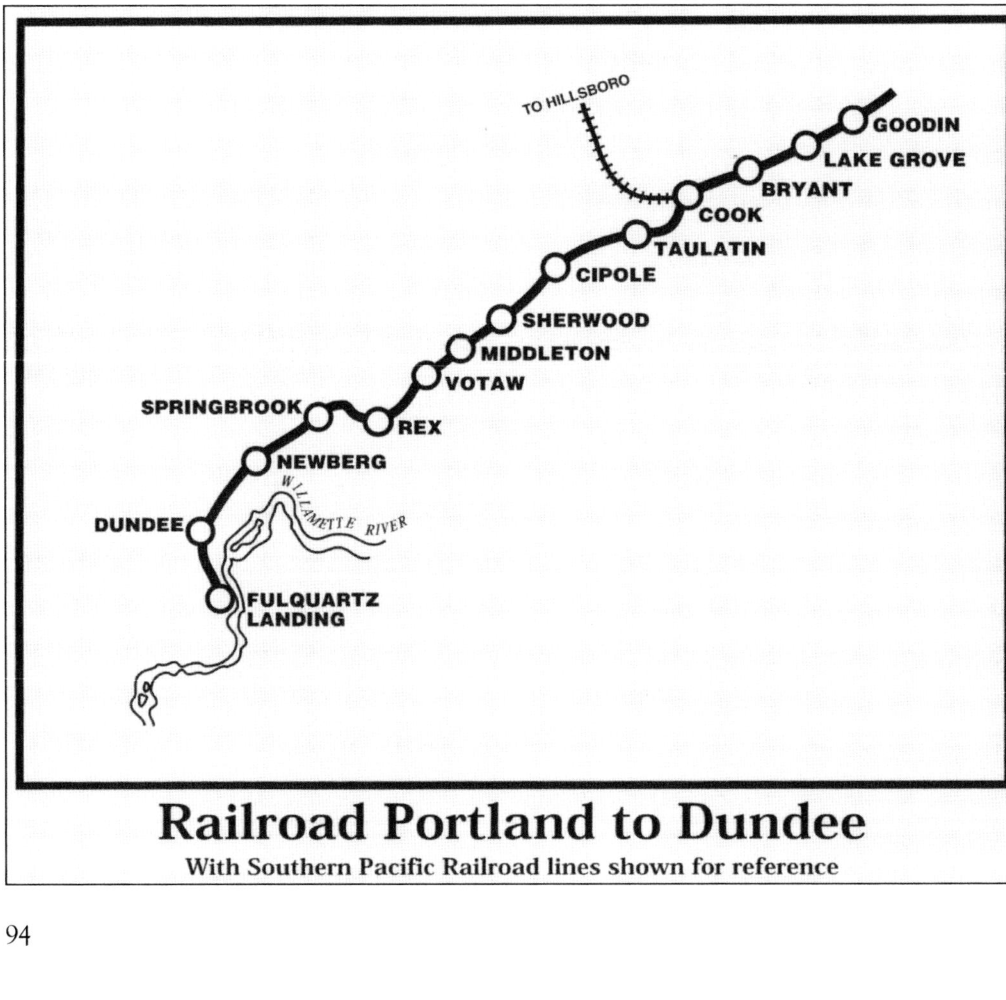

Railroad Portland to Dundee
With Southern Pacific Railroad lines shown for reference

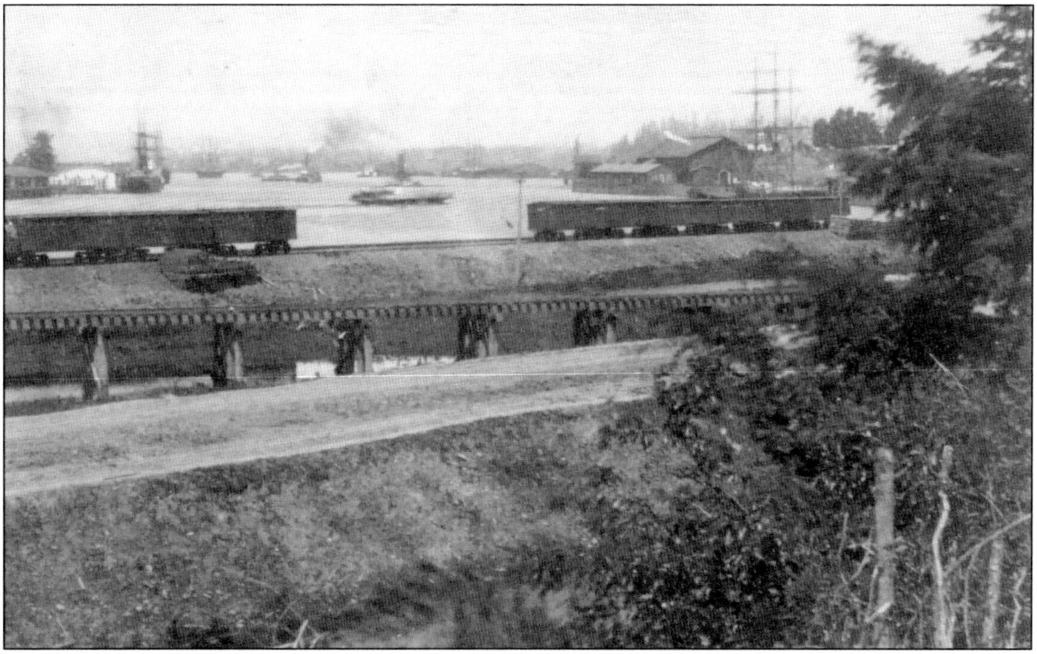

This rare view is believed to show the original narrow-gauge terminal on the public levee near Jefferson Street in West Portland around 1895. Although a controversy arose regarding the right to build on the "public" levee, the railroad elected to put its track there anyway since it provided ready access to oceangoing shipping.

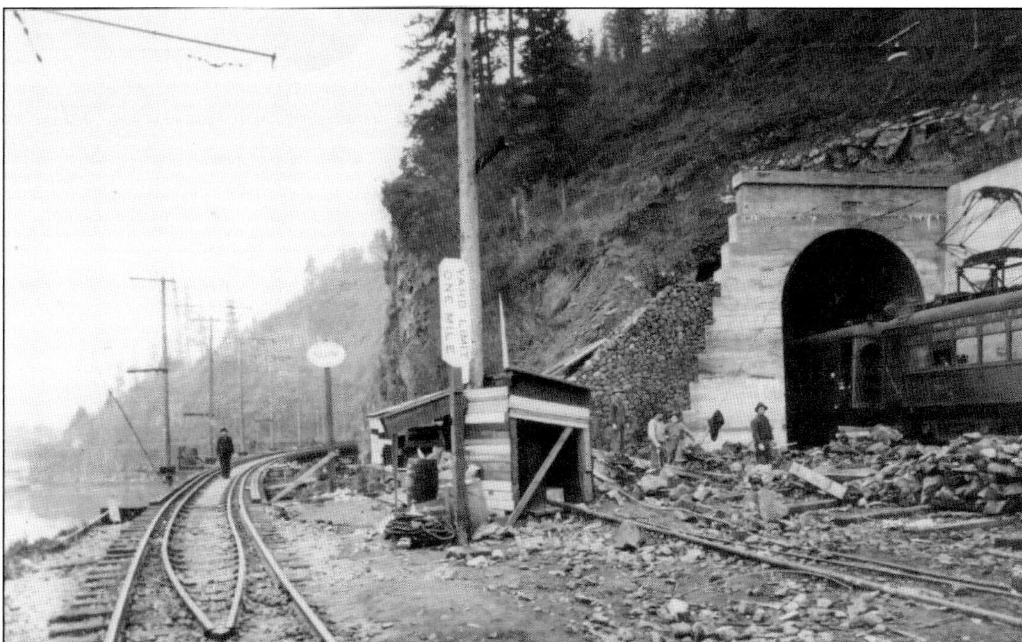

The Elk Rock tunnel was opened in December 1921, eliminating the trestle around the cliff face seen to the left. One of the SP's electric interurban trains is visible at the tunnel entrance. The photograph was probably taken shortly after the tunnel opened.

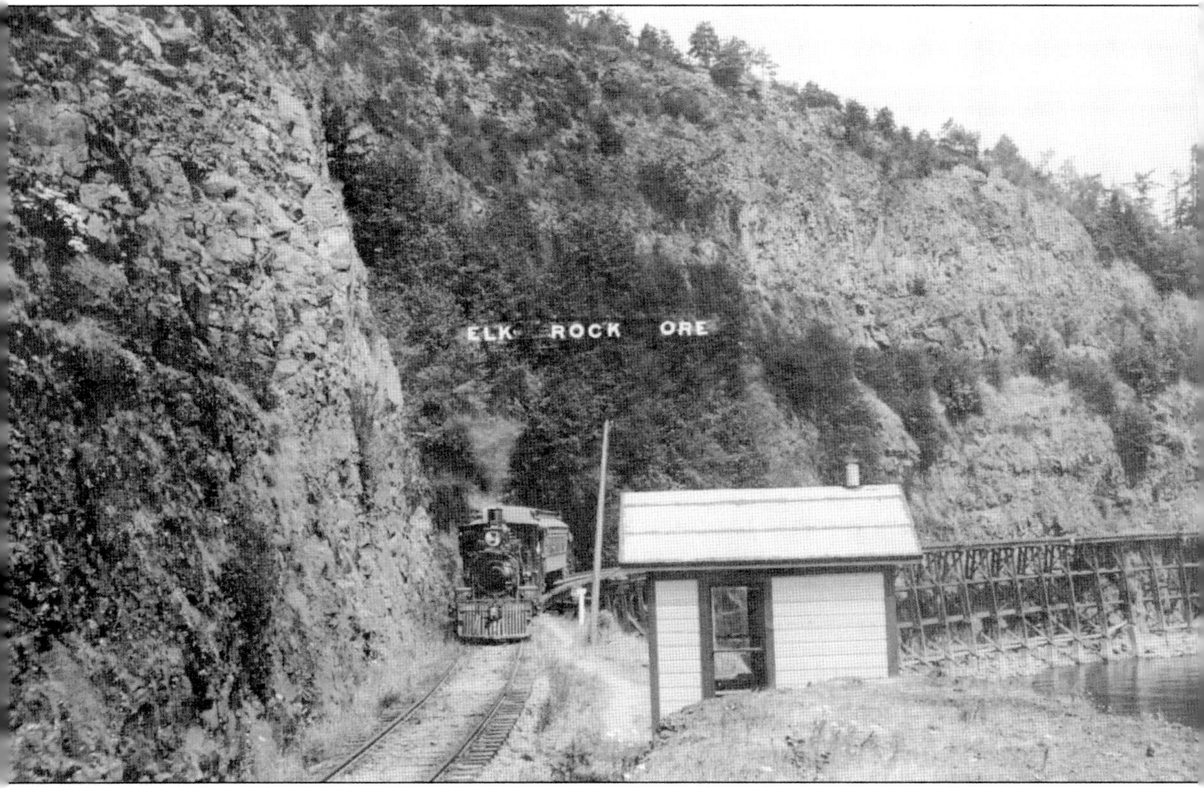

A significant barrier in the path of the Oregonian Railway between Portland and Oswego was Elk Rock. The answer was to build on trestlework, as seen here around 1900. However, falling rock along the cliff face proved to be an ongoing problem. After evaluating a number of options, a tunnel was found to be the most cost effective alternative. This section of the railroad had been converted to electric operation in 1914, and the Elk Rock tunnel thus became the only tunnel on the Southern Pacific's electric lines in Oregon. Today, this section of the line is only used by a trolley operated primarily as a tourist attraction between Lake Oswego and West Portland.

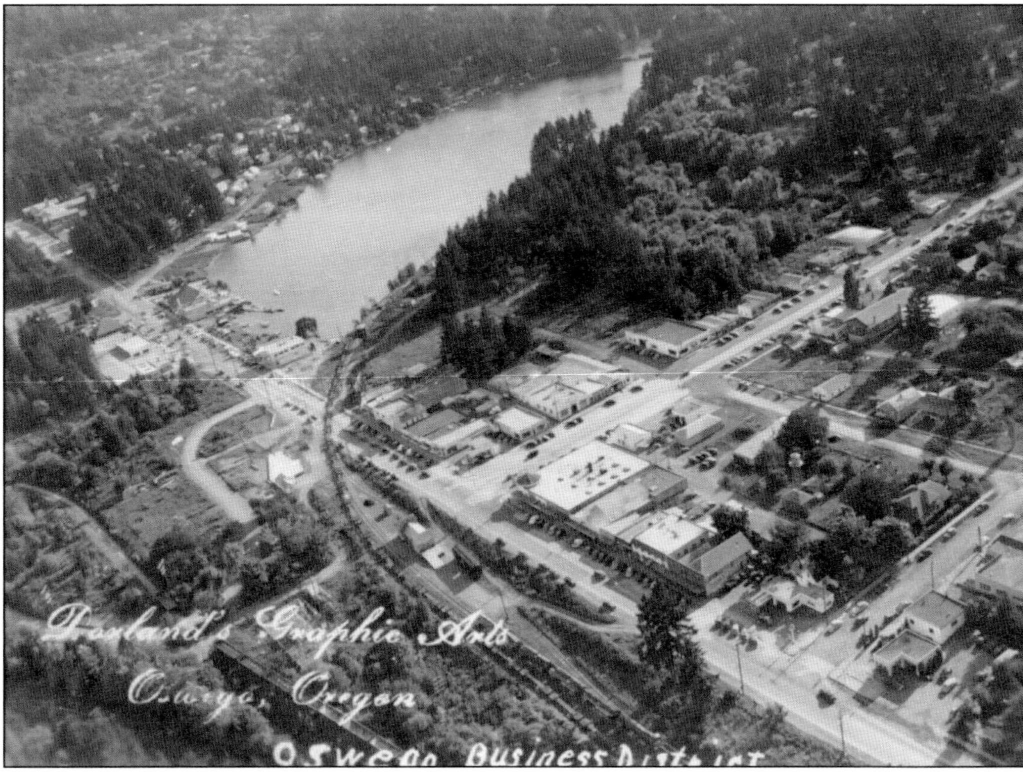

This photograph gives a good overview of Oswego around 1940. The original narrow-gauge route is clearly defined by the railroad seen curving from the bottom up to the lake and disappearing behind the trees. This line continues to St. Joseph via Newberg and Dundee. The track at lower left leads to the site of the old Oregon Iron and Steel Co. and Oregon Portland Cement Co.

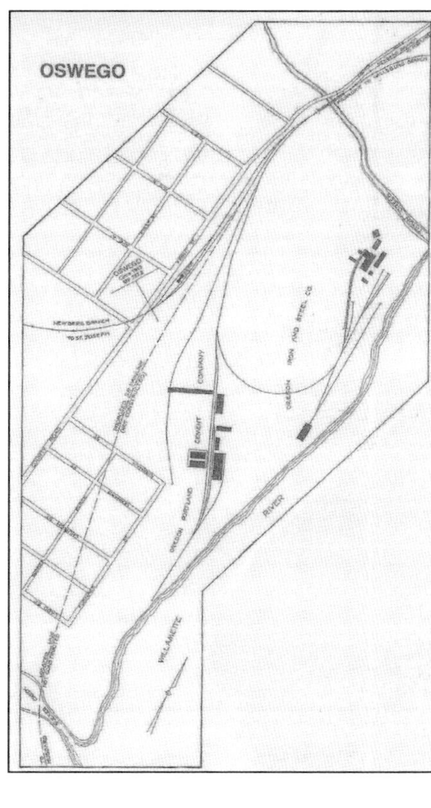

This map drawn directly from a Southern Pacific Railroad plat map gives a detailed view of the track arrangement at Oswego around 1913. Both the Oregon Iron and Steel Co. and the Oregon Portland Cement Co. are shown.

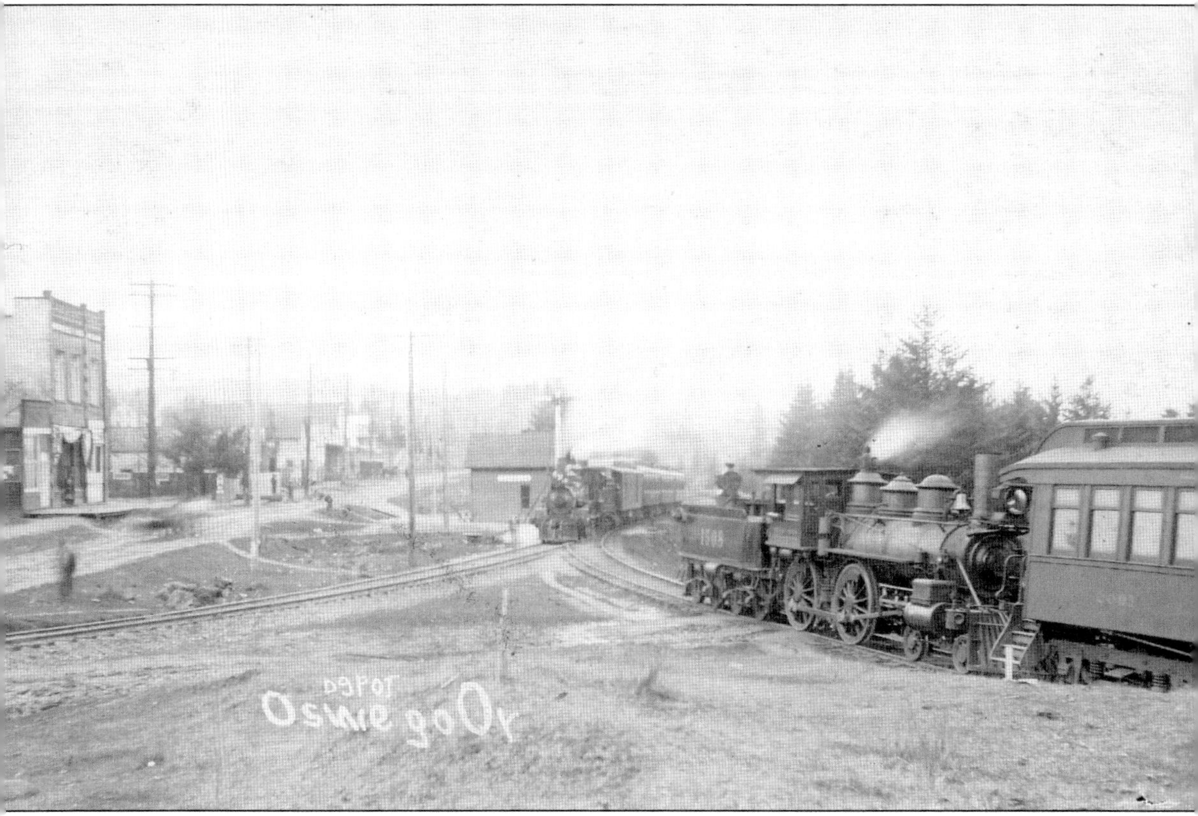

Looking toward Portland a few years earlier, this track would have been narrow gauge. Now, around 1906, standard-gauge SP train No. 77, the *Dallas Passenger*, is at the Oswego depot while a suburban passenger train waits in the clear on the spur to the Oregon Iron and Steel Co. Train No. 77 had left Portland at 7:40 a.m. and arrived at Oswego at 8:05 a.m. After a brief stop, it would continue to Dallas, arriving there at 11:10 a.m. SP 4-4-0 No. 1508 left Portland with suburban passenger train No. 93 at 7:30 a.m. and ran just 10 minutes ahead of Train No. 77 all the way to Oswego. At 8:10 a.m., No. 1508 will depart Oswego with train No. 96. The lack of turning facilities at Oswego dictates that No. 1508 will run in reverse for her run back to Portland, where train No. 96 is due to arrive at 8:35 a.m. Around this time, the SP was running 34 passenger trains daily between Portland and Oswego, with 17 in each direction except for Sunday, when only 30 trains ran.

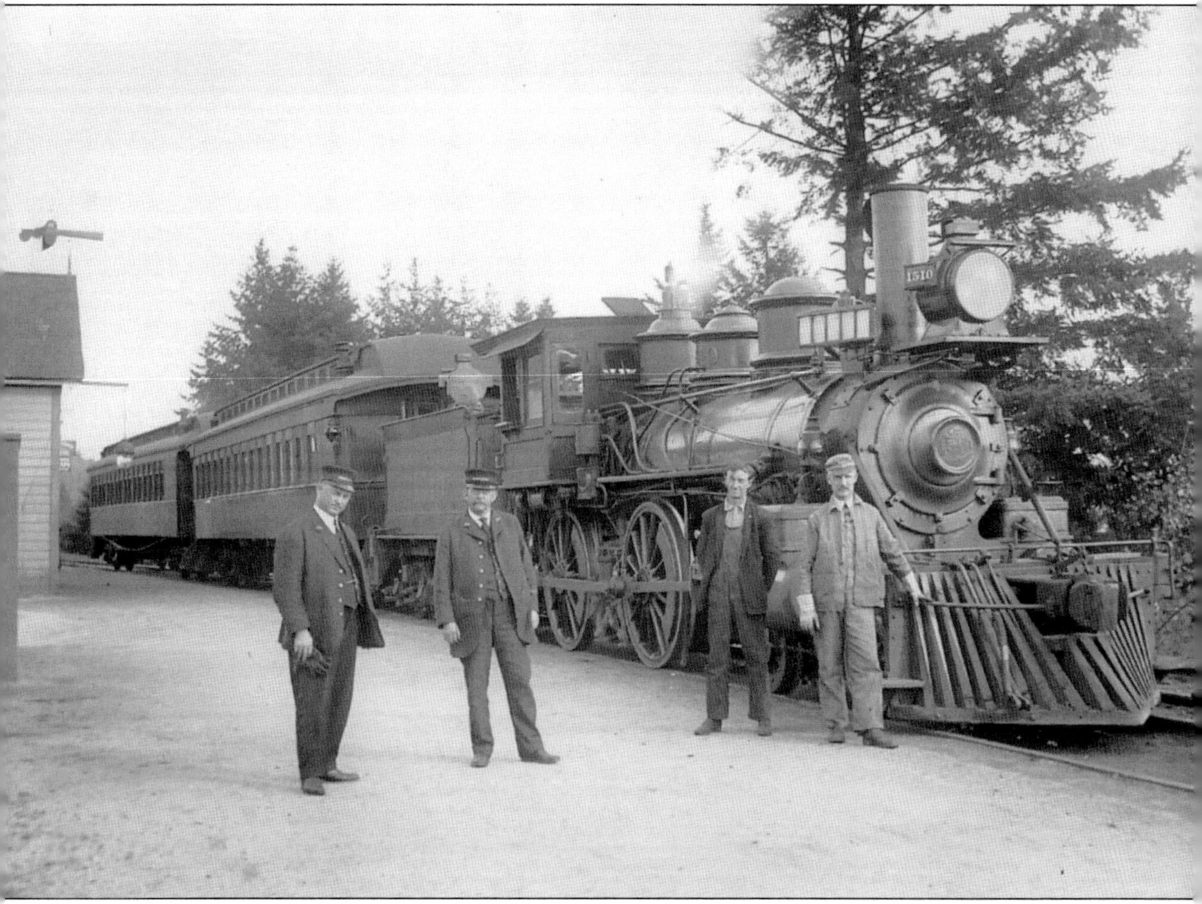

Pictured here is a typical suburban passenger train that has just arrived at Oswego around 1910. The classy little 4-4-0 was built for the Oregon & California Railroad as its No. 19 by the Baldwin Locomotive Works in 1879. She was renumbered as SP No. 1510 in December 1906 and retired in November 1913. She was finally cut up for scrap at Portland in May 1920.

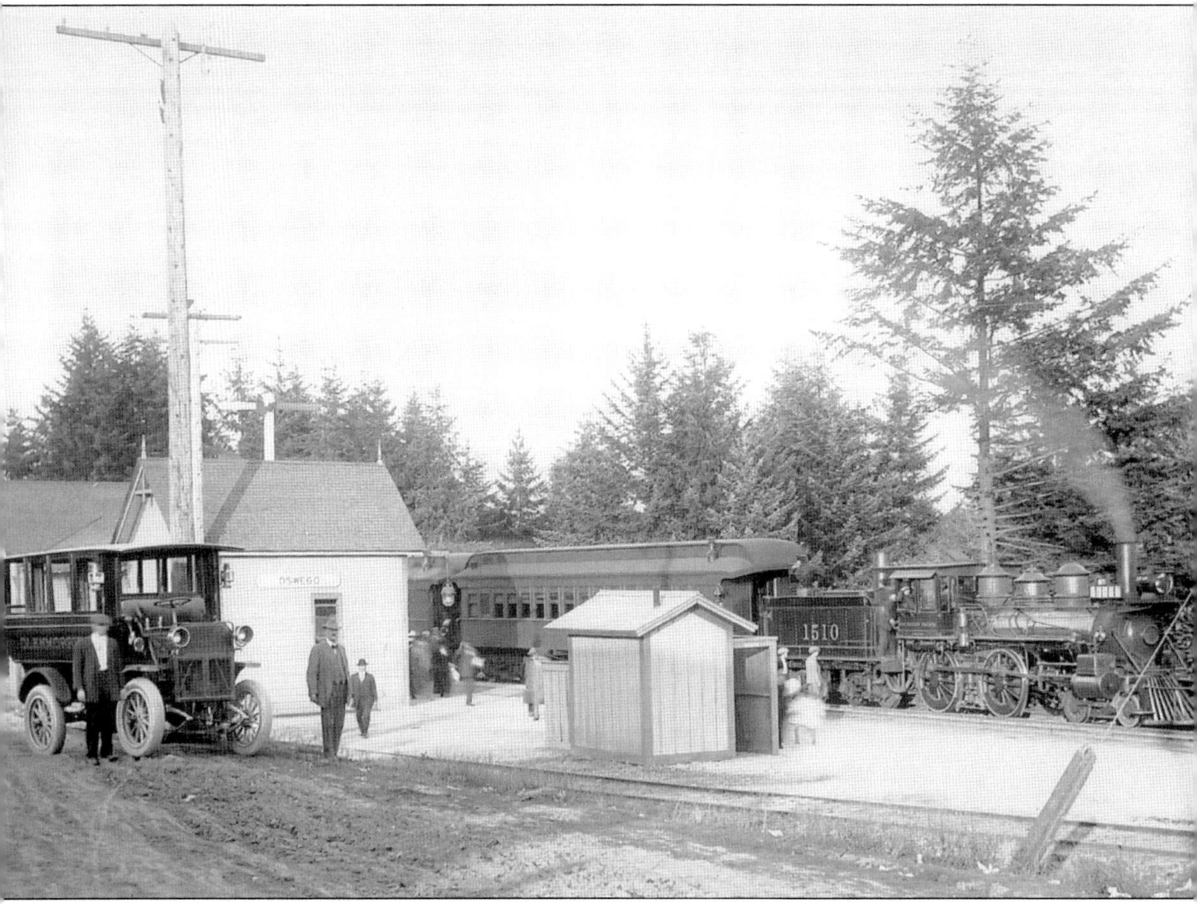

Another view of the same train gives a better overview of the facilities at Oswego, including the outdoor "facility" seen in the foreground. The Glenmorrie Bus, seen to the left, was operated for the convenience of Glenmorrie residents, giving them a direct connection to the Oswego depot and thus Portland. Glenmorrie began as a private estate in 1893 noted for the extensive variety of native and non-native trees planted on the grounds. However, by 1911 the family was selling one-acre tracts intended to make Glenmorrie into a park-like residential development. Under SP control, suburban passenger trains such as seen here were the primary traffic between Jefferson Street and Oswego until the route was electrified in 1914.

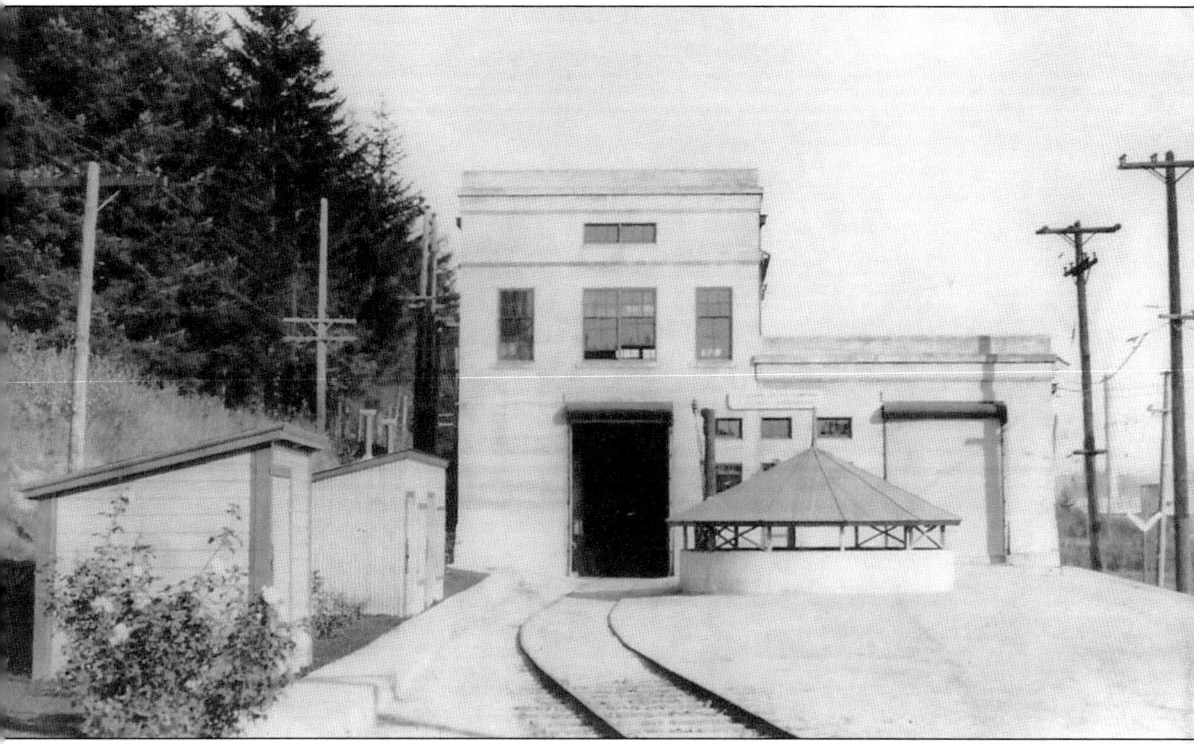

In 1912, the Southern Pacific undertook an extensive project to provide electric interurban service on many of its lines in Oregon. The project was never fully implemented, but the line from Jefferson Street through Dundee did receive overhead wire allowing for electric operation. Power for the initial electric system was purchased from the Portland Railway, Light and Power Co. and transmitted to the Oswego substation at 55,000 volts. Here, the voltage was reduced to 13,200 volts and re-transmitted to the Dundee and Forest Grove substations where it was converted to the 1,500-volt DC current used by the electric cars. The Oswego substation is seen here around 1914.

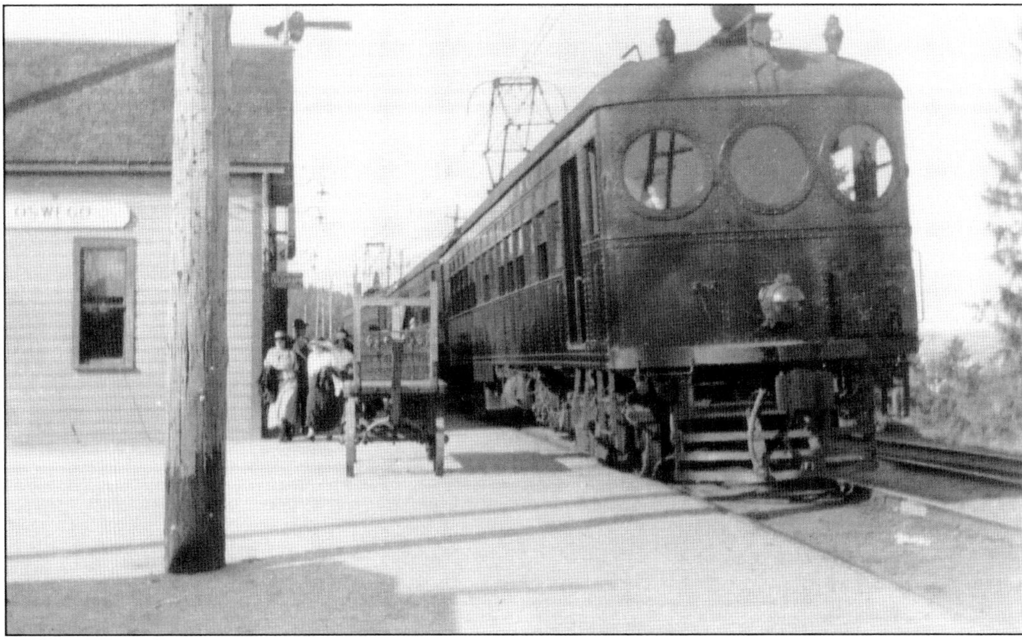

From 1914 until 1929, passenger traffic from Portland through Dundee to McMinnville and Corvallis was handled by SP's Red Electric interurban cars, as seen here at Oswego around 1920.

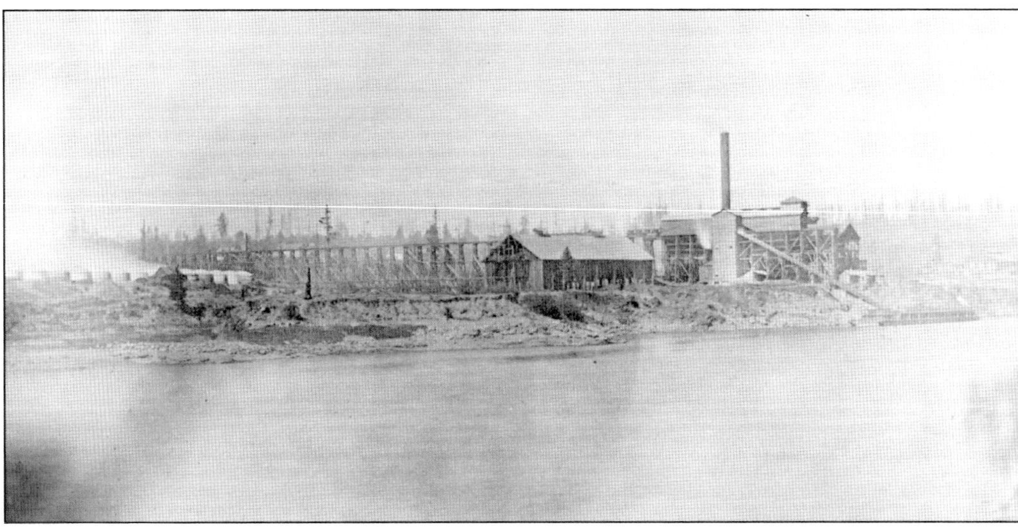

In 1865, ground was broken for the Oregon Iron Company, intended to be the "Pittsburgh of the West." In 1867, the company produced its first pig iron; one year later, cast iron pipe was being shipped to Portland from Oswego. However, the company struggled financially, and, in 1882, the property was acquired by the Oregon Iron and Steel Company with the intent of enlarging the operation into profitability. The Portland & Willamette Valley Railroad brought narrow-gauge rail service to the area between 1886 and 1888, but still the dream was not to be realized. Production was drastically curtailed in 1892 and ended completely around 1920.

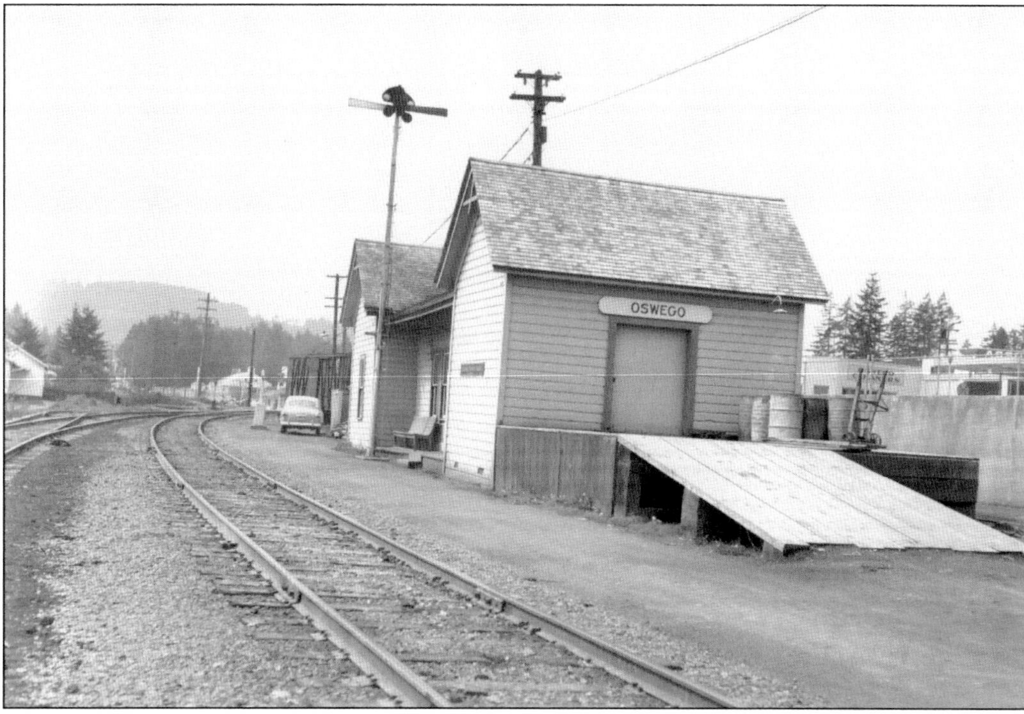

According to Southern Pacific records the unique Oswego passenger and freight depot was built in 1901, although it may have been built earlier. Passenger service to Oswego ended around 1930, but the depot was not retired until June 1958. It was replaced by a utilitarian concrete block structure.

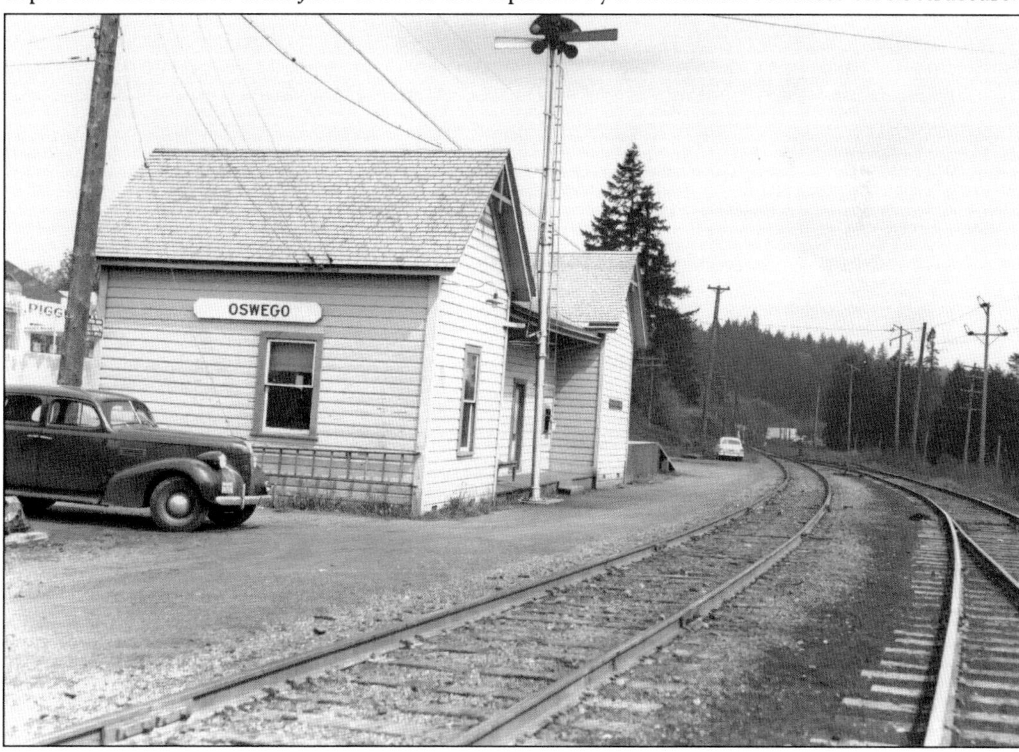

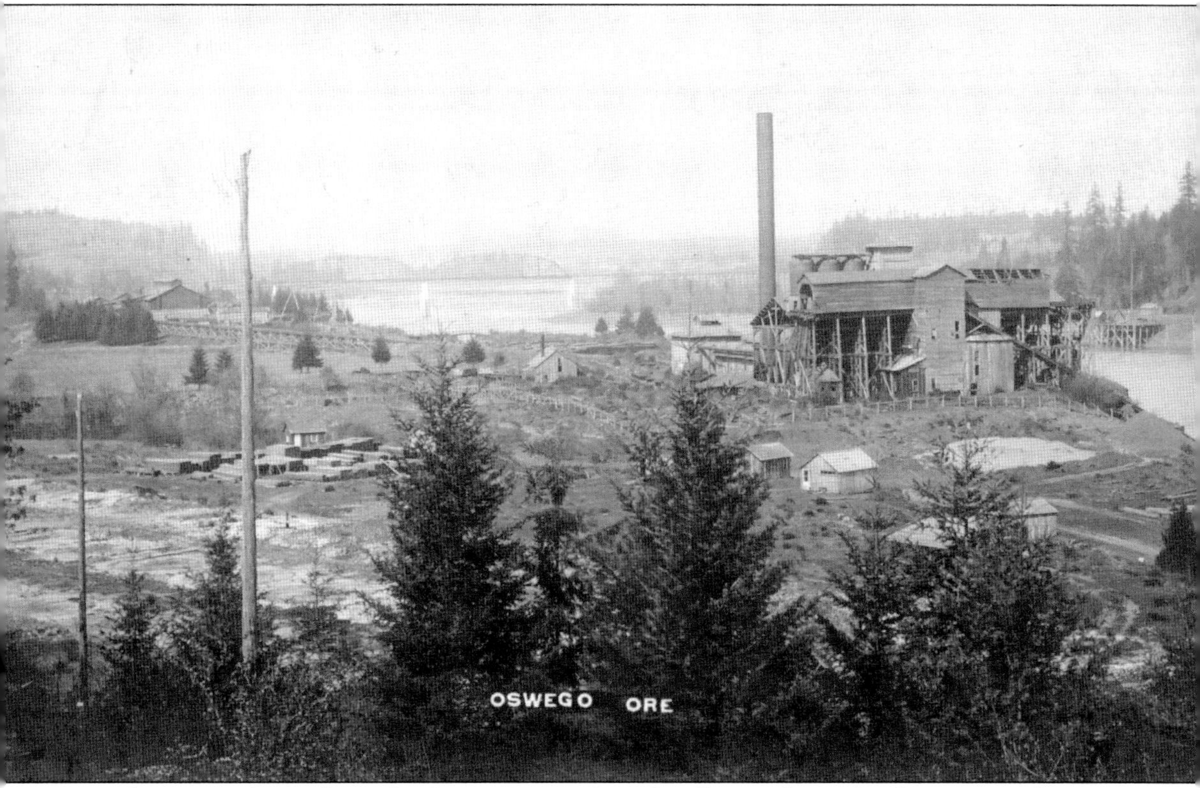

This postcard view shows the Oregon Iron and Steel Mill around 1911. By this time, production at the plant had all but ceased. The Southern Pacific railroad bridge visible in the background across the Willamette River was completed in 1910 as part of a more direct link between the SP mainline in East Portland and the SP Westside line at Oswego. The bridge remains in use in 2014.

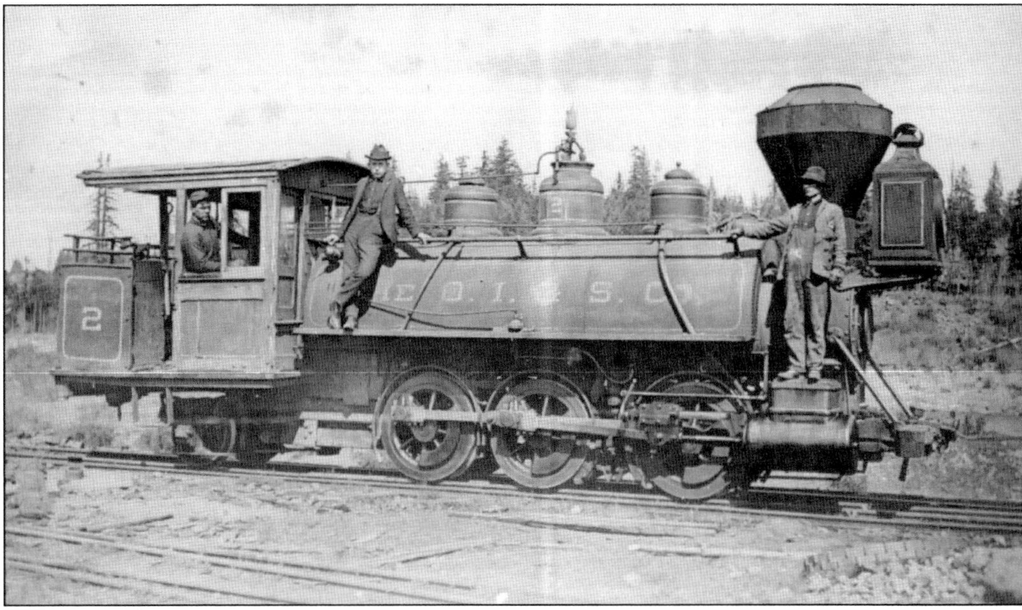

These small, narrow-gauge locomotives served the Oregon Iron and Steel Co. working within the plant complex to handle ore and finished products. Note the dual-gauge track allowing standard-gauge cars and locomotives to operate on the same track.

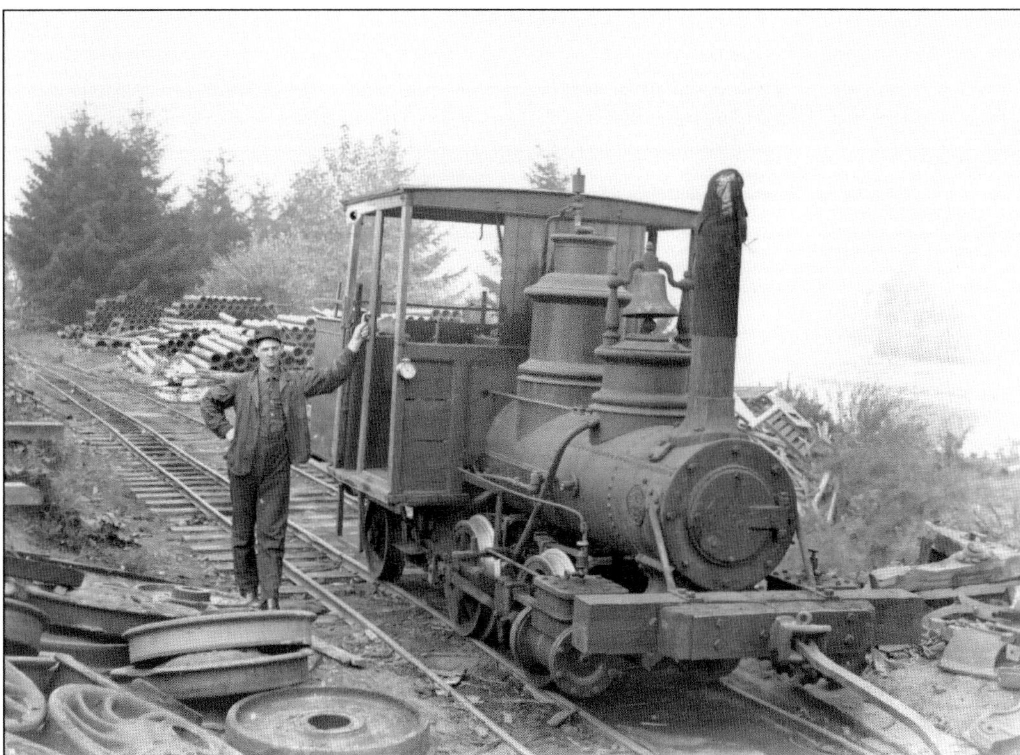

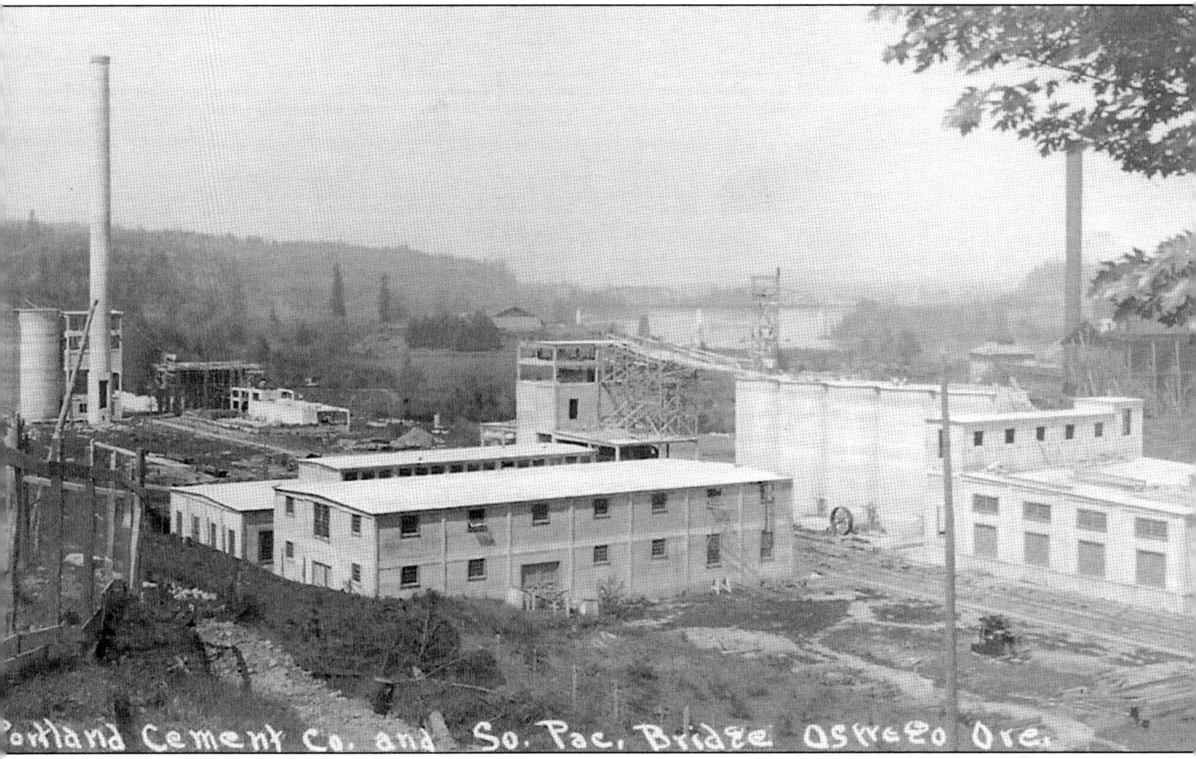

In 1909, the Portland Cement Co. was incorporated with plans to build a large cement production facility at Oswego. Initially, financing was slow in materializing and it was not until June 1916 that the first cement was produced. By then, the name had been changed to the Oregon Portland Cement Company. The plant is seen here while under construction in 1915. During the first few years, the plant's situation was tenuous, but by the 1920s the venture was prospering.

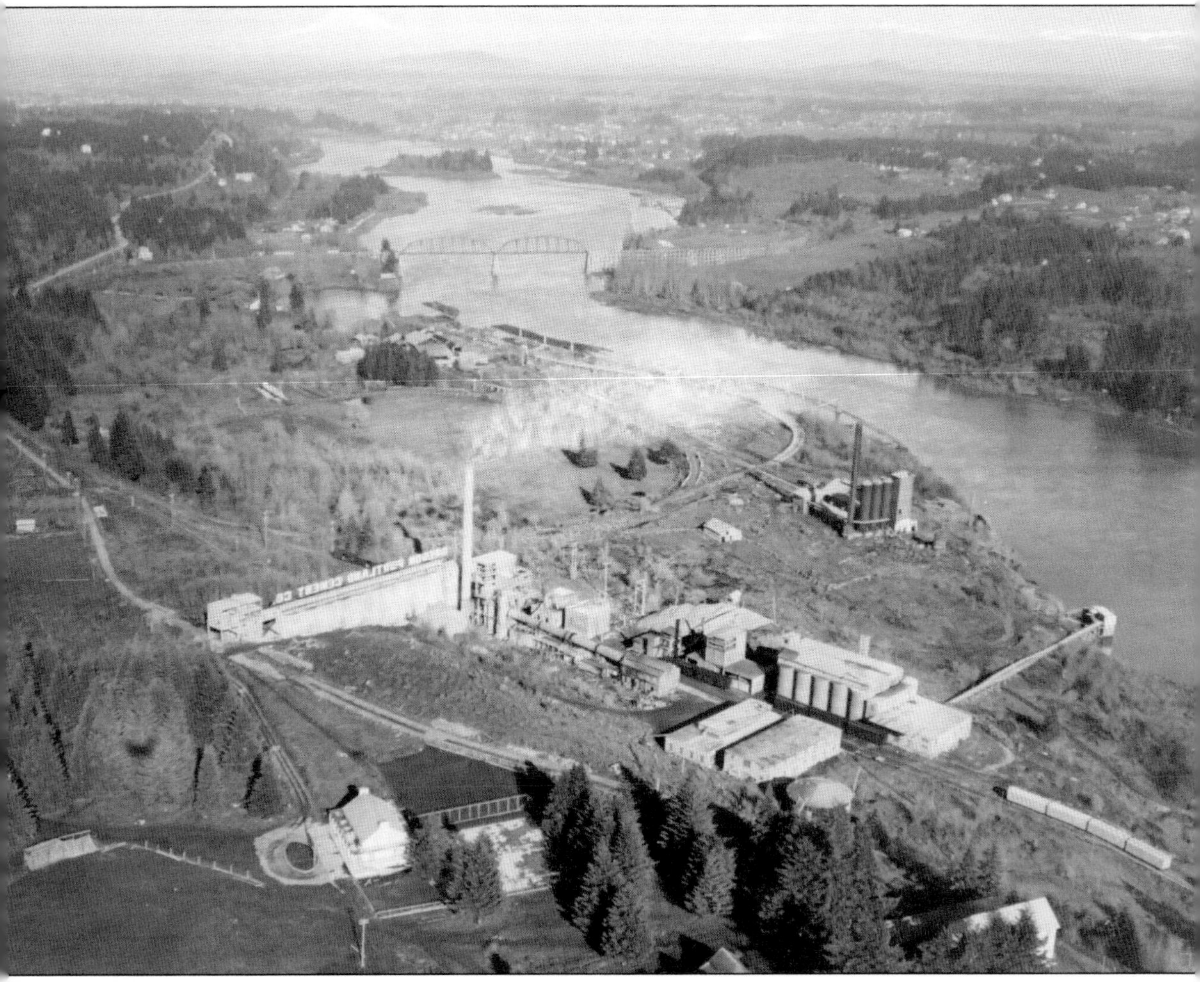

In 1916, the Acme Cement Plaster Company built a plant at Lime, Oregon, to produce plaster. In 1921, the Sun Portland Cement Company bought the Lime plant and added facilities for producing Portland cement. This company merged with the Oregon Portland Cement Company in 1926, and as demand for cement continued to increase, both plants grew accordingly. The Oswego plant is seen here looking toward the northeast in 1927. The SP railroad bridge is visible in the distance. The original narrow-gauge route continued along the left bank of the Willamette River to Jefferson Street in West Portland.

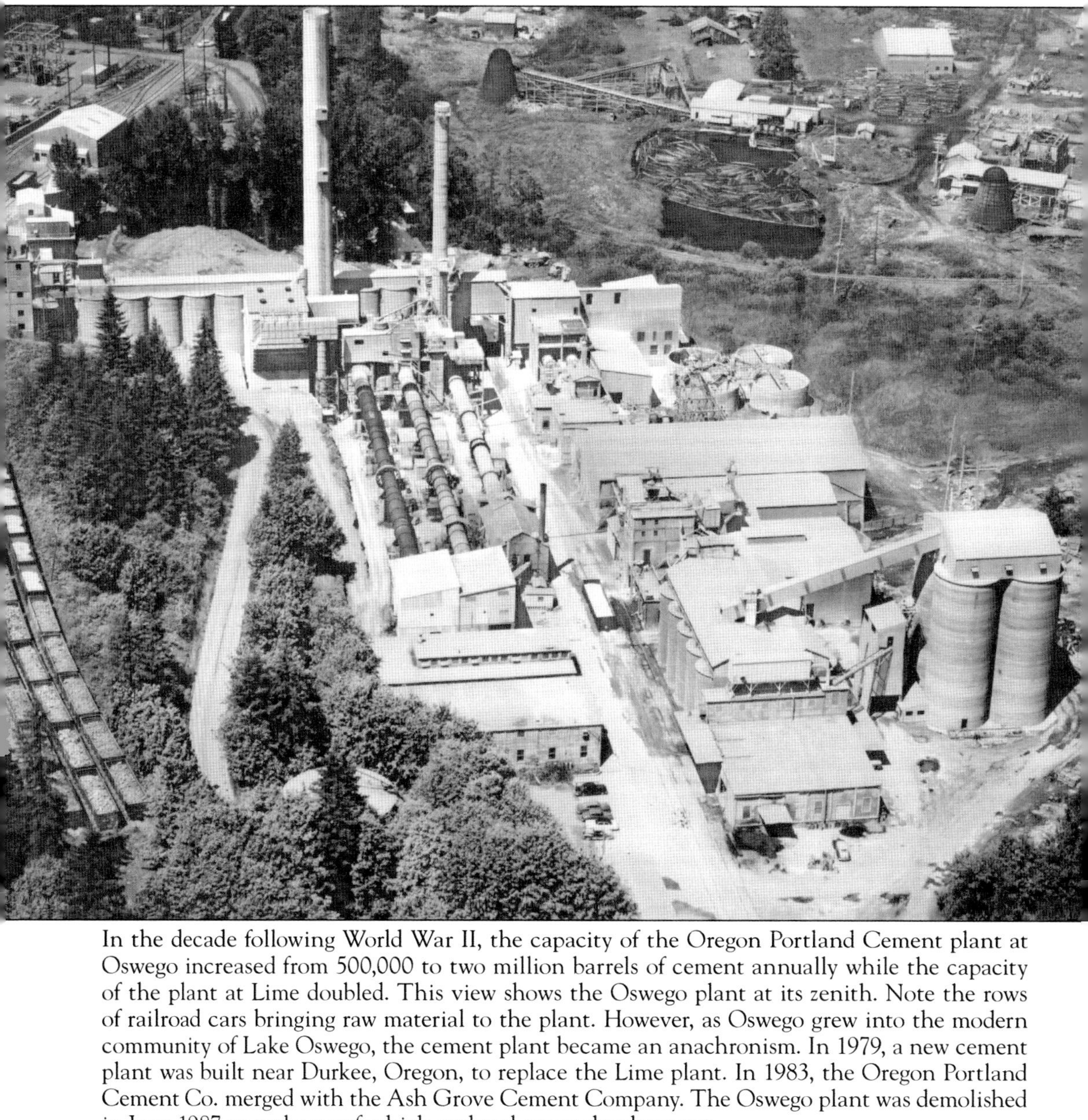

In the decade following World War II, the capacity of the Oregon Portland Cement plant at Oswego increased from 500,000 to two million barrels of cement annually while the capacity of the plant at Lime doubled. This view shows the Oswego plant at its zenith. Note the rows of railroad cars bringing raw material to the plant. However, as Oswego grew into the modern community of Lake Oswego, the cement plant became an anachronism. In 1979, a new cement plant was built near Durkee, Oregon, to replace the Lime plant. In 1983, the Oregon Portland Cement Co. merged with the Ash Grove Cement Company. The Oswego plant was demolished in June 1987 to make way for high-end real estate development.

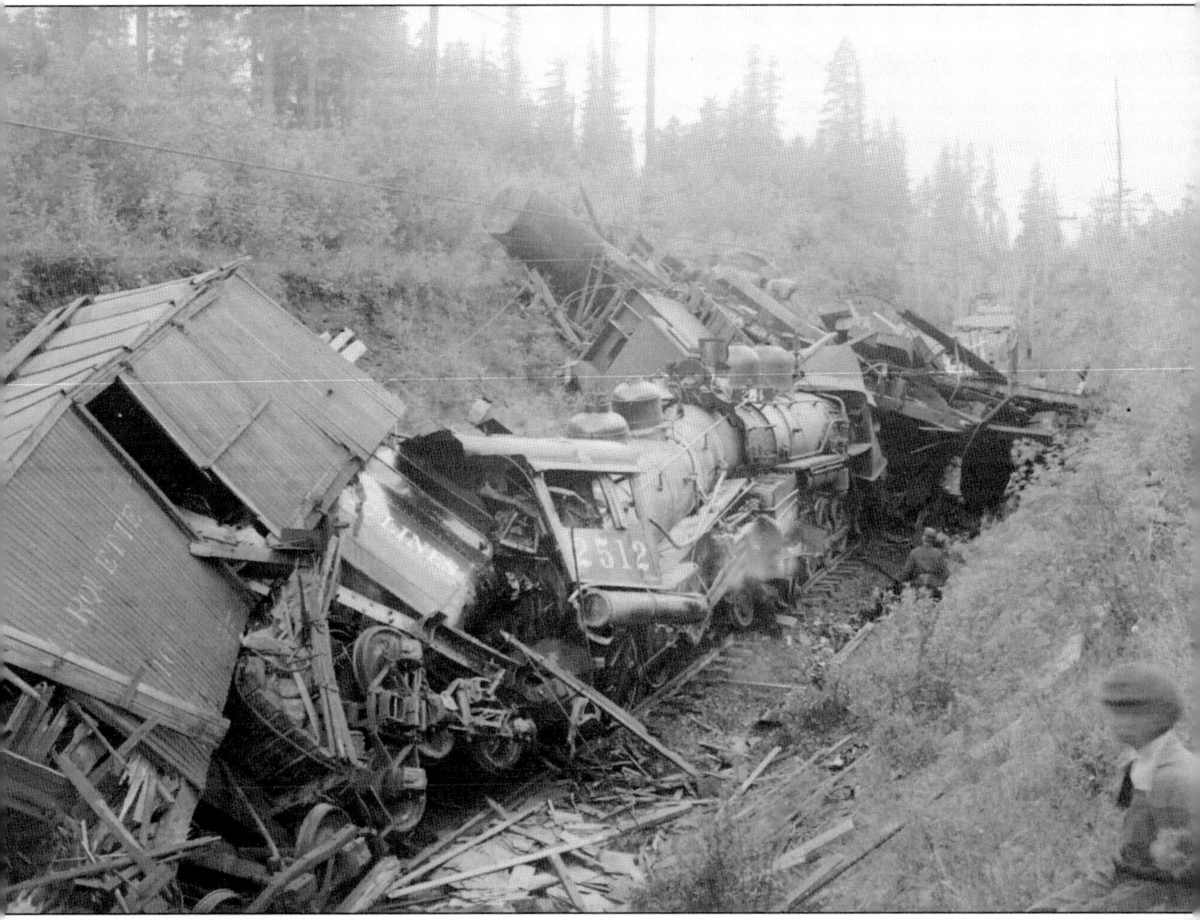

Accidents do happen, as was the case on May 31, 1918, when two Southern Pacific trains attempted to pass without the benefit of a siding. The unfortunate result is seen here near Goodin, which is located between Oswego and Cook. This section of the SP line followed the original narrow-gauge route through a heavily wooded area, which, along with curvature, limited visibility and probably contributed to the crash. Amazingly, the only fatality was engineer Willis Knight, who was on the train facing the photographer.

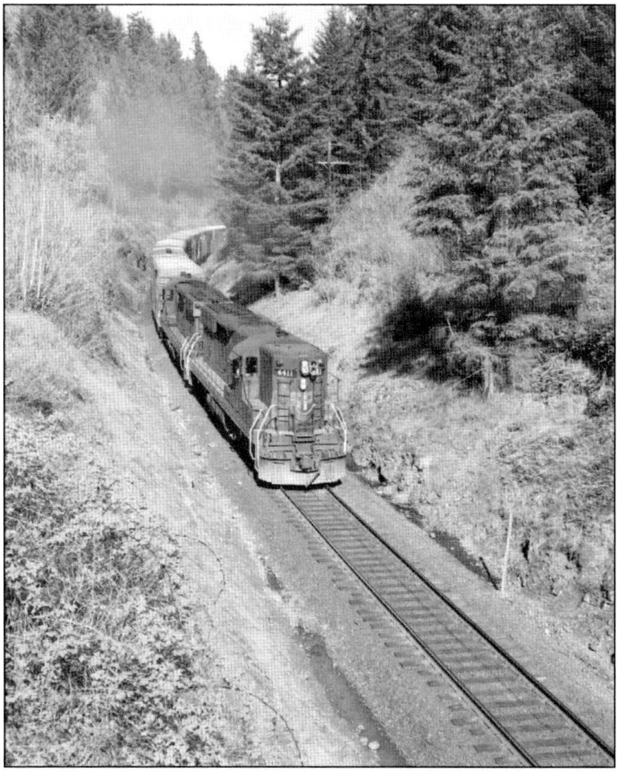

Except for the locomotives, not much has changed in the 55 years since the wreck seen in the previous photograph occurred near Goodin. It is now April 1983, and a pair of Southern Pacific SD-9s is leading the Yamhill Turn back to Portland after working on the line through Cook and Newberg. These were the days when cabooses still marked the end of a train.

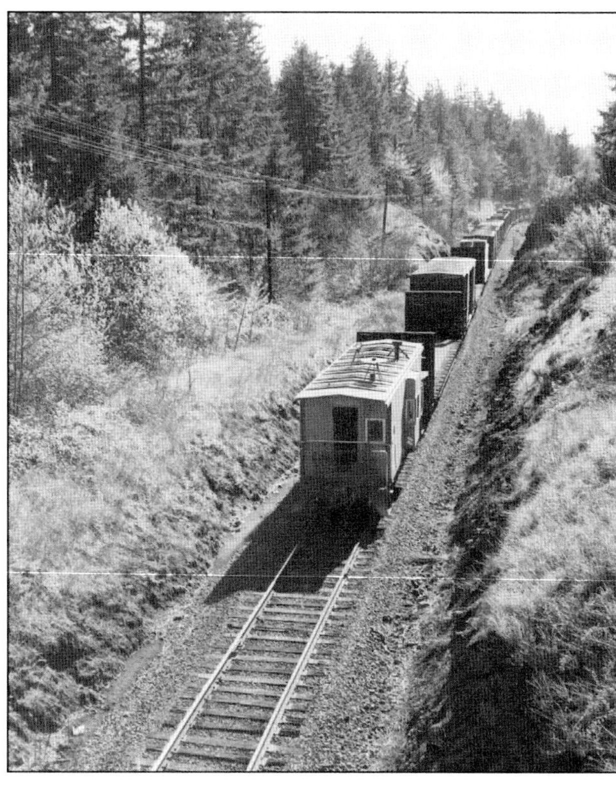

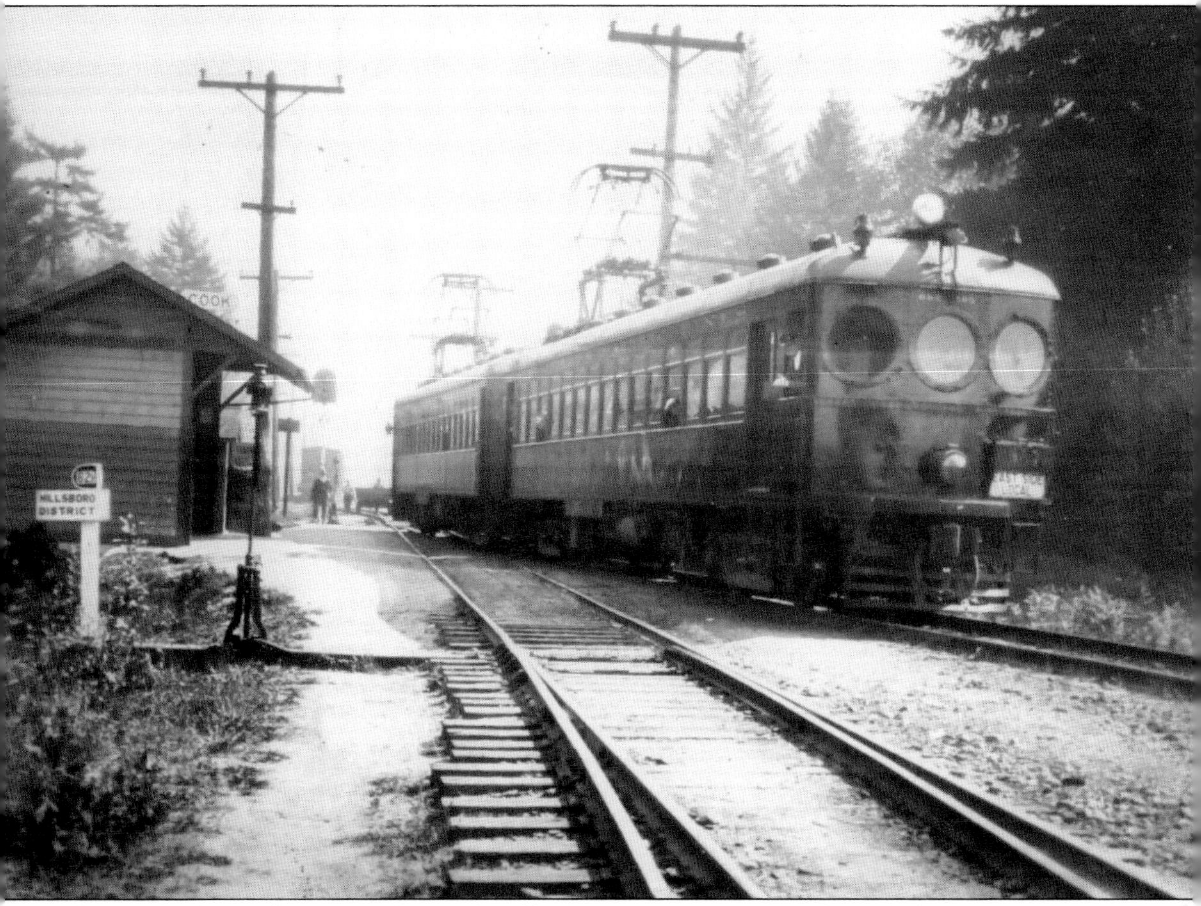

The Portland & Willamette Valley Railroad built its narrow-gauge line through this area in 1886. However, it wasn't until July 1910 when the SP built a connection from Cook to Beaverton that Cook became a significant point on the route. A wye located at Cook allowed trains to pass to and from any route. In 1914, these routes were electrified, thus leading to this view of the electric Eastside local train No. 357 stopped at Cook in 1925. Train No. 357 is on the line to Newberg. The line in the foreground is the north leg of the wye leading to Beaverton.

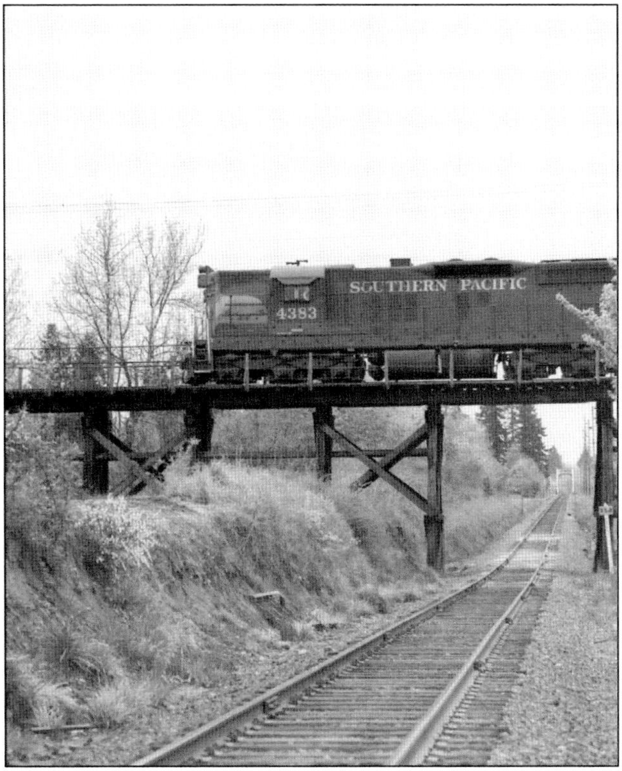

When the Oregon Electric Railway constructed its line from Salem to Portland in 1907, it was necessary to cross the old narrow-gauge route in the vicinity of Tualatin. By slightly depressing the Oregon Electric line and slightly raising the SP line, a crossing at grade was avoided. The old Oregon Electric line became part of the Burlington Northern in 1970. Here, the SP *Whiteson Turn* is crossing over the BN line on April 28, 1984.

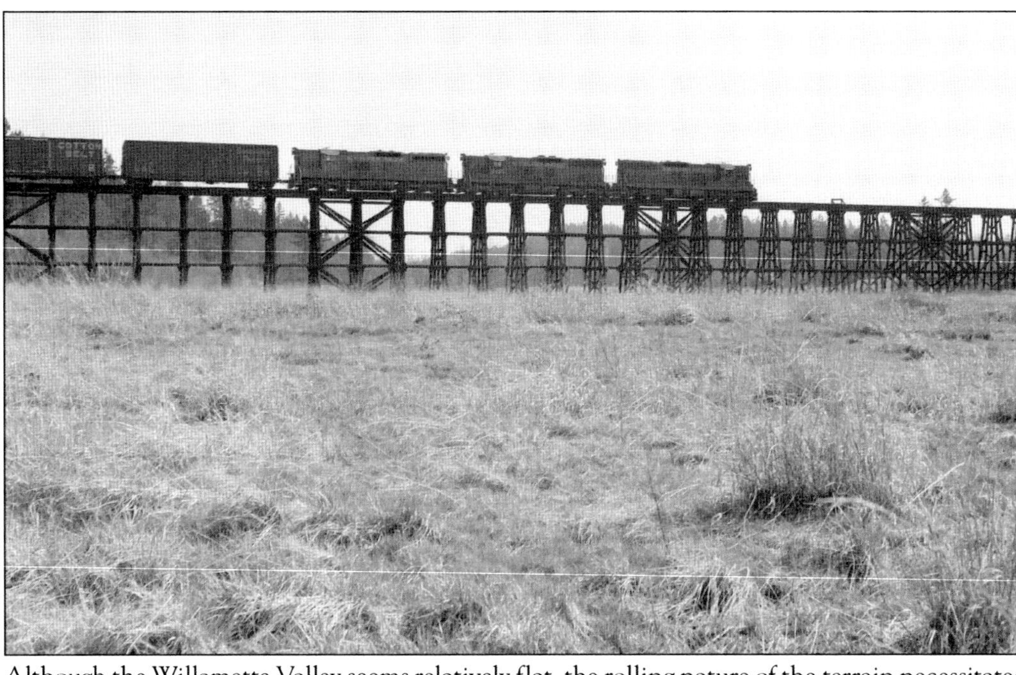

Although the Willamette Valley seems relatively flat, the rolling nature of the terrain necessitated building many timber trestles. March 7, 1982, finds the SP *Westsider* rumbling across one such trestle near Sherwood. The *Westsider* was a Southern Pacific local freight bulletined to run between Portland and Eugene via Oswego, Newberg, McMinnville, Corvallis, and Albany.

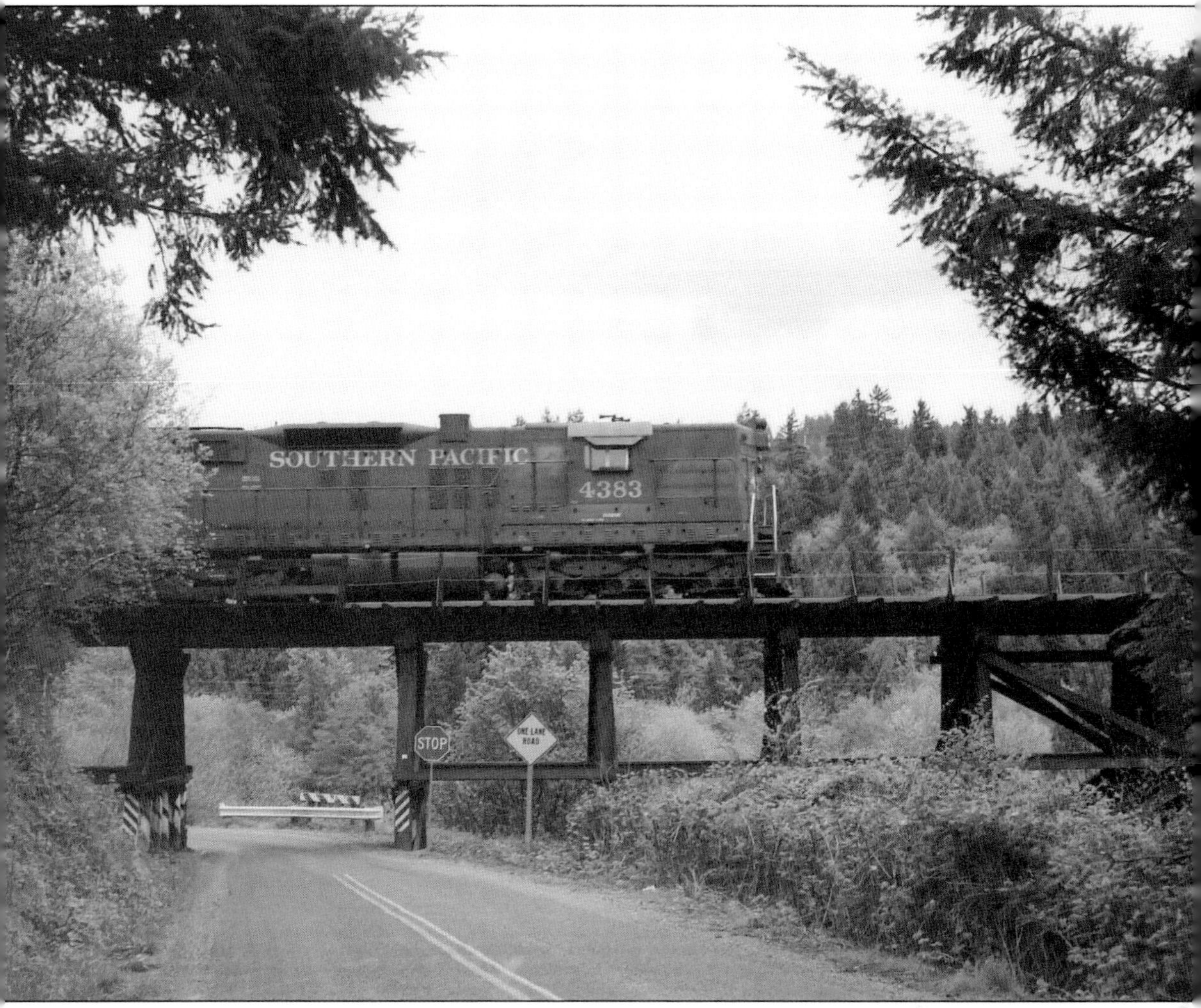

With grades approaching two percent in both directions, Rex Hill, located between Sherwood and Newberg, was the most imposing obstacle to operation in the path of the Portland & Willamette Valley Railroad between Portland and Dundee. One can only imagine tiny, narrow-gauge 2-6-0s struggling to lift minimal tonnage over the summit. Even relatively modern diesel locomotives like No. 4383, seen here climbing Rex Hill in 1984, were challenged in moving trains over this route. Not only was adequate tractive effort required to move tonnage up the grade on one side, but adequate braking ability was equally important when descending the other side.

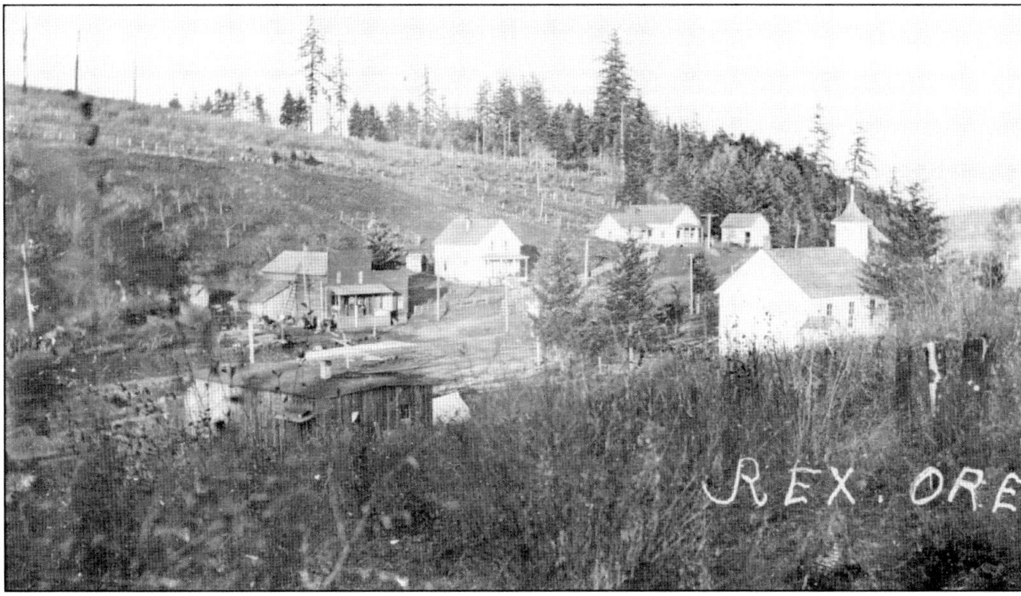

The community of Rex was located at the summit of Rex Hill. The railroad crested the summit at an elevation of 426 feet with a two-percent grade from the east and a 1.92-percent grade from the west. One urban legend suggests that the name "Rex" was selected to denote the number of wrecks the railroad would incur on the hill. However, the record of train service on Rex Hill does not support this story.

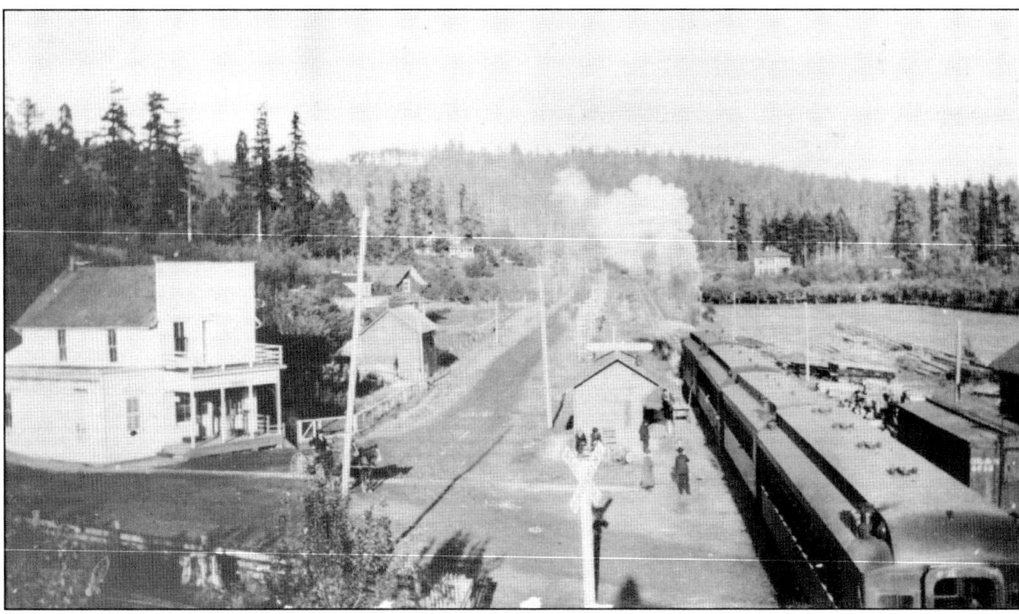

Springbrook was located on the west side of Rex Hill at the foot of the 1.92-percent grade. Although never rating an actual depot, Springbrook was provided with the standard Southern Pacific passenger shelter seen in this c. 1905 view. The afternoon lighting suggests it is 4:28 p.m. and this is train No. 76, the *Dallas Passenger*, about to attack Rex Hill as it continues toward Portland. Train No. 76 was scheduled to depart Dallas at 3:50 p.m. for a 5:45 p.m. arrival at Portland.

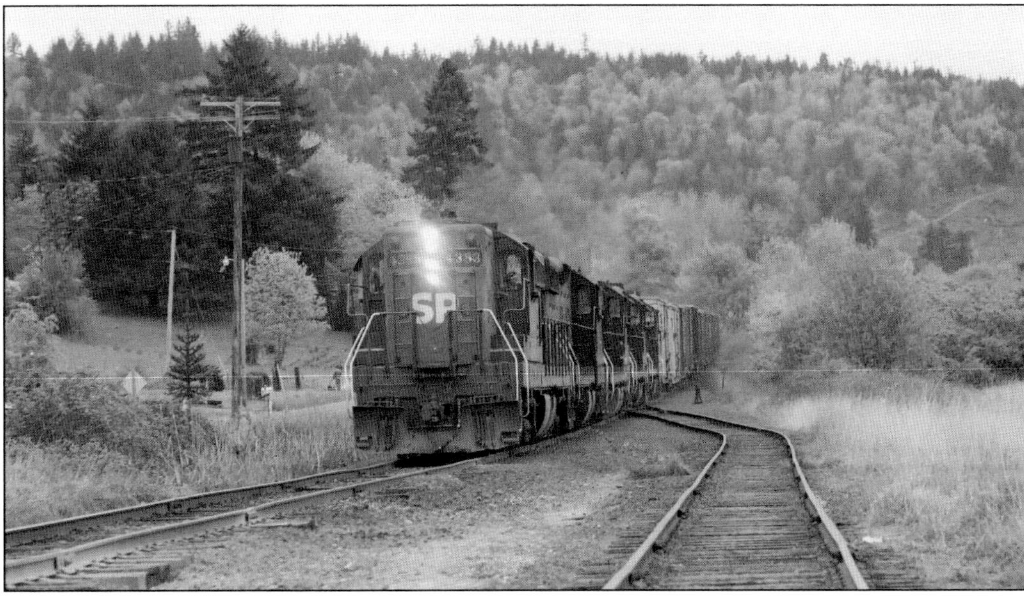

This photograph was taken from approximately the same location at Springbrook as the previous view. However, it is now 1984 and the *Whiteson Turn* has just successfully descended Rex Hill en route to Newberg and McMinnville. The crew of the little steamer leading train No. 76 in the previous view from 70 years earlier could never have imagined locomotives like the five leading today's train. Nor could they ever have imagined handling the amount of tonnage in today's train.

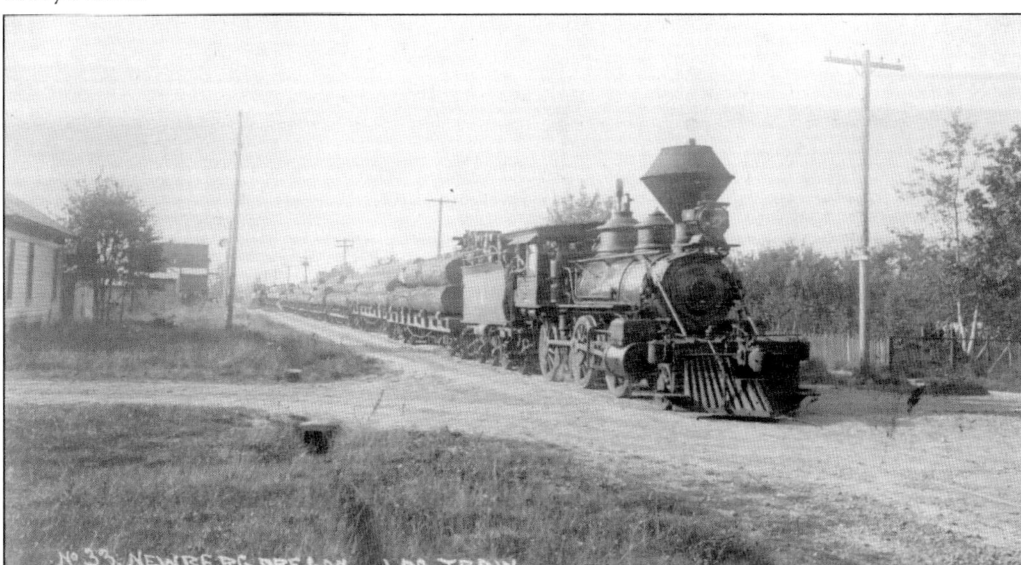

Under Southern Pacific control, operation of the former narrow-gauge line past Newberg was not limited exclusively to SP trains. The Salem, Falls City & Western Railway obtained trackage rights allowing it to operate log trains between Derry Junction (later Gerlinger) and Newberg over SP tracks. Here, Salem, Falls City & Western 2-6-0 No. 6 is leading just such a train around 1912 to the Spaulding Lumber Company mill at Newberg. Spaulding maintained a short rail line connecting the mill to the SP railroad.

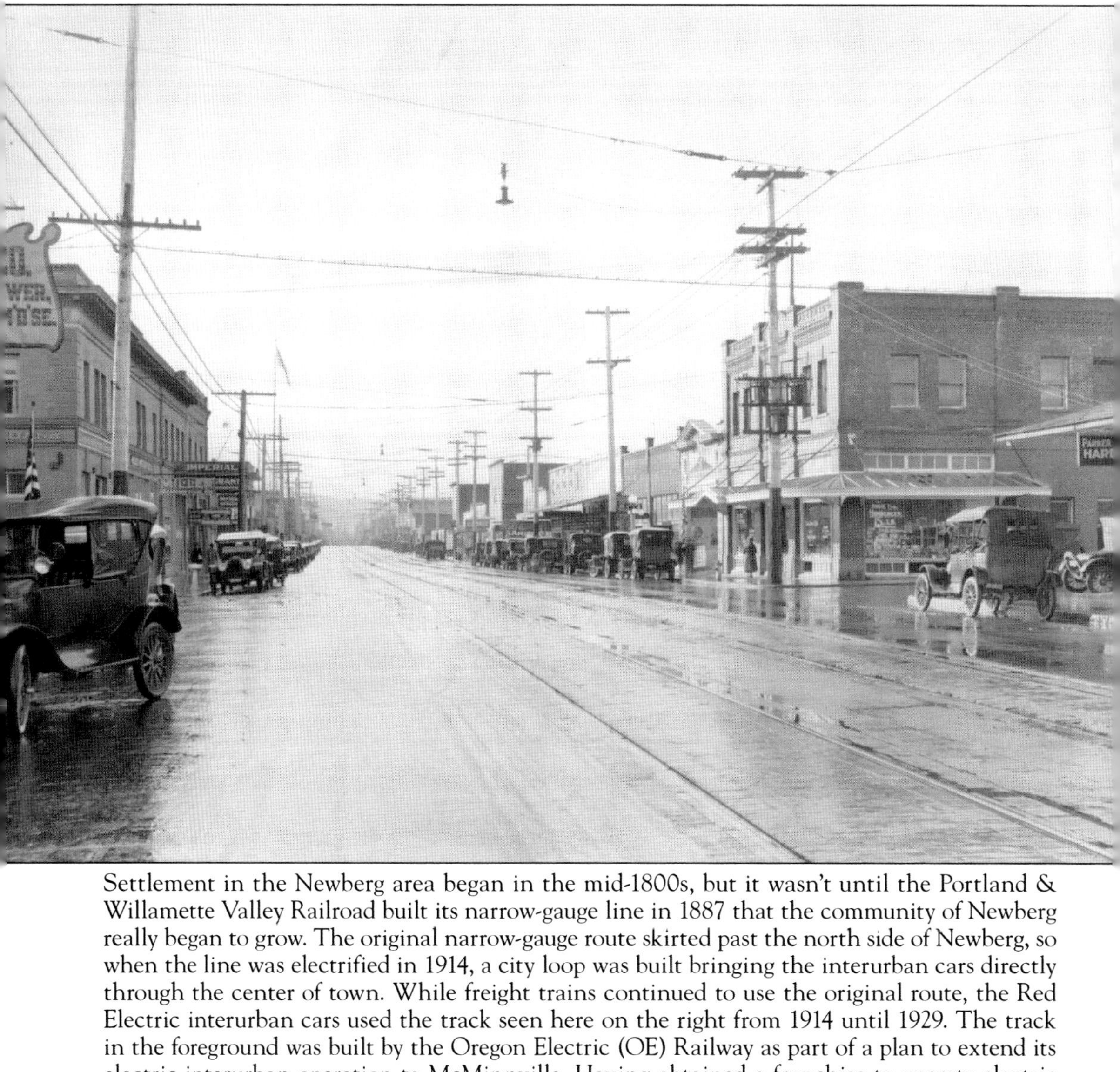

Settlement in the Newberg area began in the mid-1800s, but it wasn't until the Portland & Willamette Valley Railroad built its narrow-gauge line in 1887 that the community of Newberg really began to grow. The original narrow-gauge route skirted past the north side of Newberg, so when the line was electrified in 1914, a city loop was built bringing the interurban cars directly through the center of town. While freight trains continued to use the original route, the Red Electric interurban cars used the track seen here on the right from 1914 until 1929. The track in the foreground was built by the Oregon Electric (OE) Railway as part of a plan to extend its electric interurban operation to McMinnville. Having obtained a franchise to operate electric interurban trains through the center of Newberg, the OE built 3,300 feet of rail line parallel to the SP line. However, plans changed and the OE line to McMinnville was never built. Subsequently, the line seen here on the left was abandoned without ever being used.

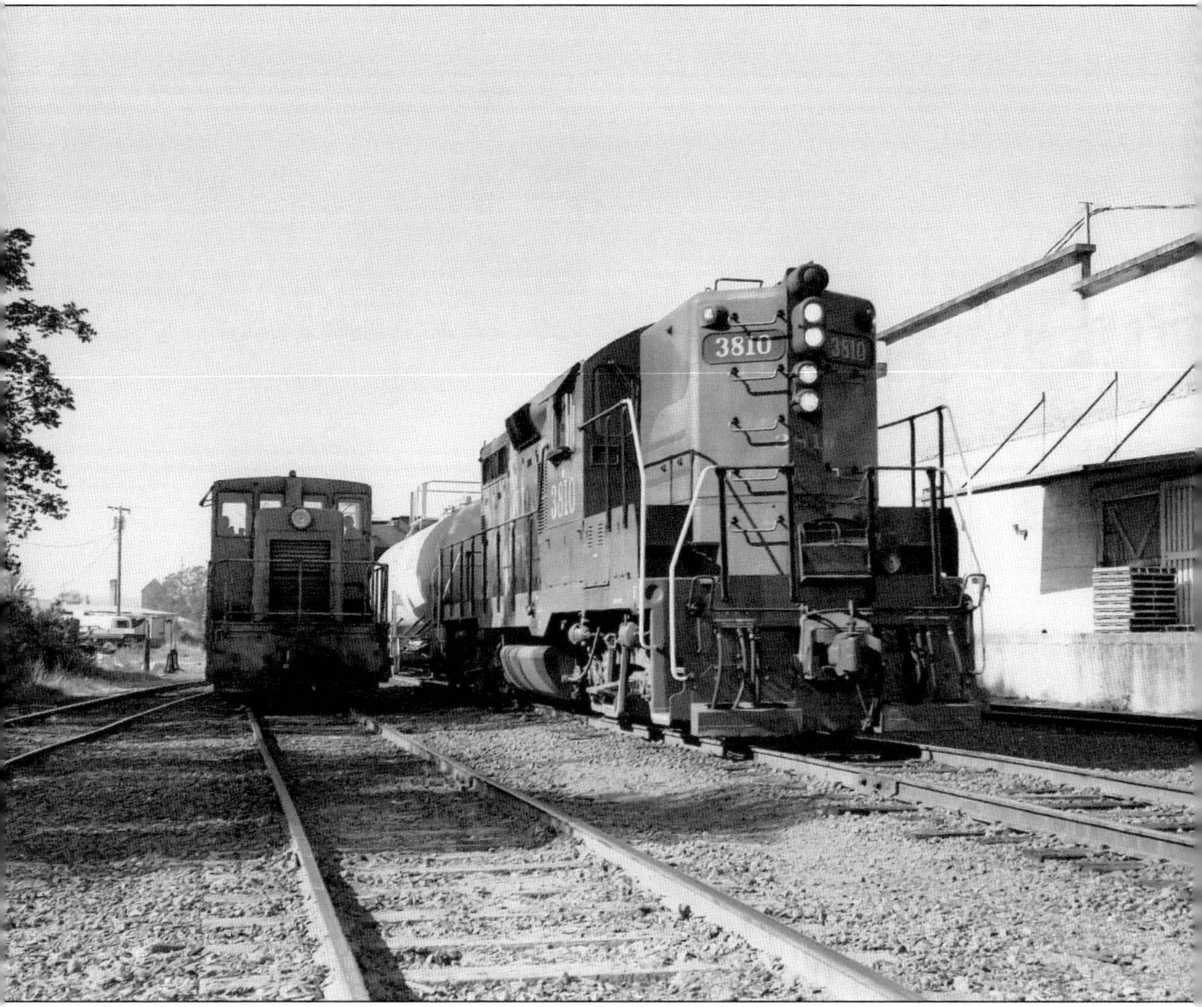

In 1927, the Spaulding Lumber Company mill at Newberg became the Spaulding Pulp & Paper Company, which by the early 1970s had become Publishers Paper Company. Although it had changed owners a couple more times, the paper mill and its railroad were still functioning, albeit on a limited basis, in 2012. In this view from October 1978, the Publishers Paper locomotive on the left is waiting for empty cars being delivered by the SP *Newberg Switcher*, which has just arrived from McMinnville. After a bit of switching, No. 3810 will return to McMinnville with loads from the paper mill while the small center cab diesel will return to the mill with empty cars ready for tomorrow's loads.

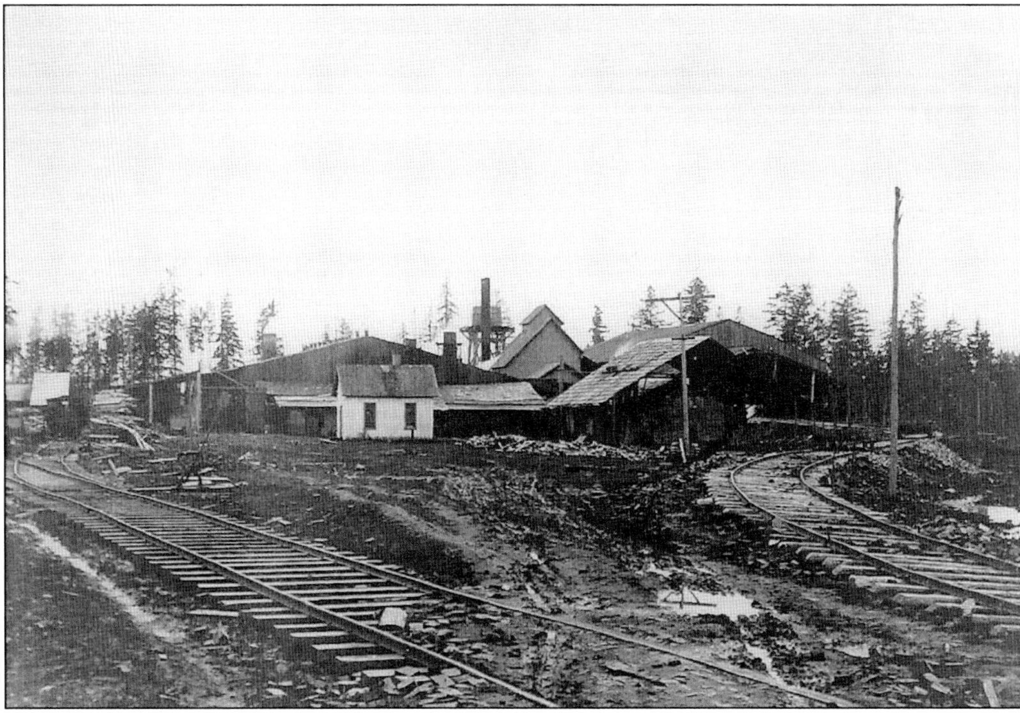

Newberg was also home to two tile and brick plants located to take advantage of natural materials available in the area. Here is the Pacific Face Brick Company plant in 1907.

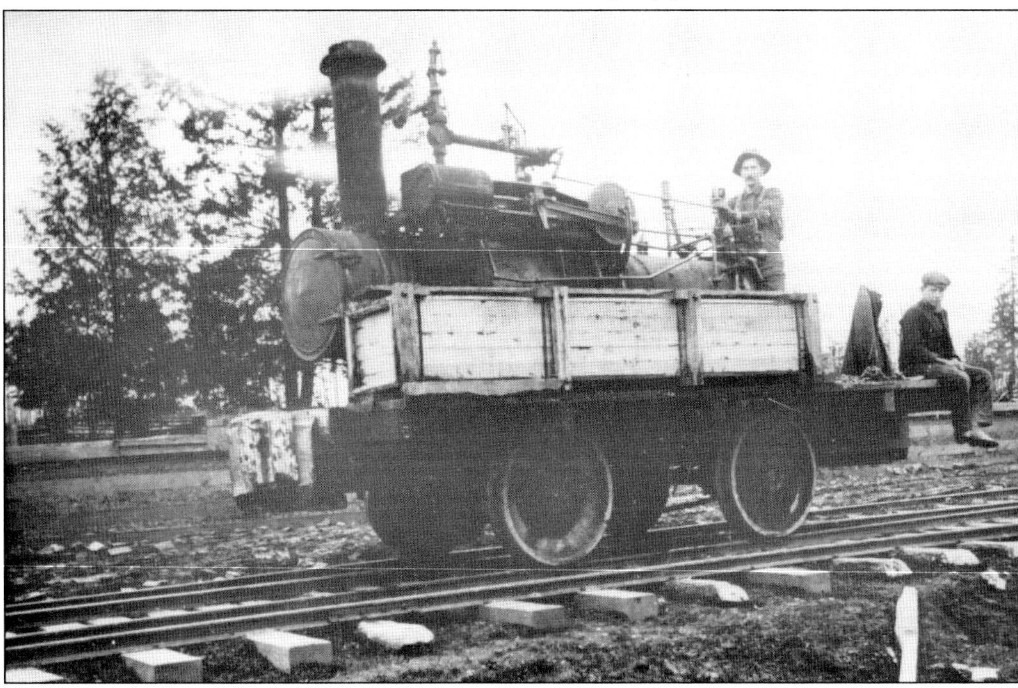

This rather unique, if not ungainly, homemade locomotive, seen here in 1907, served the Pacific Face Brick plant running between the plant and the SP railroad line at Newberg. With careful observation, the same locomotive can be seen at far left in the previous photograph.

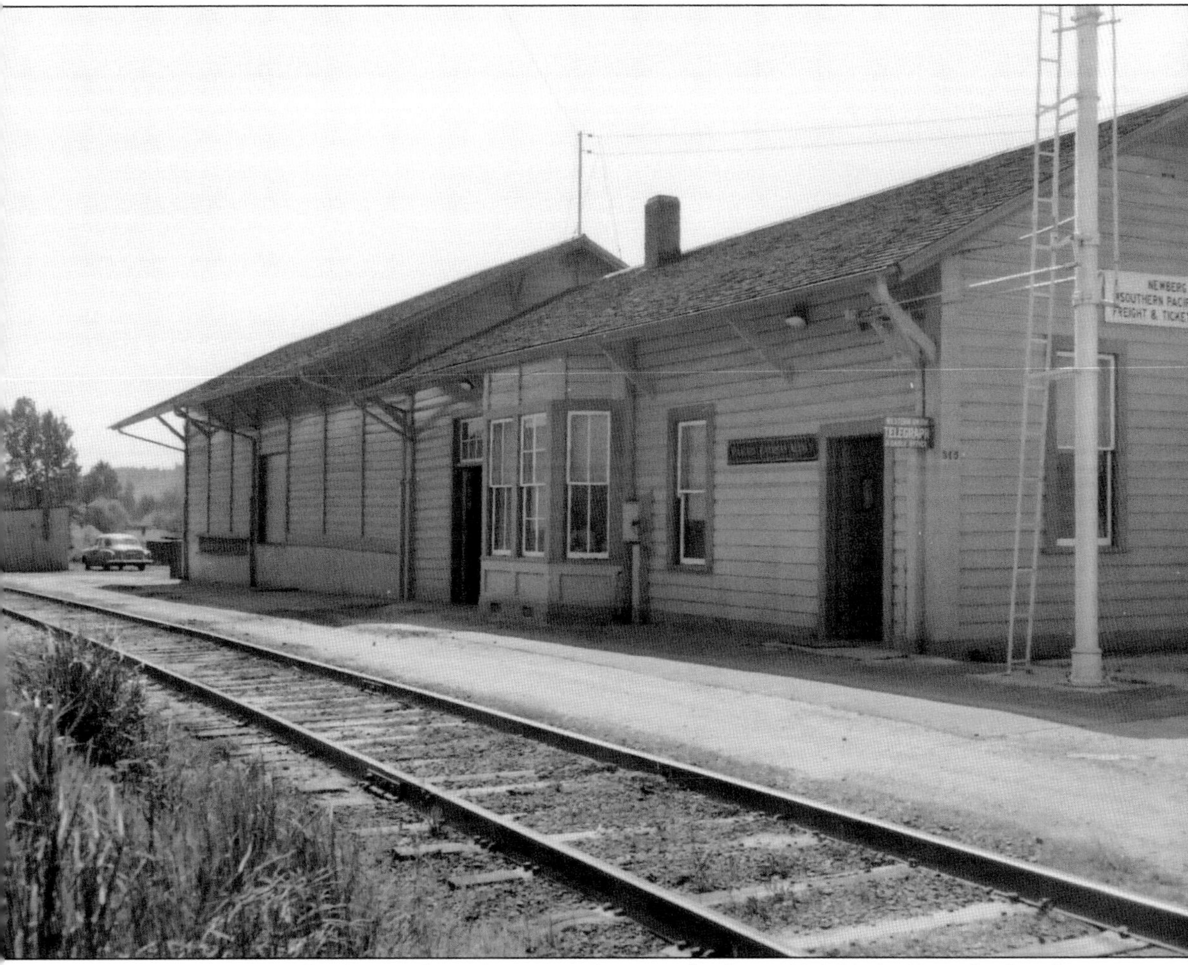

According to SP records, the Newberg depot seen here was built in 1906. Unfortunately, this date is suspect since the building was probably actually built before SP controlled the old Portland & Willamette Valley Railroad. In any case, the building measured 20 feet by 106 feet and served as a train order station between 1892 and 1932, and again between 1936 and 1965. The train order office was reactivated again between 1967 and 1977. The depot was finally retired in 1980 and demolished soon after.

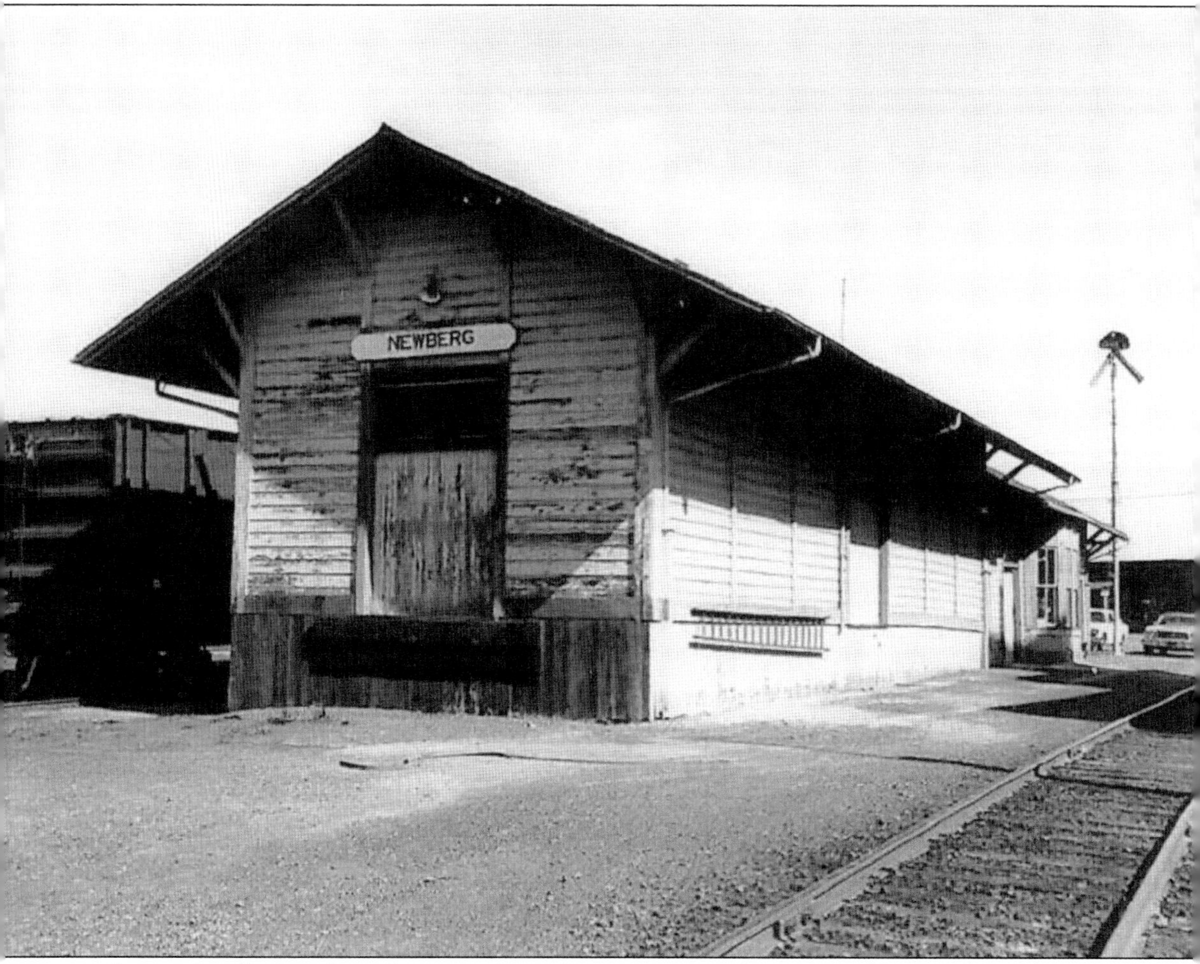

Pictured is the Newberg depot in the early 1970s. Note the train order signal standing next to the depot. The position of the semaphore blades would indicate to the train crew if they needed to pick up orders at the depot. In this case, the blades are pointing down, which on the SP indicated that the operator had no orders for this train. (Photograph by the late Don Still, author's collection.)

Construction and Roster Statistics

Summary of Construction of the Willamette Valley Narrow Gauge

The Dayton Sheridan & Grande Ronde Railroad Company
November 17, 1877–June 2, 1879
Mainline: 22.95 miles from Dayton via Whites (Whiteson and Sheridan Junction (Broadmead) to Smithfield
Branchline: 7.24 miles from Sheridan Junction (Broadmead) to Sheridan

The Willamette Valley Railroad Company
September 9, 1878–April 2, 1880
No new construction was undertaken by this company.

The Oregon Railway Company Ltd. (Oregon)
February 21, 1880–December 11, 1880
Mainline: 4.0 miles from Smithfield to Dallas

Oregonian Railway Company Ltd. (Scotland)
May 4, 1880–November 1, 1889
Mainline: 24.03 miles from Dallas to Airlie
Mainline: 89.24 miles from Ray's Landing via Woodburn and Silverton to Coburg
Branchline: 5.65 miles from Dayton Junction (near Dayton) via Dundee to Fulquartz Landing

Oregon Western Railroad Company
October 29, 1889–May 20, 1890
No new construction was undertaken by this company.

Oregonian Railroad Company (SP)
May 20, 1890–July 31, 1893
No new construction was undertaken by this company.

Portland & Willamette Valley Railroad Company
January 19, 1885–August 5, 1892
Mainline: 28.34 miles from Dundee Junction (near Dundee) via Rex Hill and Newberg to Jefferson Street (West Portland)

Portland & Yamhill Railroad Company
June 14, 1892–July 31, 1893
No new construction was undertaken by this company.

Total Mileage Operated As Narrow Gauge

Mainline: 168.56 miles
Branchline: 12.89 miles
Total narrow-gauge mileage: 181.45 miles

Locomotive Roster of the Willamette Valley Narrow Gauge

The Dayton Sheridan & Grande Ronde Railroad Company
No. 1 2-4-0 *Pioneer* National Locomotive Co. No. 259 ,May 1878
31-inch drivers / weight 21,200 pounds / tractive effort?
disposition unknown

No. 2 2-4-0 *Progress* National Locomotive Co. No. 260, May 1878
31-inch drivers / weight 21,200 pounds / tractive effort?
sold to Albert Johnson Logging Co. (Prosper Mill Co.), 1903
to Seely & Anderson
to Sturtevant & Crane

Oregonian Railway Company Ltd. (Scotland)
No. 3 2-6-0 *J.W. Ladd* Porter No. 292, February 1878
36-inch drivers / weight 36,000 pounds / tractive effort ?
owned by Walla Walla & Columbia River
leased from Walla Walla & Columbia River, 1880 to 1883
to Columbia & Puget Sound No. 6, August 1883

No. 4 2-6-0 Brownsville Pittsburgh No. 430, July 1880
38-inch drivers / weight 37,500 pounds / tractive effort ?
sold to SP of Cal No. 1025, February 1905
sold to McKenzie Shipyard, Oakland, September 1906

No. 5 2-6-0 Porter No. 374, June 1880
35.5-inch drivers / weight 36,000 pounds / tractive effort ?
sold to Sierra Valley No. 3, July 1899

No. 6 2-6-0 *Dallas* Porter No. 375, July 1880
35.5-inch drivers / weight 36,000 pounds / tractive effort ?
sold to Sierra Valley No. 1, January 1895

No. 7 2-6-0 *Scio* Porter No. 376, August 1880
35.5-inch drivers / weight 36,000 pounds / tractive effort ?
sold to Sierra Valley No. 2, January 1895
wrecked June 1899, scrapped

No. 8 4-4-0 *Portland* Baldwin Locomotive Works No. 5748, August 1881
44-inch drivers / weight 43,000 pounds / tractive effort ?
renamed *C.N. Scott* in 1885
sold to SP of Cal No. 1026, December 1903
sold to C.D. Bunker, August 1906

No. 9 4-4-0 *Dundee* Baldwin Locomotive Works (order cancelled June 1881)

Portland & Willamette Valley Railroad Company
Note: P&WV No. 1 (first) was ex–DS&GR 2-4-0 No. 1

No. 1 (second) 2-6-0 Baldwin Locomotive Works No. 5121, May 1880
44-inch drivers / weight 39,000 pounds / tractive effort 6,557 pounds
acquired 1887, ex–Utah & Northern No. 19
sold to Ilwaco Railway & Navigation Co. No. 4, April 1906
to OWR&N No. N-2, 1915
scrapped April 1931

Note: P&WV No. 2 (first) was ex–DS&GR 2-4-0 No. 2

No. 2 (second) 2-6-0 New York Locomotive Works No. 21, April 1883
48-inch drivers / weight 65,600 pounds / tractive effort 14,960 pounds
acquired by Portland & Willamette Valley in 1887
ex–Cincinnati Northern No. 8
ex–Toledo, Cincinnati & St. Louis No. 48
sold to South Pacific Coast No. 24, April 1897
scrapped January 1902

No. 3 2-6-0 New York Locomotive Works No. 22, April 1883
48-inch drivers / weight 65,600 pounds / tractive effort 14,960 pounds
acquired by Portland & Willamette Valley in 1887
ex–Cincinnati Northern No. 9
ex–Toledo, Cincinnati & St. Louis No. 49
sold to South Pacific Coast No. 25, April 1897

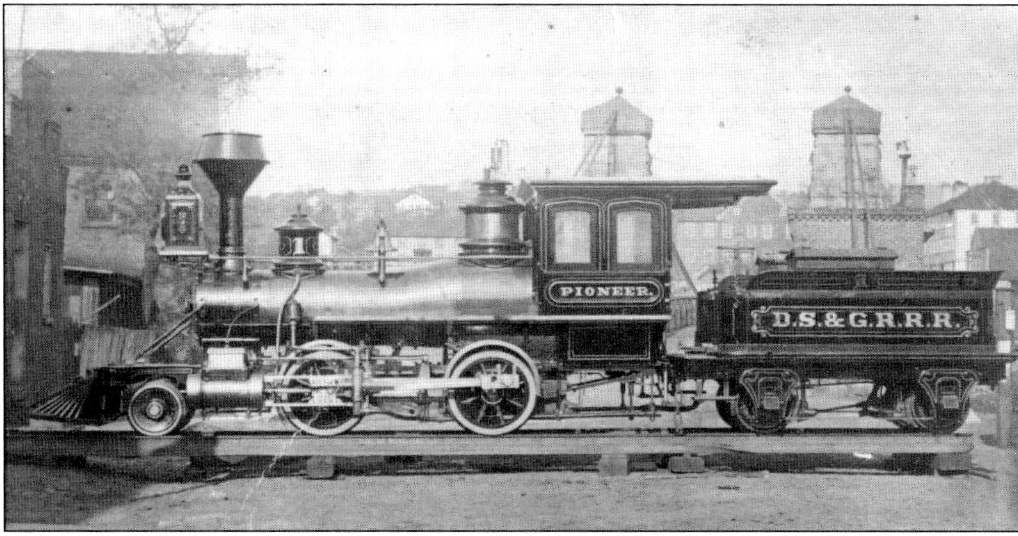

The Dayton, Sheridan & Grand Ronde Railroad's first locomotive, the *Pioneer*, poses for its builder's photograph at the National Locomotive Co. factory in Connellsville, Pennsylvania, in May 1878. The diminutive 2-4-0 was completed in May 1878 weighing 21,200 pounds and riding on 31-inch drivers. The National Locomotive Co. specialized in constructing narrow-gauge locomotives between 1871 and 1878. Photographs of the *Pioneer* and her sister *Progress* in service are extremely rare. What eventually became of the *Pioneer* is unknown.

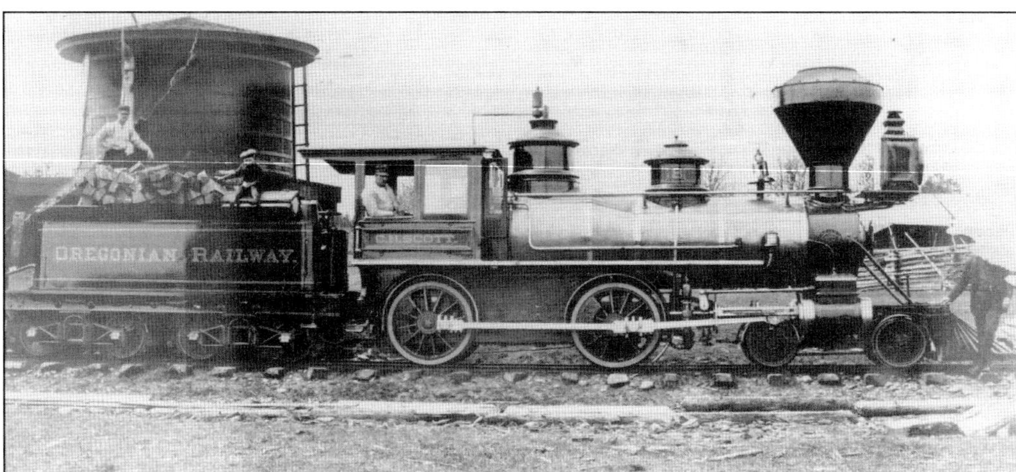

Only two narrow-gauge 4-4-0s were ordered by the Oregonian Railway and only one was actually delivered, the order for the second locomotive being cancelled in June 1881. Built by the Baldwin Locomotive Works in August 1881, she weighed 43,000 pounds, had 44-inch drivers, and arrived carrying the name *Portland*. However, she was renamed *C.N. Scott*, as seen here in 1885. She was sold to the Southern Pacific of California in December 1903 and resold to C.D. Bunker in August 1906.

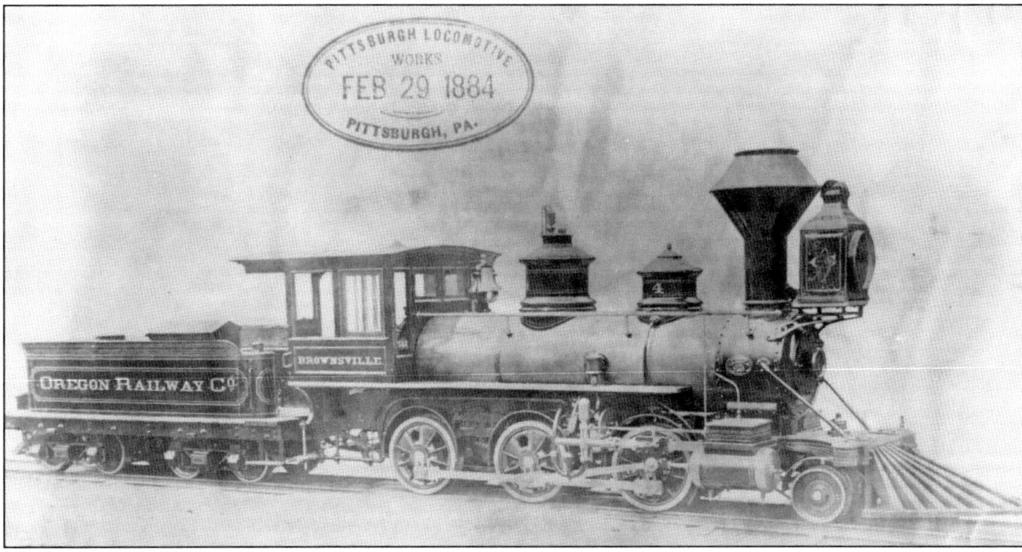

Although the early 2-4-0s were unique and the 4-4-0s were high steppers suited to passenger service, it was the 2-6-0 wheel arrangement that accounted for the bulk of the work done by steam on the Willamette Valley narrow-gauge railroad system. This builder's photograph gives a look at 2-6-0 No. 4, the *Brownsville*, as she rolled out of the Pittsburgh Locomotive Works factory in 1884. Of eight 2-6-0s that worked on the Willamette Valley narrow-gauge system, only No. 4 was built by Pittsburgh. Note the straight boiler, which differentiates No. 4 from her sisters built by Porter.

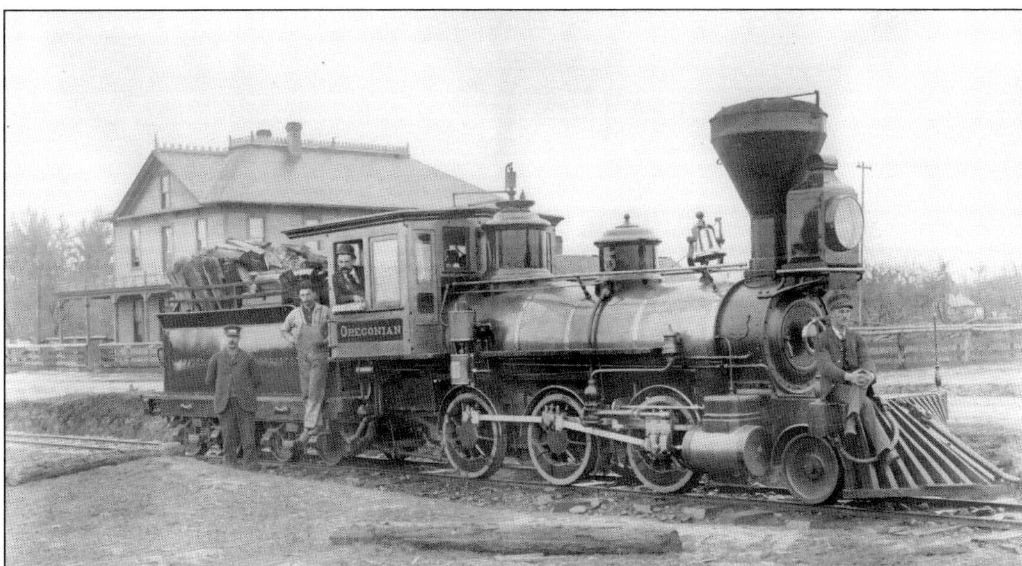

H.K. Porter Inc. built locomotive No. 5 in June 1880 under construction No. 374. She was one of three basically identical 2-6-0s turned out by Porter for the Willamette Valley narrow-gauge lines that year. Each weighed 36,000 pounds and all three rode on 35.5-inch drivers. No. 5 is seen in this early glass-plate view at Whiteson on the Oregonian Railway's Westside Division. When No. 5 and her sisters were built in 1880, air brakes were not yet in use on the Willamette Valley narrow-gauge system. However, the air pump seen just ahead of No. 5's cab indicates the Oregonian Railway was adopting this new safety feature when the photograph was taken.

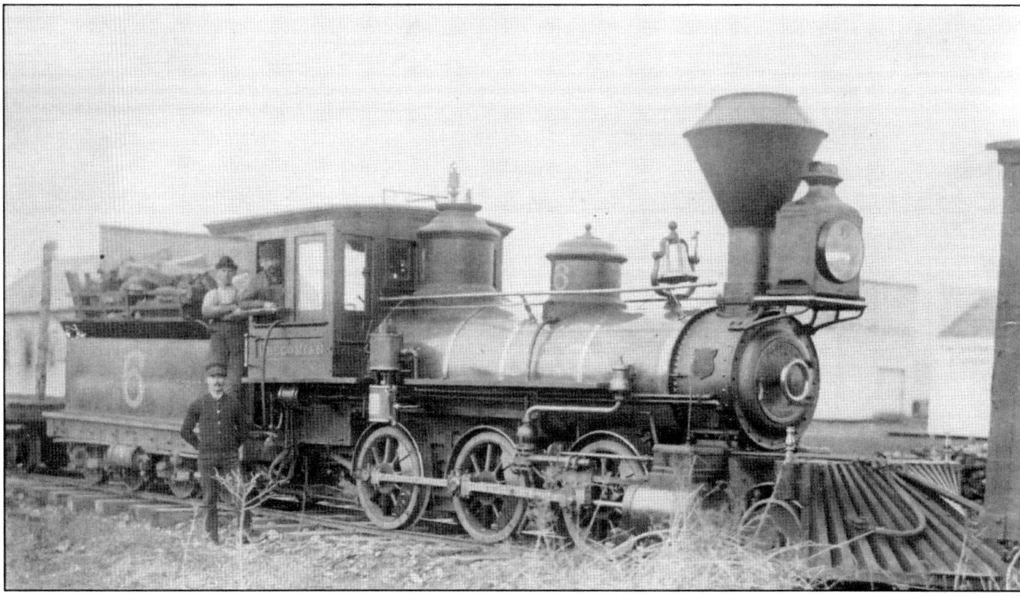

Oregonian Railway No. 6 was another of the 1880-built Porter 2-6-0s. Like No. 5, she had been upgraded with an air pump by the time this photograph was taken. Note the tapered boiler with the steam dome sitting high in front of the cab. Also note the air hose draped across the wood pilot, confirming the use of air brakes. When No. 6 was delivered in July 1880 she carried the name *Dallas*, but by the time of this photograph names were no longer being applied to Oregonian Railway locomotives.

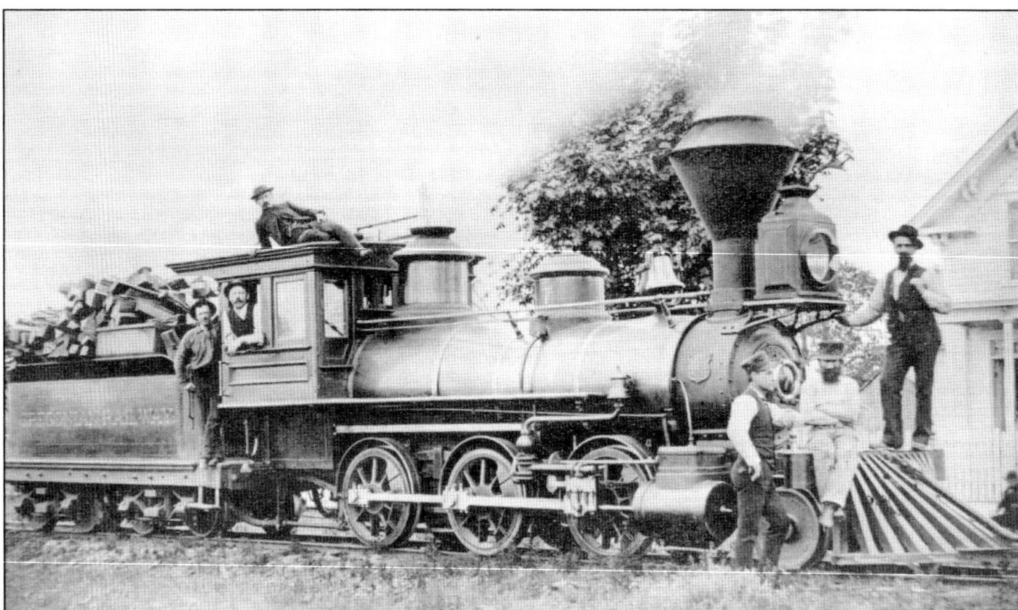

The last of the 2-6-0s H.K. Porter built for the Willamette Valley narrow-gauge system was No. 7. She was delivered as the *Scio* in August 1880 and is seen here prior to being upgraded with air brakes as witnessed by the lack of an air pump or air lines. All three of the Oregonian Railway's Porter-built 2-6-0s were sold to the Sierra Valley Railroad between 1895 and 1899. No. 7 was subsequently wrecked and scrapped in June 1899.

Additional Reading

Austin, Ed and Tom Dill. The Southern Pacific in Oregon. Pacific Fast Mail, 1987.
———. The Southern Pacific in Oregon Vol. II. Pacific Fast Mail, 1993.
Diebert & Strapac. S.P. Steam Locomotive Compendium. Shade Tree Books, 1987.
Dunscomb, Guy. A Century of Southern Pacific Steam Locomotives. Dunscomb, 1967.
Nash, Wallis. OREGON There and Back in 1877. Oregon State University Press, 1976.
Oregon Historical Society Quarterly vol. 20 No. 2.
Robertson, Donald. Encyclopedia of Western Railroad History Vol. III. Caxton, 1995.

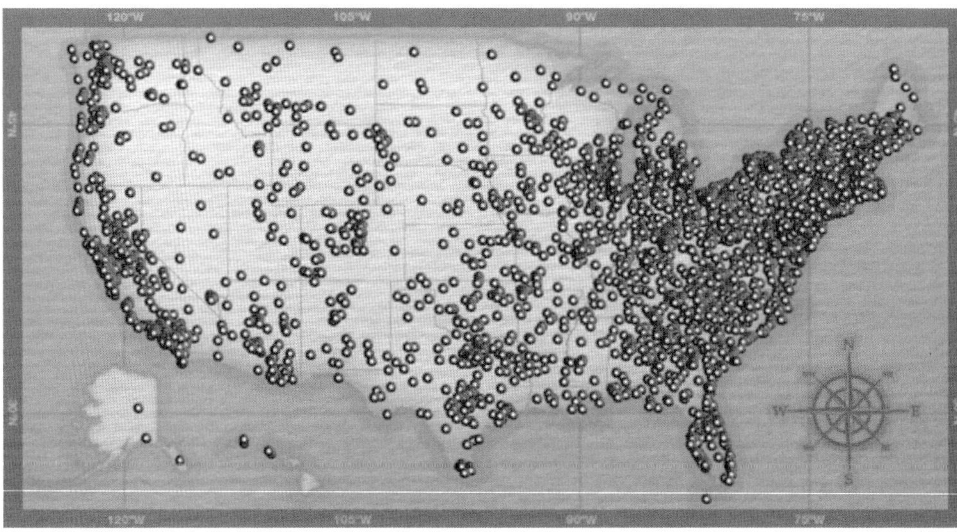